CIRCLES OF CENSORSHIP

CIRCLES OF CENSORSHIP

Censorship and its
Metaphors in French History,
Literature, and Theory

NICHOLAS HARRISON

CLARENDON PRESS · OXFORD
1995

Oxford University Press, Walton Street, Oxford OX2 6DP
Oxford New York
Athens Auckland Bangkok Bombay
Calcutta Cape Town Dar es Salaam Delhi
Florence Hong Kong Istanbul Karachi
Kuala Lumpur Madras Madrid Melbourne
Mexico City Nairobi Paris Singapore
Taipei Tokyo Toronto
and associated companies in
Berlin Ibadan

Oxford is a trade mark of Oxford University Press

Published in the United States
by Oxford University Press Inc., New York

British Library Cataloguing in Publication Data
Data available

Library of Congress Cataloging in Publication Data
Harrison, Nicholas.
Circles of censorship : censorship and its metaphors in French
history, literature, and theory / Nicholas Harrison.
Includes bibliographical references and index.
1. French literature—19th century—Censorship. 2. French
literature—20th century—Censorship. 3. Censorship—France—
History. 4. Psychoanalysis and literature. I. Title.
PQ283.H364 1995 840.9'007—dc20 95-6489
ISBN 0-19-815909-9

1 3 5 7 9 10 8 6 4 2

Typeset by Best-set Typesetter Ltd., Hong Kong

Printed in Great Britain
on acid-free paper by
Biddles Ltd, Guildford and King's Lynn

Acknowledgements

❧

This book has benefited from the help of numerous people. In particular I want to thank Malcolm Bowie, Andrew Brown, Peter Collier (who supervised my Ph.D.), Rosamund Davies, Marian Hobson-Jeanneret, and Simon Whiteman, for reading the whole thing at different points in its genesis and pointing out ways in which it might be improved; Jeremy Pettitt and John Stanton-Ife, for providing useful advice concerning my work on metaphor and jurisprudence respectively; Simon Gaunt, for his advice about publishing; and the master and fellows of St Catharine's College, Cambridge, for awarding me the research fellowship during which this project was completed.

Two organizations whose publications have been very useful to me and who do valuable work in documenting and campaigning against censorship are Writers and Scholars International Ltd, Lancaster House, 33 Islington High Street, London N1 9LH, who publish *Index on Censorship*, and Article 19 (International Centre Against Censorship), 90 Borough High Street, London SE1 1LL.

I would like to dedicate this book to the memory of Peter Saunders.

N. D. H.

Contents

✽

Note on the Text

❧

Most of the translations in this book are mine. Reference is made to a published translation if I am aware of one (a date and page number are given after those applying to the French text), but more often than not my quotation is different from the published version. Sometimes this is because I think the translation is inaccurate, but often it is because an alternative version provides the emphasis I am looking for.

Throughout the book italics in quotations are those of the author quoted, unless I indicate otherwise.

In general I use the Harvard (author–date) system of reference, except for those texts listed below for which I use abbreviations. In the case of Freud, I give the original date of publication, and then the volume and page numbers from the *Standard Edition*.

BPI	Bibliothèque Publique d'Information
ÉÉÉ	Pierre Guyotat, *Éden, Éden, Éden* (Paris: Gallimard, 1970)
LI	Pierre Guyotat, *Littérature interdite* (Paris: Gallimard, 1972)
OC	D. A. F. Sade, Marquis de, *Œuvres complètes* (Paris: Cercle du Livre Précieux, 1966–7)
SASDLR	*Le Surréalisme au service de la revolution*
SE	Sigmund Freud, *The Standard Edition of the Complete Psychological Works of Sigmund Freud*, ed. J. Strachey (London: Hogarth Press, 1953–66)
SFL	Roland Barthes, *Sade, Fourier, Loyola* (Paris: Seuil, 1971)
TQ	*Tel Quel*

Introduction

༄❀༅

CENSURE est un de ces mots commodes dont notre époque fait une grande consommation, parce qu'ils permettent à peu de frais de se situer du côté des bien-pensants, c'est-à-dire avec tout le monde aujourd'hui. À gauche, à droite comme au milieu, il est entendu que l'on est *contre* la censure, *contre* la guerre, *contre* le racisme, *pour* les droits de l'homme ou la liberté d'expression. Grandes convictions qui ne résisteront pas trois secondes ensuite à l'épreuve des circonstances.[1]

(Jean-Jacques Pauvert, *Nouveaux (et moins nouveaux)
visages de la censure* (1994: 7))

In 1947, at the age of 20, Jean-Jacques Pauvert started to publish Sade's complete works. For a decade these works were seized by the police, until finally in 1956 legal proceedings were launched against Pauvert on the grounds that Sade's novels constituted an 'outrage aux bonnes mœurs' (the closest English equivalent of which would be an 'affront to public decency'[2]). At the trial in December of that year he was found guilty, but was effectively acquitted the following year in the Court of Appeal. From that point on, Sade's work became increasingly widely available in France. Not only was it never again prosecuted, but it also came quite rapidly to occupy a fully accredited position in the canon of great French literature. It would seem, in the light of this, that the Pauvert trial and subsequent appeal not only marked an important moment in the gradual process by which Sade, viewed by many as the final frontier of literary freedom of expression, became more acceptable and more widely read, but also more actively set in motion a new phase

---

[1] 'Censorship is one of those convenient words which are widely used today because they allow people to seem, with a minimum of effort, decent and right-thinking, the same as everyone else these days. The Left, the Right and the Centre all agree that one should be *anti*-censorship, *anti*-war, *anti*-racism, *pro*-human rights or freedom of expression. These are impressive convictions, which don't last five minutes when they are put to the test.'

[2] *Les bonnes mœurs*, according to the Robert dictionary, means 'respect for virtue and the practice thereof (*respect et pratique des vertus*)'. It has specifically sexual connotations—colloquially, *les mœurs* means the vice squad.

in this development. From one point of view the 'Sade Affair' could be seen as the last shudder of a system of censorship which was grinding to a halt, but from another it was an active factor in a continuing history of censorship which had shaped, and continued to shape, the ways in which Sade was read and the kind of audience he reached.

Pauvert himself has turned into the grand old man of censorship issues in France, his most recent thoughts on the topic appearing in the book whose opening words provide my epigraph. He (like many French intellectuals, I believe) has tended to look at the Sade affair, and censorship in general, exclusively from the former point of view, treating censorship as a phenomenon of oppression which, behind its different 'faces', has remained essentially the same throughout history. His own experiences have left him with an impressively single-minded attachment to freedom of expression and an understandable impatience with those whose ready opposition to the principle of censorship turns out to be less than steadfast in practice. Looking at the subsequent course of Pauvert's successful career, however, one has to ask how oppressive in practice the censorship was which he suffered in the Sade affair or later in connection with other books, since there can be little doubt that in the long run it proved beneficial to him in many respects.

Pauvert is apparently struck by the readiness with which people declare themselves against censorship, and regards this impulse as basically a sound one, and to that extent my starting-point is the same as his. I want to suggest, though, that in deriding those whose opposition to censorship is not absolute, Pauvert is inclined to ignore the genuine complexities of the field of censorship and so fails to see that often the 'épreuve des circonstances' detaches people from the rhetoric of freedom of expression, not so much because they were not truly attached to it in the first place, as because that rhetoric overlies a history of substantive practical contradictions of which it is, by its nature, unable to take account. My project in this book is to examine the notions of censorship and of freedom of expression in a particular historical context and to cast new light on the issues which they raise, issues which the very terms 'censorship' and 'freedom of expression' often serve to obscure.

My study is centred on France, whose Revolution of 1789 was crucial in establishing the basic rhetoric of human rights with which we are familiar today. More specifically, it is concerned above all with French literary culture since the Revolution, and the role which the concepts of freedom of expression and censorship have played in that culture. Literary culture is of particular interest in that it is frequently assumed to be the arena in which freedom of expression is at its most unconditional: this assumption will be questioned in the course of Chapter 1 of this book, which deals with the general history of censorship in France and seeks to establish a historicized understanding of the notion of freedom of expression which shows that even literary culture has been historically subject to and influenced by a wide range of constraints. I focus on literature that has been considered immoral or obscene, looking particularly at the *Madame Bovary* trial of 1857 and Pauvert's trial a century later, and then use feminist critiques of pornography and its relation to the law to question the place of pornographic literature within the freedom of expression. The relationship of the censor to the object of censorship may fall prey to a disturbing circularity, I will argue, within which the censor and the object of censorship may in important respects be complicitous rather than oppositional.

If I come to concentrate on moral rather than overtly political censorship, this is for various reasons. Partly it is because the motives for political censorship and the power relationships it involves are usually relatively clear and do not call for elaborate theoretical models, and because debates about moral censorship— especially in connection with pornography—are particularly lively at the moment. It is also because the history of literary culture itself seems to encourage a movement in that direction, a movement which is doubtless a sign of the influence of censorship upon it. I am also interested, however, in the ways in which various literary writers in twentieth-century France have attempted to overcome censorship and to politicize their writing. A crucial factor in this was the impact of Freudian theory, which offered a new way of conceiving of censorship and its relevance to the self and to literature. In order to understand this impact one needs a thorough understanding of the Freudian theory of censorship on which these writers drew, and to this end in Chapter 2 I examine Freud's use of the term 'censorship' and its relation to the political and social contexts from which it was drawn.

From each of these first two sections, then, there emerge discourses on censorship, the first of which one might term legal-historical, the second psychoanalytic. My aim in Chapter 3 is to show how these two discourses have intersected in modern French literary culture, most conspicuously in the work of the Surrealists and the *Tel Quel* group. This point of intersection is the site of a discourse of 'counter-censorship' (a (supposedly) radical opposition to, or subversion of, censorship) which is my principle concern in this third Chapter. The enthusiasm displayed in certain strands of thought for writing such as that of Sade, I will argue, has been profoundly shaped and to some degree was created by what I am terming the discourse of counter-censorship, generated at the point of intersection I have located; but a more sophisticated understanding of both political and psychic censorship suggests that this enthusiasm is ill founded in important respects.

It will be gathered that in the course of this study, my focus narrows. Even when I am engaged in an analysis of the Surrealists' attitude to sex, however, or in a close reading of Barthes's writing on Sade, I hope to make it clear that broader political, psychic, and artistic issues are at stake. *Tel Quel* on the one hand and the Surrealists on the other are chosen as objects of attention precisely because their respective projects represent two distinctive moments in French history at which discourses on political, psychic, and artistic freedom were intertwined, and because their cultural impact, in France and beyond, is still felt today. Having said this, I am not claiming that literary censorship is more important than the other types I discuss, nor that moral censorship is more fundamental than political censorship. A great many factors can create a form of 'censorship' and a great many issues are relevant to the question of freedom of expression, including issues such as literacy (most fundamentally of all), education, racism, and structures of media ownership and finance, for instance, as well as perhaps more obviously relevant issues such as State secrecy, regulations regarding privacy, or the extraordinary powers governments have always granted themselves during wars.

Many of these issues I can deal with only briefly, if at all, and only in Chapter 1. It is an awareness of limitations of this sort which has prompted me to cut across the book's forward and unifying motion by introducing a major division before its latter two sections, which are grouped under the title 'Metaphors of Censorship'. I will indicate in due course what I mean by 'metaphor' in this connection, but should note at this point that the division of Part One from Part Two is not intended as a division of practice from theory, nor of politics from culture, nor even necessarily of the literal from the metaphorical, but as a gesture signalling in a provisional way my resistance to the idea that, as one moves towards psychoanalysis and further into literature and into questions of sex and sexuality, one is approaching profound truths which are more 'real' than contingent political issues. Time after time, writers on Sade, for instance, have suggested that they have uncovered the *true* reasons for the censorship of his work, and have discovered what his *real* crime was, and those writers have frequently forgotten, in the process, the fact that many people have found his books offensive and upsetting and that Sade's 'real crime' included real crime. These facts are not the whole story, of course, but they should not be devalued according to some spurious hierarchy of realities. The metaphors of censorship which I discuss are also real, I will argue, are intimately linked with politics in the complex circles of censorship I will describe, and are worthy of detailed attention; but they are not more real or more worthy of attention than many other areas of censorship which fall outside the scope of this book.

PART ONE

Censorship

1. *Freedom of Expression in History and in Theory*

✦

In December 1793, in the midst of the post-Revolutionary Terror which lasted from June 1793 to July 1794, Sade wrote a letter on the day which turned out to be the last of a spell spent out of jail: the next morning he was arrested and imprisoned, and subsequently escaped the guillotine only through good fortune. These circumstances lend a particular resonance to a passage from the letter which reads:

> Beneath my window in the rue Helvétius I can hear the drunken singing of the decapitators. [. . .] 'Human rights'—decreed, you will remember, 'in the presence and under the auspices of the Supreme Being'—will doubtless provide scant protection against this rising tide. Nevertheless I can take a certain pleasure in reminding you of article 11: 'Free communication of thoughts and opinions is one of man's most precious rights; every citizen can therefore speak, write, and publish freely . . .'[1] I will break off there, since the limit of the law is reintroduced at that point, and that is something I do not wish to consider. (In Sollers 1992: 48–9)

The *Déclaration des droits de l'homme et du citoyen* to which Sade refers was made on 16 August 1789 and formed the foundation of the constitution of 3 September 1791. The discourse of freedom of expression which it instituted has proved enduring in modern liberal thought: the European Convention on Human Rights of 1950, which followed fairly closely the Universal Declaration of Human Rights of 1948, was ratified in France in 1975, and its tenth article restated the basic principle of what was by then generally termed *liberté d'expression*. It also set out the various rubrics under which this right might be considered less than absolute, such as government regulation of broadcasting, State security, libel, and so on.

---

[1] In French, the article reads: 'La libre communication des pensées et des opinions est un des droits les plus précieux de l'homme; tout citoyen peut donc parler, écrire, imprimer librement, sauf à répondre de l'abus de cette liberté dans les cas déterminés par la loi.'

While the basic formulae of today's constitution concerning this issue are close to those of the original *Déclaration*, the underlying notions concerning the nature of the citizen's participation in and accountability to her or his society, the criteria by which certain uses of the right are deemed abuses (the phrase which Sade omitted was 'sauf à répondre de l'abus de cette liberté dans les cas déterminés par la loi', meaning that 'abuses' of the right as defined in law would be actionable), the nature of the authority possessed by those placed to make such judgements, and the range of individuals considered worthy of the freedom, have been far from constant. Those who appeal to the freedom of expression frequently share Sade's aversion to recognizing the limits which the law has always imposed upon it; and too often they have failed to recognize that, as Sade suggested, the right can ring a little hollow if political circumstances are unfavourable to its being exercised. As I hope to show in this chapter, the *Déclaration*'s rhetoric of freedom of expression, despite its endurance and its undoubted importance to post-Revolutionary consciousness, has been repeatedly reinterpreted and compromised, and cannot be fully understood without some sense both of the historical context out of which it emerged and of the shifting uses to which it has subsequently been put.

THE CIRCUMSTANCES OF FREEDOM

The Prehistory of Freedom of Expression

If it is a mistake to think of the *Déclaration* as having made freedom of expression an absolute and unchanging right, it is also a mistake to think of it as having defined itself against a tradition of absolute unfreedom. In the area of freedom of expression as in others, 1789 did not mark the complete historical break which it has come to stand for, not least through the *Déclaration* itself. I want to begin by discussing the closing decades of the *ancien régime*, which are particularly instructive in this respect for their complex and shifting layering of repressiveness and tolerance. Before doing so, however, I want to make a few points about the traditions of censorship from which the modes of censorship practised in those decades evolved.

The first printing press in France was installed at the Sorbonne in 1470. Censorship in the early decades of printing was the responsibility primarily of the Church, and was correspondingly concerned above all with religious orthodoxy. By the mid-sixteenth century the censors' attentions had broadened to include all books available in France, and responsibility was moving fitfully towards the Crown. Thus, by the middle of the seventeenth century, censorship had been officially 'secularized' in that it was carried out under the Crown's authority. The Church continued to play an important role, however, not least via its *Index Librorum Prohibitorum*, whose prohibitions were intended to be binding throughout Christendom and which, having appeared for the first time in 1559, was not officially suppressed until 1965.

The *Index Librorum Prohibitorum* was the embodiment of one particular discourse of censorship, in which an agent of absolute, metaphysically guaranteed authority must be *seen* to carry out censorship, and so clearly to delimit the bounds of acceptable thought and behaviour. The straightforward contours of this model, which I will refer to as exemplary censorship, are those against which the freedom of expression stands out most clearly, and against which it is still often pictured. A fairly cursory look at the history of the model's operation reveals greater complexity, however. First, the lack of perfect harmony, and the shifts in the balance of power, between the Crown, the Parliament, and the University, meant that this absolute authority was not monolithic, and that the weight of the State did not automatically fall in line with the Church's guidelines. Secondly, even in the sixteenth century it was apparent that censorship never operated as a purely negative, repressive force, in that it frequently proved (counter-)productive in terms of the interest it generated in a potential readership, and also in that the censor's non-opposition to a work began inevitably to be seen as a more active form of endorsement. Censorship, in other words, was an active factor in the reader's understanding of the text. Thirdly, books were not only vehicles for ideas but also commodities which as such occupied an ambiguous position in relation to those ideas and their 'freedom'. As of 1537, for instance, control of the presses was concentrated in the hands of a select band of master publishers, *maîtres-libraires-imprimeurs*, who were chosen by the king and who shared an interest with the latter in suppressing clandestine literature and literary piracy which undercut their monopoly. Thus it was partly in response to publishers' requests for protection from counterfeiters that censorship was effectively bolstered in 1563, when Charles IX made the right to publish a matter of royal *privilège*, a system which had existed in less rigorous form for some time. Similarly, a system of registration of copyright, the *dépôt légal*, was instituted in 1537, which meant that copies of all published works were held officially and were systematically dated and attributed. The proclaimed aim of the *dépôt légal* was to reinvigorate and protect the literary domain, and this answered a genuine need, since Renaissance humanists were frequently interrupted in their researches into ancient letters by texts which were mutilated, incomplete, distorted by copyists, or simply lost, but the system also, of course, made life easier for the censor.

Under the pressure of factors such as these—the instabilities and contradictions of supposedly monolithic power, the 'productive' powers of censorship *vis-à-vis* readers, and the demands of commerce—the increasingly unwieldy and diverse machinery of exemplary censorship started to pull itself apart from the inside. By the early years of the eighteenth century there were already both general and local versions of the *privilège*, and there were additional forms of endorsement called *permissions simples* and *permissions de Sceau* which could be obtained more cheaply but offered fewer guarantees. In both cases, the name of the censor was printed. From 1718, however, a still lower level of endorsement, the *permission tacite*, was also awarded, occupying an equivocal, paradoxical position in relation to authority and the law. If a publisher received a *permission tacite* for one of his books, he was expected to use an imprint which gave the impression that it had been published abroad; and such books were included in an official list of foreign books whose sale was permitted in France.

By around 1730, at a time when there were about 300 *privilèges* a year, maybe a dozen books appeared with a *permission tacite*, but this balance shifted until by the end of the *ancien régime* there were more books with a *permission tacite* than with a *privilège*. Furthermore, the fact that Voltaire, for example, hoped to persuade the police to turn a blind eye to his *Lettres philosophiques* of 1733, even though it was made absolutely clear that official tolerance was out of the question, suggests (despite his failure) that there was some play in the machinery of censorship at more than one level. It was no doubt inevitable that a large amount of unofficial publication, most of which was carried out abroad—three different editions of that particular work by Voltaire, for instance—should slip through the net and into circulation, and by now it was widely recognized by both writers and censors that a book tended to be all the more widely read if officially forbidden.

Between 1750 and 1760 the convoluted system of *permissions tacites* was supplemented by one involving clandestine, oral permission of which there was no official record. Thus an agreement would be made, for example, that inspectors from the censorship office would forewarn printers of police raids on their premises, so that they could conceal any evidence of their 'clandestine' printing, and could otherwise work undisturbed. Malesherbes, perhaps the most famous Director of the Book Trade under the *ancien régime*, actually favoured the abolition of censorship except for works threatening public order and those which were indecent or defamatory, and when he was ordered in 1752 by the royal council to seize manuscripts, plates, and copies of the second volume of the *Encyclopédie* (which was not a clandestine publication, but was, of course, a very controversial one), he tipped off Diderot before the police arrived and offered his own house as a hiding-place for the offending material. He may have acted partly out of some feeling of class loyalty, but he was also genuinely interested, it seems, in the threatened material itself. Indeed, in his *Mémoires sur la librairie* of 1809 Malesherbes cited the *Encyclopédie* in support of his remark that a man who read only those books which had received official blessing would be almost a century behind his contemporaries (cited by Hermann-Mascard 1968: 97).

These various administrative compromises marked so many crucial moments in the changing relationship between, on one hand, writers, printers, and their audience, and on the other, a fragmenting authority, with a contestatory space opening up which it was ever harder to control. Public opinion was emerging as a force to be reckoned with, and the different types of semi-official semi-permission provided a buffer between this new force and the censors, at the same time splitting the very principle of censorship into spheres of power, authority, and action which could now be considered separately. Whereas full official permission for a book entailed responsibility for it on the part of the censors, a *permission tacite* distributed anonymously by the *Bureau de Librairie* (the government office controlling the book trade) meant that if a public debate arose around a work, then the government could simply disown a particular censor, whose name was unknown to the public, and ban the book as one which had entered circulation without authorization.

In practice this anonymity was far from guaranteed, however, which was why the system of oral *permissions* came into being. The measure of personal responsibility attaching to individual censors was clearly something which weighed heavily on them: one censor complained, for example, that it was 'very unfair that people associate the censor with all the author's opinions' (cited by Cerf 1967: 17). A *permission tacite* was usually given to works which were obviously provocative because of their approach to conventional religion or morality, those which contained personal allusions, those dealing with recent history or politics, and those concerning foreign countries which might take offence if criticism of them were officially approved, but censors would sometimes give one to a work which did not risk being controversial but which they considered aesthetically mediocre and so not worthy of official approval. They would also frequently equivocate and leave an ultimate decision up to the minister, especially if, as was not uncommon, the author of a work managed to contact them personally and to contest their decision.

Despite all these developments in the system from the mid-seventeenth century and despite the peculiar flexibilities it comprised, the apparatus of censorship remained formidable. The risks were still great for publishers, writers, and others connected with the book trade: almost 1,000 spent a spell in prison between 1659 and 1789, and thousands of books met with prosecution. For this reason, many writers and printers chose to work just outside French borders. For all its flexibility, then, the censorship system was less than successful even in economic terms. Those who suffered most were doubtless, as Robert Darnton has argued, journeymen, lowly distributors, and so on, but those in high cultural circles were far from invulnerable: Diderot, for instance, was imprisoned for 102 days in 1749 after publishing his *Lettre sur les aveugles à l'usage de ceux qui voient* ('Letter on the Blind for Those who can See'), even though it was published anonymously, and even though he did his best to convince the authorities of his contrition and offered to give them the names of the printers and booksellers who had been involved.

There is no doubt that the vagaries of the censorship system left their mark on publications themselves. The division between the acceptable and the unacceptable continued to function as more than a cut-off point and actively affected not only the way books were read but also the way they were written. In the case of novels (which from 1737 to 1750, according to Georges May (1963: ch. 3), were officially prohibited altogether as a genre because of their immorality), this meant, for instance, that authors tended to frame their narratives with moralistic meta-narratives of the type one still finds, towards the end of the century, in many of Sade's works. It was also argued by Diderot in his *Lettre historique et politique sur le commerce de la librairie* ('Historical and Political Letter on the Book Trade') of 1763 that, if authors felt they were unlikely to measure up to official standards, then they wrote with complete abandon, seeing no reason to exercise self-restraint. Printers, too, had the opportunity to respond to the censor: in the case of the *Encyclopédie*, Le Breton, the work's main printer and seller, secretly rewrote or eliminated passages (mainly about Catholicism) in more than forty articles in the last ten volumes. Diderot discovered this for certain only in 1764, and was convinced that the articles were spoilt. It was also true, however, that material was often cut out by the writers of the *Encyclopédie* themselves before they submitted their work to the censors: according to one historian, the *encyclopédistes* were 'often their own most stringent censors' (Kafker 1964: 47 n.), and their wariness translated stylistically into their use of irony, allusiveness, and ambiguity. These devices represented another manner, in other words, in which censorship could act productively on reading, encouraging the writer and reader to meet in a subtextual space beyond the censor's reach yet given its shape by the latter's preoccupations. The *encyclopédistes'* hope was, of course, that this space would one day become public: as d'Alembert put it in a letter to Voltaire of 21 July 1757, in his comments on a contribution entitled 'Magie, magiciens et mages', 'We are simply asking your heretic's permission to be more circumspect in places where he has been a little too bold [. . .] In time people will distinguish what we actually think from what we have said' (in Voltaire 1971: 105–6).

The first edition of the *Encyclopédie* was eventually completed in 1772 only after it had been campaigned against by the *anti-philosophes* movement and by Jesuits, had been put on the *Index*, and had twice had its *privilège* revoked. In the end, however, it was one of the century's best sellers: according to Darnton, there were about 24,000 copies of it in circulation by 1789, of which perhaps 11,500 were in France. By the mid-1750s, the system of *privilèges* was working not to threaten but to protect the *Encyclopédie*'s publishers, and the publishing battles were not between the *encyclopédistes* and the censors but between different commercial concerns vying for a profitable market (Darnton 1983: ch. 6). Again, this may suggest a growing liberalism on the part of the censors, and may indicate that the influence of religious orthodoxy was diminishing, but it was also a sign of the Crown's increasing complicity with those who valued a thriving economy above all else. Publishing was still dominated by the corporation of élite master publishers, who had a financial stake in the system of *privilèges* since it helped them to drive smaller competitors out of business and to combat counterfeiters. This was not necessarily in the longer-term interests of the Crown, however, given the resentment it generated, and given that the master publishers tended also to have a stake in the shady market of *livres philosophiques*. This category included not only what we might consider philosophy, but also pornographic and political texts and images, many the aggressive, iconoclastic outpourings of unknown writers with no stake in the status quo. All of these seemingly reached a wide audience, and one perhaps ill equipped, on the whole, to distinguish between philosophy, fact, and fiction.

Though the looseness of the term *livres philosophiques* may initially have been a product of the censor's need to make crude binary distinctions between the acceptable and the unacceptable, the linking of politics, philosophy, and pornography was appealing for writers and readers of such works, too. It was in this period that, as Hunt argues, 'pornography developed democratic implications because of its association with print culture, with the new materialist philosophies of science and nature and with political attacks on the powers of the established régimes' (Hunt 1993: 43–4). This association was partly the result of substantive connections, but it was partly a matter of temporal coincidence. If this period saw a French pornographic tradition take shape which has placed pornography, as DeJean notes, 'at the intersection of sexual explicitness or obscenity and political dissidence' (in Hunt 1993: 121), this tradition has tended to betray what DeJean analyses as 'a desperate desire to define pornography as a force for the political subversion of the French tradition from within' (in Hunt 1993: 122), and to ignore the history of this coincidence *as* mere coincidence. The question of the place of pornography within democratic culture is one to which I will return later.

The appointment of censors had finally been set on a firmer footing in 1742 with the creation of the *corps des censeurs royaux*, which gave them a fully recognized place in the civil service and tried to take account of the difficulties they faced before the ever more daunting weight and variety of published material. Under the new system, a total of seventy-nine official positions were subdivided by specialization, thirty-five dealing with literature, ten with theology, ten with jurisprudence, one with marine jurisprudence, ten with medicine, natural history, and chemistry, two with surgery and anatomy, eight with mathematics, one with geography, navigation, and travel, one with painting, engraving, and sculpture, and one with architecture. By 1785 the total had increased to 183. The increase was not a sign of increased severity, however, so much as a reflection of the continuing growth of book production (and, beyond that, of literacy, which doubled in the eighteenth century (see Darnton 1983: 18)).

Although this list of censors seems exhaustive and is a sign that some sort of complete control of the printed word was still hoped for by the administrations of Louis XV and Louis XVI, its very diversity and its recognition of discrete categories of specialized knowledge were inevitably at odds with a traditional conception of a univocal moral code which could be imposed unreflectively from above. Indeed by its very nature this diversified system implied that politics was not limited to overtly political institutions and that political potentialities infused a whole spectrum of discourses and practices. This conception of knowledge and this analysis of the political process were also, of course, fundamental tenets of a certain Enlightenment vision of a population who, exposed to a whole panoply of ideas, opinions, and systems of knowledge competing freely for popular endorsement, would become capable of rational self-government, a vision which was fundamentally at odds with the traditional model of exemplary censorship.

Inconsistency on the part of the censors was therefore inevitable, and this was as much because of, as despite, any attempt to organize them into a rational system. The royal censors were in general relatively Enlightened men: indeed, thirteen of the fifty-two censors for literature in 1758, for instance, were also contributors to the *Encyclopédie*. Nevertheless the Church, even without statutory powers, continued to exert a considerable reactionary influence, and the Parliament too could still impose bans. If only out of sensitivity to these bodies of opinion, censors were inevitably somewhat conservative in their official role, whatever their personal convictions: in one report from towards the end of the century, a censor wrote that, 'As a reader, I enjoyed the work. But it is a question of publishing it as a censor' (cited by Cerf 1967: 19).

The royal censors' reports generally displayed a willingness—even a compulsion—on their part to justify their positions in a way previous occupants of their role had never done, nor been expected to do. Rather than mere thoroughness, it was at times a genuine excitement about the material in hand which seemed to motivate them to write reports several pages long; one censor, for instance, describing Mercier de la Rivière's *De l'instruction publique*, which argued for free schooling and for the establishment of a kind of civil catechism, noted approvingly that it was very philosophical ('tout philosophique') and concluded, 'It is soundly written and I think that a society in which men are governed according to these principles will come as near as is possible to happiness' (cited by Cerf 1967: 12). Conversely, there was disappointment if the material was merely inoffensive and was in no way instructive.

Goldgar has argued that attitudes such as these were the product of the substantial overlap of the activity of censorship with that of writers and critics who saw themselves as part of a republic of letters whose values they sought to uphold. A sizeable proportion of censors also worked for journals and revues, and it is not a matter of chance that the censors' reports were filled with the idioms of literary criticism and evaluation. Manuscripts were sometimes turned down solely on aesthetic grounds by men for whom evaluation, censure, and censorship (the latter both covered by the term *censure* in French) were closely related. In this context, one Abbé Geinoz, who worked both as a journalist for the *Journal des sçavans* and as a censor, could make his case to Malesherbes for a censor's pension on the grounds of his 'zeal for the censorship of books and for literature in general' (cited by Goldgar 1992: 104). For Geinoz and his colleagues, Goldgar concludes (1992: 104), 'censorship and literature were part of the same enterprise'.

The complexities of the censors' position are a powerful indication that one can easily take too simple (and perhaps too optimistic) a view both of the politics of Enlightenment and of the philosophy of the Revolution. Sade, for one, seemingly felt that Enlightenment *philosophie* and the agents of power spoke the same language (see Roger 1976: 203–4). On the one hand, Enlightenment writers clearly did represent a challenge to the old order in important respects, and the responsiveness of the censors to ideas promoting social change was indeed in conflict with the conservative basis of the system in which they worked. On the other hand, as Robert Darnton argues throughout *Bohème littéraire et révolution*, Enlightenment philosophy was past its heyday by 1789 (indeed, Voltaire, Rousseau, Diderot, Condillac, d'Alembert, and Mably all died between 1778 and 1785), and by the end of their lives many *philosophes*—such as those employed as censors—nad a significant investment in the *ancien régime*'s inequalities and idiosyncracies. Paradoxical as it may seem, Enlightenment thought flourished under the *ancien régime*, and, as I will show later in this section, the exchange of ideas and opinions which the freedom of expression was designed to protect and facilitate was arguably more vigorous in certain respects at the end of the old regime, before the right was declared, than at the beginning of the new one.

The Rhetoric of Freedom

The pre-revolutionary history of censorship in the age of printing, to summarize briefly what has gone before, saw a significant shift, as what I have termed exemplary censorship (which aimed for a perfect fit between its public discourse and its practice) was undermined by its own inherent contradictions and by social, economic, and ideological changes. Thus, whereas for a sixteenth-century censor any hint of doctrinal double standards was potentially an embarrassment, for a late-eighteenth-century censor multiple standards were the norm. For the latter, notably, the public and the private were split, and only in public discourse could heterodoxy not be admitted. This shift, in other words, was a shift in the material reality of censorship, over an extended period during which the discourse of censorship, though losing credibility, remained basically constant. The *Déclaration*, then, marked a break with the discourse of censorship of the *ancien régime*, (seemingly) embracing heterodoxy and instituting a powerful new discourse of freedom which has dominated the modern period, without ever fully displacing the earlier discourse. I now want to examine briefly the rhetoric used in the *Déclaration* before looking at censorship after 1789.

One feature of the original *Déclaration* which was to have a profound effect on the way in which it was subsequently interpreted was the inordinate faith it betrayed in the immediate power of its own legal formulations. The present tenses ('La libre communication des pensées et des opinions *est* un des droits les plus précieux de l'homme; tout citoyen *peut* donc parler, écrire, imprimer librement' (emphasis added)) facilitated a slip from a general statement about a right that was assumed to be essentially pre-given and universal, to a performative political utterance whose very articulation was assumed to guarantee its reality. This slip was not an avoidable ambiguity, however, nor a temporal event, but the condition of the non-transcendental, universal legitimacy which the *Déclaration* hoped to achieve.[2]

Hints of transcendence crept into the *Déclaration*, however, in the text's visionary rhetoric. The *Déclaration* presented itself as offering the hope of collective salvation by revealing, 'en présence et sous les auspices de l'Etre Suprême', rights which were deemed 'natural, inalienable and sacred': furthermore it was first printed in the format of a breviary, and prompted various commentaries which treated it as a catechism, such as Mirabeau's *Catéchisme de la Constitution* or Le Vasseur's *Catéchisme de la Liberté*. The religious vocabulary was chosen no doubt partly to appease the clergy, and partly to help win over a largely Catholic populace: but also partly because transcendent legitimacy seemed more persuasive than any non-transcendent type, and because a particular Christian framework of thought (summarized by Certeau (1978: 195) as 'messianic, evangelical and crusading') had been unconsciously inherited even by those Revolutionaries who favoured secularization.[3] In any case, leading figures of the Enlightenment

---

[2] Bennington argues (1985: 170) that the space in which any such legal utterance takes place is that of the *après-coup*, that of 'the narrative dimension of history which it [law] implicitly denies, on which it depends for its necessity, and which guarantees its insufficiency [. . .] The political is implicitly recognized to be a radically inconclusive realm.'

[3] The significance of this framework for contemporary understandings of the freedom of expression and of secularism is an issue I raise in my essay 'Freedom of

such as Voltaire quite consciously adopted a double standard as regards religion, considering it to have an important function in keeping the uneducated masses and even educated women in check. Enlightenment was an élite affair in certain respects, and in certain respects deliberately so.

Despite the persistence of a particular religious framework after the Revolution, opponents of the *Déclaration* who considered it, unsurprisingly, to mark too radical a break with the past expressed fears that the rights it affirmed in the abstract were not sufficiently securely anchored in actual social structures, and that the mass of French subjects would not measure up to the *Déclaration*'s vision.[4] Again, as Bennington points out, this tension is inbuilt: in his words, 'in order to understand the legislator's language and accept his wisdom, the people would *already* have to be what they can only become through the laws which the legislator formulates' (1985: 169). The position of the moderate Right at that time, as summed up by Jacques Marx in an essay on political opposition to the *Déclaration* (in Haarscher 1989: 35–55), was that to create something out of nothing in politics, rather than relying on the 'long-term accumulation of institutional experience, distilled in judicial precedents, institutions, and so on', was a dangerous gamble. There was a fairly widespread fear that rights instituted in the abstract would damage individuals' sense of their social responsibilities, and Jacques Marx argues that the notion of a 'natural politics' indeed laid the ground for the Terror in some way.

Nevertheless, subsequent debates have most frequently accepted the *Déclaration* on its own terms, sharing the latter's assumption

Expression: The Case of Blasphemy' (Harrison 1994). This essay deals with the uses of the discourse of freedom of expression made in connection with Godard's *Je vous salue, Marie*, Scorsese's *The Last Temptation of Christ*, and Rushdie's *The Satanic Verses* in the France of the 1980s.

[4] It seems that Freud, too, considered the changes which the Revolution sought to effect in this respect to be too abrupt. In *The Future of an Illusion* (1927) he imagines the following objection to his rationalism in the face of religion: 'have you learned nothing from history? Once before an attempt of this kind was made to substitute reason for religion, officially and in the grand manner. Surely you remember the French Revolution and Robespierre? And you must also remember how short-lived and miserably ineffectual the experiment was? The same experiment is being repeated in Russia at the present time, and we need not feel anxious as to its outcome. Do you not think we may take it for granted that men cannot do without religion?' (*SE*: xxi. 46). Though Freud presents these remarks as the point of view of an imaginary other, it is fairly clear he believed that the French and Russian revolutions were indeed chastening examples.

that the text itself was a sufficient precondition for rights such as freedom of expression to exist in reality, and failing to take into account significant material factors (of types I will discuss later) untouched by that particular legislation. Apocalyptic assessments of the contemporary state of affairs in this area, and nostalgic glances at earlier eras (or at the *Déclaration* itself), are symptomatic of this approach, as is any discourse on free expression, I would argue, which treats freedom of expression as something (ever) already achieved (though perhaps in need of a certain amount of protection), rather than as an imagined horizon to be worked towards. The rhetoric of freedom of expression, in other words, is necessary but insufficient to the freedom it describes. As Benjamin Constant (who did not draw out the full implications of his own words) put it in 1815,

All the constitutions which have been given to France guaranteed the liberty of the individual, and yet, under the rule of these constitutions, it has been constantly violated. The fact is that a simple declaration is not sufficient; you need positive safeguards. You need bodies sufficiently powerful to be able to employ, in favour of the oppressed, the means of defence sanctioned by the written law.[5] (1980: 408; 1988: 289)

The 'individual' protected by the *Déclaration* was implicitly of a certain type—primarily (and, in some instances, legally) male, upper or middle class, white and Christian—who was considered to be pre-equipped intellectually and politically to participate in society (which was necessarily seen, from the same perspective, as fundamentally static). The fact that women were initially excluded from this paradigm was made explicit in November 1789 when Louise de Kéralio, a writer and the daughter of a royal censor, wrote to the administration announcing her intention to open a new printing shop, and was refused royal approbation partly on the grounds that she was a woman (see Hesse 1991: 30–1). Perhaps the first, proto-feminist critique of the fact that the 'man' whose rights had been declared in the *Déclaration des droits de l'homme et du citoyen* really was male came in the shape of Olympe de Gouges's

---

[5] A similar point is made by Foucault in the following, more general terms: 'Liberty is a *practice* [. . .] The liberty of men is never assured by the institutions and laws that are intended to guarantee them. This is why almost all of these laws and institutions are quite capable of being turned around. Not because they are ambiguous, but simply because "liberty" is what must be exercised [. . .] I think it can never be inherent in the structure of things to guarantee the exercise of freedom. The guarantee of freedom is freedom' (1991: 245).

Déclaration des droits de la femme et de la citoyenne of 1791, where she bemoaned the fact that all that women seemed to have gained from the Revolution was the increased disdain with which they were treated by their newly 'liberated' menfolk. She also attempted to set out some of the specific female freedoms (concerning maternity, for instance) which the *Déclaration* in practice failed to guarantee, and claims to which its purported universalism worked to undermine. It is notable in this connection that the period from 1789 to 1792, as Norberg points out (in Hunt 1993: 243), saw the re-emergence of an old form of 'prostitute literature' (which may have functioned as pornography in the modern sense), namely almanacs listing prostitutes' addresses, prices, and specialities and, in a provocative instance of a masculine twist to the Revolution's rhetoric, describing these women as 'very active *citoyennes*' who 'know all the Rights of Man'.

(De)limiting the Freedom of Expression

However decisive the *Déclaration* may have been in instituting an enduring rhetoric of what it termed the right to the free communication of thoughts and ideas, it can be seen that beneath this discursive break there were substantial continuities in the practices of censorship, understood in a broad sense, and in social inequalities which served to undermine supposedly universal rights. The case of Louise de Kéralio is doubly instructive in this respect, since her plans were thwarted not only because she was a woman but also because it was argued that *liberté d'expression* did not necessarily extend to the freedom to acquire a print shop. This was symptomatic of the fact that many of the powerful players in pre-revolutionary publishing managed to hold on to their privileged position after 1789, and, through protecting their commercial interests, to exercise a form of censorship more restrictive, according to Restif de la Bretonne in 1789, than that of the royal censors (see Hesse 1991: 5–6). Furthermore this mechanism, as Hesse notes (p. 55), was deliberately used as a form of censorship by the government, which in 1790 solicited the services of the Paris Book Guild to monitor books and pamphlets arriving in the capital in order to identify and suppress counter-revolutionary material.

In some respects, the period immediately after the Revolution was nevertheless one in which freedom of expression was relatively far-reaching. Despite the continuing power of much of the old guard, many new publishers emerged on to the scene. About 300 new papers and journals appeared between July 1789 and July 1790, a good number of which, according to Darnton (1983: 41), were real newspapers, whereas in the 1770s the few periodicals available had carried very little news. This was perhaps above all a period, however, in which 'the liberation of disrespect knew no bounds', as Schama puts it (1989: 521), and there was a profusion of ephemeral literature of the type which described Marie-Antoinette's purported debauchery, for instance, a topic which was extremely popular both before and after the Revolution. Publications of this sort, which doubtless helped to dissipate the monarchy's sacred aura, were distinguished not only by their combination of politics, 'philosophy', and pornographic material but also, it should be noted, by the misogyny which this combination brought to the fore. Unsigned editions of *Justine* (which Sade publicly denied he had written) were also readily available at this time, and sold well.

Though the *Déclaration* no doubt helped to make all this possible, it is important to note that a year *before* the Revolution, in the summer of 1788, censorship was actually at a low point, political leaflets appearing at a rate of perhaps ten a day by September of that year, and that the first legal sanction of the abstract principle of press freedom came in a royal ruling of December 1788 (see Hesse 1991: 20). This signalled the beginning of what Schama has described as 'an unprecedented explosion of politics in speech, print, image and even music—that broke all the barriers that had traditionally circumscribed it' (1989: 859). From one perspective, the *Déclaration* could itself be seen as a *part* of this explosion, an instance of the sort of unbridled oratory (cf. Schama 1989: 532) with which successive waves of revolutionary politicians staked their claim to political legitimacy only to find that once they were in power such oratory made governance palpably more difficult, and that freedom of expression was hard to guarantee. So it was that as early as August 1789 the revolutionary government was proving at least as severe as the *ancien régime* in its actions against journeymen, news-stand holders, and the like, those associated most closely with the scurrilous popular literature which still felt subversive to those in power. Before long there was more overt political censorship, too: by August 1792 royalist pamphlets were being eliminated, their authors referred to as 'poisoners of public opinion' in the Commune's decree on the matter (cited in *Communications* 1967: 156), and things got worse under the Terror.

From Robespierre's execution in July 1794 until Bonaparte's seizure of power in 1799, liberalism and repression (especially of royalist and Jacobin pamphlets) alternated, although books generally escaped constraint. Book publishing for much of this period was far from healthy, however, struggling to find its way amidst administrative confusion and disrupted and changing markets. Hesse concludes, in her study of book publishing in Paris between 1789 and 1810 (see Hesse 1991: 241), that 'far from representing the commercial triumph of Enlightenment culture, the Revolution represented its undoing', and that 'the cultural complicity between market capitalism and cultural programme of the Enlightenment' which had held in the latter decades of the *ancien régime* collapsed after 1789. It is certainly clear that, as far as the Enlightenment ideal of freedom of expression was concerned, the Revolution proved less than a complete triumph. The rest of this section will give a brief account of areas in which pre-censorship persisted even after the Revolution, as successive governments sought to delimit (and limit) that freedom.

The constitution drawn up under the Consulate in 1799 did not mention the press, but this seems to have provoked little protest. This may have been because it was felt that the press's right to freedom was implicitly recognized, and it may have been, as Gabriel-Robinet suggests, that the French public's top political priority at this point was stability. Napoleon himself apparently saw the press as a great threat, and on reaching power remarked, 'If I give the press free rein I won't last three months in power [. . .] Freedom of the press? Absolutely not. They can't have it' (cited by Gabriel-Robinet 1965: 50). The number of papers authorized during Napoleon's years in power was to drop as low as four, and even these were closely monitored. Sade, meanwhile, had apparently sent Napoleon a deluxe copy of *Justine et Juliette*, but Napoleon reportedly threw it away (or, on other accounts, burnt it). Sade's books had been readily available from 1791 until 1797, though it was partly because of *Justine* that Sade was arrested in December 1793 and that the book's printer was executed in January 1794. Once Napoleon reached power, Sade's novels disappeared further underground, to resurface only in the twentieth century. Sade, who already had a monstrous reputation, had come under attack in August 1799 in the press by writers who stressed that *Justine* was widely read and claimed that in Paris a group of *débauchés* were using it as a sort of textbook, that it was undermining *les bonnes mœurs* of France as a whole, and that both Sade and his books deserved to be burnt (see Lély 1982: 534–7). These accusations, according to Roger (1976: 69), were to prove highly influential, and in March 1801 Sade was again arrested and was made a *prisonnier d'État*, which is to say that he was imprisoned without a trial. Some writers have suggested that Napoleon himself was behind this and that the falsely attributed *Zoloé* was the immediate cause, though Jean Tulard rejects this argument in his essay 'Sade et la censure sous le Premier Empire' (in Aix-en-Provence 1968: 209–15). However that may be, it seems that, unlike in previous cases, it *was* because of his obscene literature that Sade was imprisoned in this instance.

The level of repression of the printed word represented by Napoleon's measures was greeted with widespread resentment, which Napoleon sought to allay by bluffing, declaring via his paper *Le Moniteur* in 1805 that there was no censorship in France and that, in the paper's words, 'Freedom of thought is this century's foremost achievement: the emperor wishes it to be upheld' (cited by Garçon 1985: 202). Unconvincing as such a declaration must have been to his sceptical people, however, both the reference to 'freedom of thought' (*la liberté de pensée*) and the very fact that Napoleon's brand of censorship attempted to cover its tracks are indications of the extent to which the *Déclaration* had succeeded in redefining the discourse of government in this area.

It is fairly clear that in Napoleon's case the need to consolidate power was experienced as a stronger force than the post-revolutionary consciousness to which he paid lip-service. He did recognize that the disadvantages of official censorship included the way it made him ultimately responsible for the many foolish opinions which made their way into the press, and the way it gave inept clerks power over intellects greater than their own (see Goblot 1959: 57), but he continued to see publishing above all as a political weapon which was dangerous if it fell into the wrong hands. His remarks on these matters suggest that what he found difficult was not the principle of censorship so much as the delegation of power, and that he would have had few qualms about censorship if he could have done it all himself. The kind of control he wanted proved unattainable, however, a nation-wide homogeneity of criteria and their application as elusive as ever. Thus Madame de Staël's *De l'Allemagne*, for example, was pulped, and Madame de Staël exiled, only after the book had already been allowed to appear in expurgated form by the censors.

The nation's resentment of Napoleonic censorship was sufficiently manifest that, when Napoleon abdicated and a new constitutional charter was signed by Louis XVIII in 1814, it contained an article stating, 'The French have the right to print and to publish their opinions, within the bounds of the laws necessary to suppress abuses of this freedom' (cited by Garçon 1985: 203), and the Senate, in explaining Napoleon's exile, explicitly (and hypocritically) evoked his abuses of press freedom, alluding both to his censorship and to his propaganda. In spite of these declarations, Louis XVIII immediately imposed restrictions on newspapers. By this time Napoleon had seemingly decided that the price of censorship in terms of popular support was too high, and may also, as Gabriel-Robinet argues, have been genuinely won over to a more liberal position: later, in 1821, Napoleon remarked 'my son will be obliged to rule with freedom of the press. It is a necessity today' (cited by Gabriel-Robinet 1965: 56), and he quashed Louis XVIII's measures after he escaped from Elba and seized power briefly in 1815.

The inception of the second Restoration half-way through 1815 marked the beginning of a period which lasted until the establishment of the July Monarchy in 1830, during which the law regarding freedom of expression and the official commissions implementing it changed constantly. Innovations of this period included a measure introduced in 1819 which replaced the publisher's *déclaration préalable* (a 'prior declaration' which had been a legal requirement since 21 October 1814) with a system of financial deposits—a symptom of a growing tendency to trust in the market as a moral mediator; and the newspapers' new practice of printing blanks and dots to indicate censorship, which began in response to new censorship laws of 1820. This in turn was doubtless successful in irritating the censors, and is to be compared with a letter written to the Minister of Police in 1812 by a dramatist named Étienne, who called for sanctions against another dramatist in whose script characters who were discussing 'five or six individuals who oversee the opinions expressed in the papers' suddenly broke off their conversation with the words 'But shh . . .'. Étienne's objection to this was that, in his words, 'this expression and the dots after it require no interpretation, and the author's intention is quite clearly to draw attention to the authorities responsible for monitoring periodicals' (cited by Goblot 1959: 54). It was the allusion to censorship and the imitation of its methods, in other words, which Étienne found offensive, and which he wanted censored.

By the 1820s the idea of censorship was so unpopular that the names of censors were a closely kept secret. It was a topic which was fiercely debated throughout the period in the Parliament and elsewhere: Chateaubriand, for instance, produced a pamphlet in 1824—itself subjected to restrictions of advertising and distribution—entitled *De la censure que l'on vient d'établir* ('On the Censorship that has just been Established'). Chateaubriand was a resolute royalist and no political radical, and like many people of his day considered post-censorship a necessity, but he was profoundly opposed to pre-censorship, especially of the press. In his pamphlet he argued that a free press was necessary to guarantee that government was representative, and that if the press abused this freedom then only the judiciary had the authority to penalize it. He concluded by appropriating the metaphor of sickness, so often applied to the effect of censorable material on the health of the body politic, using it instead to suggest that it was freedom of expression and the rule of law which were the conditions of political health, and which censorship threatened to corrupt. In his words, 'Remedy is straightforward if the disease is treated early enough, but if you allow it to develop it becomes incurable' (1824: 47). Books also came under renewed scrutiny in this period: in November 1823, for instance, *Les Liaisons dangereuses* (which was published in 1782) was condemned to destruction by a Paris court for having helped cause the Revolution of 1789.

The chief parliamentary proponent of censorship at this time was Louis de Bonald, who became president of the censorship committee in 1827 and who argued that censorship was not a question of limiting freedom of thought, since the human mind was an inviolate refuge for it, nor even of attenuating freedom of speech and writing in the private domain, but rather of necessary controls over the public domain via restrictions on publishing. As Todorov explains it,

Starting with this premise, his reasoning took the form of a rigorous syllogism. The major premise was that public speech and writing were actions: to speak was to act; one does things with words. The minor premise was that no government, no society, could accord its subjects unlimited freedom of action; otherwise it would regress to the savage state of war of all against all. The conclusion: it was inconceivable for a reasonable government to make verbal actions, which were the most important in a civilized nation, an exception to the law that it applied to all public actions. (In Hollier 1989: 617)

What was dressed up as a right of the individual was, in Bonald's analysis, an exercise of power, which functioned to judge and by extension to influence developments in the public sphere—and, unlike the institutions of legislative, executive, and judiciary power, it was uncontrolled and unaccountable, since journalists and other writers were not elected or revocable. The 'opinions' protected by freedom of opinion, argued Bonald, were not 'just' ideas and either did or did not contain material harmful to the common good, and one had to have an enforceable hierarchy of values (Christian, for him) in order to distinguish between them—especially if, as he apparently presumed, humans were at base murderous and mutually antagonistic. He proceeded from this to maintain that prevention, as with a sickness or with any crime, was better than the sort of cure represented by post-publication prosecutions, particularly since the polymorphous forms of heresy, for example, made it difficult to give an advance legal definition of the crime. In this way writers would be saved from damage to their reputations and from incurring wasted publication expenses, and would be prevented from using the judiciary to achieve perverse publicity.

Bonald's principal opponent in these debates was Benjamin Constant, in whose view pre-censorship was both 'ineffective' and 'intolerable' (Constant 1980: 508; 1988: 322). Constant's argument hinged on a different construction of the public/private distinction which Bonald used to circumscribe the appropriate field of action of the individual, emphasizing instead the appropriate limits of State power. This alternative construction was built on his analysis of the minimal degree of direct political influence most people could hope to attain, which he contrasted with his vision of the ancient republics, whose small size meant that (those granted the status of) citizens could participate directly in affairs of State through interacting in the *agora*. In nineteenth-century France, Constant pointed out, such direct participation was no longer possible, not only because of the size of the modern state (to which books and the press offered a counterbalance, a modern version of the ancients' participatory freedom), but also because, relatedly, the French people's *mœurs* were more fluid and less homogenous, and could be judged only by public opinion.

Constant, like Bonald, endorsed a certain hierarchy of values, and agreed that defamation or calls to violence, for instance, should be subject to restraint. He felt, though, that free discussion had its own worth, imposing on interlocutors the calming recognition of a shared context which made exchange possible and in which certain tones, rather than certain opinions, damaged the acceptable level of discourse which the educated, at least, had an interest in protecting. In Constant's analysis the government, as well as the individual, benefited from a pluralist press and from publishing in general, not least in that the latter helped avoid the social volatility which had characterized the revolutionary period, when it was seen that a long-standing lack of press and publishing freedom had rendered the mass of French subjects 'ignorant and gullible' (Constant 1980: 476). Further considerations were that the government would lose all credibility if never open to contradiction and would effectively be made actively responsible for publications it had only passively endorsed (as earlier censors had found), that borders would have to be closed and spies posted throughout the land, and finally, again, that unwarranted perverse publicity—making the censored popular, or even making the worthwhile unpopular through its official sanction—could not be avoided.

Constant also argued that the moderns, unlike the ancients, tended to measure their freedom in terms of their *lack* of involvement with politics. This argument touched on a tension which existed even before the Revolution of 1789 in the thought of Enlightenment philosophers concerning the reasons why freedom of expression was a desirable goal in the first place. In an essay on the politics of the *philosophes* Coleman argues that the two main trends can be located in the attitudes of Voltaire and Rousseau respectively, Voltaire seeking 'to defend private individuals against the arbitrary power of the state' and maintaining that 'public opinion operates to limit the state's prestige and authority', whereas Rousseau sought 'to maximize the citizen's identification with the political association to which he has freely committed himself' (in Hollier 1989: 496). Once whole-heartedly committed to a political association, the citizen is, in Rousseau's view, forced to be free. In the years preceding the Revolution, as opposition to the *ancien régime* grew, this current of thought was made powerful by a context in which those who desired change were not central to the processes of government, and where an attitude of detachment bore no prospect of their empowerment. Once the *ancien régime* had been overthrown, however, the need for united action from the newly empowered class was generally less acute (though this varied through successive régimes) and a historical shift was set in progress such that a position closer to Voltaire's became the more common one. One indication of this move towards autonomy as the index of freedom and as the predominant purpose of anti-censorship law is the change from the *Déclaration*'s wording on this issue, with its participatory emphasis on 'la libre communi-cation des pensées et des opinions', to today's 'liberté d'expression', which is often interpreted to mean that individuals have an absolute right to express their opinions, or simply to express themselves, irrespective of the impact this will have on their society. Constant recognized, however, that this position carried certain dangers: in his words, 'The danger of modern liberty is that, absorbed in the enjoyment of our private independence, and in the pursuit of our particular interests, we should surrender too easily our right to share in political power' (1980: 512–13; 1988: 326).

In the end, particularly draconian measures imposed in 1830, which completely eliminated press freedom, were catalytic in the revolution of that year. The last two years of Charles X's reign had seen fierce polemics in the press against religion, priests, the army, and the king, and when ferocious police action was launched against the newspapers, journalists marched in protest to occupy the presses and to defend them from the government forces. Again, the *Déclaration*'s rhetoric provided an important conceptual rally-ing-point for various strands of opinion: the Charter of 1830 pro-claimed the French people's right to publish their opinions ('The French have the right to print and to publish their opinions, within the bounds of the law. Censorship will never again be established' (cited by Garçon 1985: 203), and one clandestine republican society of the early 1830s called itself the Société des Droits de l'Homme. As far as books were concerned, freedom of expression did take a major step forward in 1830, but newspapers continued until 1881 to be subjected to an ebb and flow of repressive measures (scarcely ever recognized as 'censorship' by the authorities), with brief periods of relative freedom after the changes of regime in 1848 and 1870. Repressive measures mostly took the form of economic hurdles—deposits, stamp duty, and so on—which prevented unwealthy undesirables from publishing,[6] but they also, particularly towards the end of the Second Republic and under the Second Empire, included more direct interventions such as seizures. Under the Third Republic too, by 1877, Republican papers were frequently being seized or denied distribution. Nevertheless, it was under the Third Republic that the law concerning freedom of the press reached something close to its present-day form, when it was decided that a clean break had to be made with the huge number of laws which had accumulated over the years. The law of 29 July 1881 started from the premiss that the printed word in general was (or should be) free, and that only offences under common law should be punishable in this area. The need for advance authorization and for deposits was dropped in favour of a simple declaration of the names of the paper's manager and printer, and the continued requirement of the *dépôt légal*. This system has in principle endured, with minor adjustments, until the present day.

Compromises, Exceptions, and Problems

Even since 1881 the principle and the practice of freedom have not always coincided. This is partly because there have been cases of pre-censorship, and partly because post-censorship too can obviously restrict freedom of expression; and partly because, more fundamentally, it can be unclear in some cases how successfully, or

---

[6] Another 'economic hurdle' was the price of newspapers, which was too high for most people to afford, even supposing they were literate. There were only about 70,000 newspaper subscribers in France at this time, out of a population of thirty-five million. In 1836, however, this situation began to change rapidly when Émile de Girardin founded *La Presse*, a subscription to which cost half the standard rate and which established the usual economic basis of the modern newspaper by relying on advertising as its main source of income. This strategy was an immediate success, and other papers quickly followed suit.

in what way, the principle and the practice of that freedom can be made to coincide. It is in this light that I will be looking more closely in the last two sections of Chapter 1 at the case of literature which has been considered *contraire aux bonnes mœurs* and also at 'pornography' in a broad sense, and their relationship to freedom of expression. I wish to end this section by indicating relatively briefly some other areas in which freedom of expression has been compromised or has been subject to restrictions which, for good reasons or for bad, have meant that that freedom has not been, and is not, absolute.

To take a first example, the theatre is an area of 'expression' where post-revolutionary legislation, though linked to broad movements of repression and liberalization regarding the printed word, evolved separately, and where censorship continued until 1906. Even in the immediate wake of the Revolution there was wide agreement that the theatre needed some sort of external control, a consensus that held throughout the nineteenth century.[7] Victor Hugo challenged this consensus in 1832 when his play *Le Roi s'amuse* was closed down after its first night for 'outrage aux bonnes mœurs' (though the real motive was probably political), but the government's lawyer argued successfully that the Charter of 1830 did not extend to the right to stage a play since the theatre was not used to express opinions. In the case of most shows this was probably largely true, and any appeal against censorship later in the century tended to be made in the name of 'la liberté industrielle' or 'la liberté d'entreprise' rather than 'la libre communication des pensées et des opinions'. On the other hand, even habitual opponents of censorship welcomed the actions of the Bureau des Théâtres when faced with the type of jingoistic and anti-Semitic plays which became common at around the time of the Dreyfus affair in the mid-1890s. Generally, regard for the theatre was fairly low, and the middle and upper classes were concerned about the way it gathered together a mass of people, many of them illiterate (and for whom the theatre was potentially an important source of information and instruction), and exposed them to visual as well as verbal stimuli, which were considered likely to bypass reason and to feed directly into antisocial passions. Conversely,

---

[7] I discuss this consensus in more detail in 'Colluding with the Censor: Theatre Censorship in France after the Revolution', *Romance Studies*, 25 (spring 1995), 7–25.

books, as is suggested by their relatively early freedom from prior restraint, were usually considered less intellectually accessible and so less dangerous than journals (or later, magazines), caricatures, and so on. The nineteenth-century publisher thus came to possess a degree of respectability which earlier printer–booksellers had lacked. By the same logic, the strongest political satires in drama appeared—at first sight surprisingly—at large, respectable, subsidized theatres such as the Théâtre Français and the Odéon, which attracted a primarily bourgeois audience; and the modern system of numbered places was introduced by law half-way through the century, so as to price seats out of the range of most people. It was hoped by many in authority that popular entertainment would, meanwhile, be rendered a harmless diversion: the *cafés-concerts*, for instance, were described by a minister under Napoleon III as '*maisons de tolérance* [a term usually used for brothels] which stupefy ordinary people [*le peuple*] and stop them from thinking about politics' (cited by Krakovitch 1985: 177).

For much of the nineteenth century, theatre censors worked to build a protective barrier around *les bonnes mœurs* in the sense of an entire bourgeois way of life, systematically eliminating representations of suicide or of cuckolded husbands, for instance, and allowing only married couples to address each other as *tu* on the stage. By the end of the century, however, the censors were somewhat more relaxed, and many shows clearly set out to explore the limits of the censors' tolerance and the effects that could be achieved (including the effect of popularity) by treading the line between the acceptable and the censorable. A ground-breaking show entitled *Le Coucher d'Yvette* ('Yvette Goes to Bed'), for instance, which was staged and given a visa in 1894, consisted of a woman taking off her overclothes, getting into bed, and blowing out a candle. According to Pierre Labracherie ('La Censure au théâtre', in *Crapouillot* 1963: 35–49), its audiences tended to be disappointed at how tame it was, but another theatre nevertheless decided to follow suit. The censor who saw this second version asked incredulously at the end, 'Is that it?', and when told that it was, refused to give it a visa, exclaiming, 'Well it's not enough, and it's excessive!' (*Ce n'est pas assez, et c'est trop!*) (cited in *Crapouillot* 1963: 44). In spite of—and because of—this refusal, this second show sparked off a whole series in which women removed their clothes, including *Le Bain d'Yvette* ('Yvette Takes a

Bath'), *Le Déshabillé de la Parisienne* ('A Parisian Lady Un-
dresses'), *Fais dodo, la môme* ('Beddy-byes, Baby'), and, in a
microvariation on the theme, *Le Lever d'Yvette* ('Yvette Gets Up').
All of this provides a resounding counter-example to the theory
that censorship promotes inventiveness and creativity.

Audiences rarely complained about the obscenity of the shows
they saw, and prosecutions consequently became more difficult.
The decision to end theatre censorship was finally less a matter of
principle than a reflection of the government's awareness of the
insufficiencies and absurdities of the censors' practice, and the *de
facto* absence of theatre censorship from 1906 was endorsed legis-
latively only in 1945. By this time the censors' paternalistic fears
had long since found an alternative, more pressing object of attention—and a perennial one—in the cinema. In 1909 the Minister of
the Interior banned a newsreel which showed four condemned men
being killed, and granted mayors a power of censorship. For these
purposes cinema was classified with *spectacles de curiosité* rather
than with the theatre, and until 1912 it comprised mainly infor-
mational films and short sketches. From the early 1910s longer film
stories about crime became increasingly common, and from the
start, disapproved of by most mayors, were banned in most places
outside Paris. The mayor of Paris, on the other hand, introduced
the first visa system in 1915. Bannings elsewhere proved so unpopular, however, that many mayors came to act more toler-
antly, and in 1916 the government decided to take the matter into
its own hands by establishing a central regulatory commission,
whose brief, according to decrees of 1945, 1956, and 1961, was to
detect films which were '*contraires aux bonnes mœurs* or liable to
have a harmful effect on public morality' (Long, Weil, and Braibant
1984: 483). The existence of the commission did not (and does not)
technically annul the right of mayors to censor locally, which they
may do either on the grounds that the projection of a film threatens
to engender 'serious disturbances' (*troubles sérieux*) in the form of
reactions hostile enough to lead to violence from a particular group
of people within the mayor's administrative area, or if it can be
shown that the film will be 'detrimental to public order'
(*préjudiciable à l'ordre public*) (Long, Weil, and Braibant 1984:
485). One paradoxical implication of this seems to be that pressure
groups who sanction violence as a reaction to a film which pro-
vokes them (or perhaps, more precisely, look as if they risk becom-

ing violent if the provocation continues) should stand a better chance of achieving their goals than do those who favour non-violence and rational argument. And while violence—like another great liberal anathema, book-burning—may not be a very sophisticated way of communicating an opinion and fails to create the shared context of discussion which Constant promoted as one of the great benefits of freedom of speech, there can be little doubt that it may serve as an intense and authentic method of self-expression.

What makes the threat of violence unacceptable in this instance is the idea of *ordre public*. *Ordre public* can suggest the entire social order, the very fabric of society, rather than the limits of behaviour that is acceptable in public, but there has been an attempt to separate out a more restricted notion of *ordre matériel et extérieur* for modern legal purposes. This process has been aided by (and related to) the increasing tendency to separate the idea of 'expression' from that of action. The former's impact on society has been considered less forceful as the latter has been reduced to more quantifiable categories, mainly physical or economic. One might see the origins of this separation in the Reformation, but, as late as the seventeenth century, speech and action were effectively inseparable, so that religious heresy was considered as bad as, if not worse than, a physical attack on the church, and political crimes were considered to constitute sedition, which was equivalent to treason. Religious and political misdemeanours were, in any case, hard to separate, since both were seen as attacks on the entire social order and the profound obligations which held it together. Even in Constant's and Bonald's debate in the nineteenth century it was agreed that expression and action should be classed together for legislative purposes, although the fact they needed to assert this explicitly was a sign that a significant shift in the conceptual field had by that time taken place.

This background of a restricted sense of *ordre public*, and of a concept of 'expression' which is basically separate from that order and is guaranteed as a right, does not mean, however, that the film commission and beyond that the government no longer make their moral positions felt. Legislation introduced in 1975, for instance, limited the number of cinemas allowed to show pornography and established a higher level of tax for pornographic films, after a process of deregulation had unleashed a wave of film pornography earlier that year—nine out of ten cinemas in Grenoble, for example, having given themselves over to pornography in the wake of the deregulation. The authorities explicitly disapprove of such films, in other words, but do not feel they have the right to use their moral criteria to trump others' rights to freedom of expression and consumption. It is as a compromise that they work to reduce the total output of pornography via stringent fiscal and financial regulations, such as those introduced in 1975—and without necessarily lowering their own 'immoral earnings'.[8] On a local level, however, a film's immorality is no longer considered sufficient grounds for a mayor to restrict it once the commission has decided that it is not immoral, and, though people have the right to voice their objections to such a film, their objections are not allowed to influence the judicial authorities (see Long, Weil, and Braibant 1984: 484–5). An exception to this can be made if it can be proved that there are special local circumstances, but when dealing with an idea such as immorality which strains towards the universal, such proof is hard to establish. A ban placed by the mayor of Nice on various films was annulled, for example, after the only local circumstance he invoked in justification of the ban was 'the wave of immorality which swept across Nice at the start of 1954' (cited by Long, Weil, and Braibant 1984: 486). The fact that this idea now sounds almost quaint indicates how rapidly public opinion on these matters has changed in the last forty years.

In other areas, too, moral issues have not been exempt from the attention of censors and would-be censors in the post-war period. An important development with regard to printed material was the law of 16 June 1949, which established a Commission de Surveillance et de Contrôle des Publications Destinées à l'Enfance et à l'Adolescence, a body appointed by the Ministry of the Interior to draw up lists of publications which should be restricted because unsuitable for minors. The magazine *Olympia*, for example, whose contents consisted mainly of extracts from books which had been or still were subject to indictments, was banned forever, three days after its first issue appeared in 1961. The fact that the books in question, which included *Lolita*, *The Story of O*, and *Tropic of Capricorn*, were published by the Olympia Press in English (both in

---

[8] This strategy is reminiscent of the Riancey Amendment, one of a series of measures of 1850 limiting press freedom, which aimed to restrict the success of popular and populist serialized novels by creating a special tax for papers and journals which published fictional writing.

complete form and in the magazine) suggested not only that the application of the law designed to protect (French) minors was being overextended—and, indeed, a subsequent decision by the Conseil d'État (a central administrative tribunal) interpreted it as covering all publications sold in sealed envelopes—but also that the commission's lack of accountability had left room for something of a vendetta against the Olympia Press (see Girodias 1966: introduction).

This decision was taken, it should be stressed, not by a court but directly, and prior to publication (though not prior to printing, of course), by the commission, to whom such publications have to be submitted in advance and whose brief is to check that publications intended for a youthful audience should contain, in the words of the legal text, 'no illustrations, no fictional or factual narratives, no articles and no inserts which cast a favourable light on crime, lying, theft, laziness, cowardice, hatred, debauchery or any act considered an offence or liable to demoralize minors or to create or foster racial prejudice' (cited by Garçon 1985: 203). Children, like women in earlier legislation, can be excepted from 'universal' rights without any sense of contradiction, since it is usually considered that they, especially while still in education (which means their separation from adults is reinforced by a public/private distinction), are incomplete individuals, still passing through their 'formative years' and yet to settle on a stable set of values which will be at once their own and those compatible with the well-being of society as a whole.[9] It was for this reason that a review of *Justine* written in 1792 advised the novel's potential readers, 'Young people, [. . .] flee from this book and its dangers to your emotional and sensual wellbeing. You, men of maturity whom experience and abated passions have put beyond any danger, read it and see how far a frenzied human imagination can go' (cited by Lély 1982: 547); and it is for this reason that the text guiding the commission does not feel a need to distinguish between actual crimes, such as theft, and behaviour which is less likely to entail legal proceedings, such as laziness or cowardice. Nine years after this commission was estab-

[9] While it might be objected that children, to take one category of individuals excluded from the freedom of expression, are inherently unable to participate in society as fully as adults, the line dividing children from adults must also, inherently, remain a subject of debate, and the law has drawn that line differently at different points in history and in different contexts.

lished, an ordinance of 1958 reiterated in more general terms the same restrictions, but stipulated that it was illegal to offer, give, or sell to minors *any* publication which represented a danger to them by promoting crime or by being licentious or pornographic, thereby providing administrative would-be censors with a back-door, extra-judicial way of placing restrictions on books which were not actually intended for children but which they considered offensive. This was the case of Guyotat's *Éden, Éden, Éden*, for instance, which I discuss further in the last section of Chapter 3, and also of efforts by the Socialists in the early 1980s to combat hard and child pornography—though, in the latter case, few objected to the abuse of the law which these efforts represented.

In the area of politics, too, the law of 1881 evidently did not put an end to all government censorship. Drastic curtailments of press freedom have occurred at times of war, including, most obviously, the two world wars, the French Vietnamese war and the Algerian war, but also more recently during the Gulf war, when President Mitterrand stated categorically that press freedom was no priority. This was the same Mitterrand who, as a presidential candidate in 1980, had declared 'all censorship of information will be abolished', and who in 1990 claimed the lack of governmental pressure on the media as a major success of his first term of office (Favier 1990: 198).

Wars are not the only case where, if 'state security' is at stake, the government is still capable of taking extra-judicial action. In 1987, for example, 60,000 copies of Laurent Gally's *L'Agent Noir*, a book containing information on the French intelligence services, were seized on the orders of the Interior and Defence Ministries, and the publishers (Éditions Robert Laffont) were told to cut twenty-four pages from the text. A total of 17,191 copies were subsequently burnt. In some cases, of course, such decisions may be taken in a grey area where different rights and duties clash—those of *discrétion personnelle* and *réserve*, to which civil servants submit, for instance, as against the exigencies of investigative journalism and the right to hold political opinions. Privacy law, likewise, could be seen as a necessity which is open to abuse, particularly in that privacy has come to be recognized as a right, and in that French courts have not adopted a ruling of the European Court of Human Rights stipulating that politicians' right to privacy is more

restricted than that of people not in public office. Similar ambiguities mark the special status of foreign publications, which were
classed separately in the Act of 1881 and in its amendement by a
decree of 6 May 1939, which gave the Minister of the Interior the
right to ban their distribution, circulation, and sale. This provision
was used during the Cold War against foreign communist journals,
and has been used more recently against hard-core pornography
and against anti-Semitic and 'revisionist' literature (Errera 1993:
62). The Conseil d'État ruled in 1954 that a foreign publication was
one which was 'materially and intellectually of foreign origin' (cited
by Article 19, 1989: 12), but this has in practice previously included
even journals published in French in France, when the proprietor
did not possess French citizenship.

Before returning in the next section to my central concerns regarding literary censorship, I want to make a few further points
about an issue I raised in connection with the revolutionary period,
namely the continuing significance for the freedom of expression of
the commercial conditions under which it is exercised. Particularly
since the Revolution, courts have often regarded the market as a
mediator of morality, on the assumption that socio-financial and
moral elevation are indissociable—or, on a slightly different interpretation, have tended to privilege the demands of the market
over those of morality. This tendency was alluded to earlier in
connection with the institution in 1819 of a system of financial
deposits for newspaper publishers, and the eventual abandonment
of that system in 1830 arguably made little actual difference to the
question of who was likely to publish a paper, in view of the capital
required to establish one. Marx, for one, criticized this aspect of the
French press as a form of 'material censorship' (Marx 1975b: 167),
in an essay of 1842 where he argued that 'to make freedom of the
press a class of freedom of the trades is to defend it in such a way
as to kill it with the defence [. . .] *The first freedom of the press
consists in not being a trade*' (Marx 1975b: 174–5). Indeed, the
commercial structure behind many contemporary papers is such
that their primary function is not to disseminate information or
opinions so much as to create, willy-nilly, a mass readership to 'sell'
to a lucrative advertising market. Even beyond this, we are, in
Jansen's analysis, in an era of 'information capitalism' in which the
very production of information or knowledge (as opposed to the

media through which it is made public) is frequently shaped by considerations of profit.

The economic structure of book production is clearly rather different, but the market has nevertheless been appealed to quite explicitly, on occasion, in the context of moral control. Baudelaire, for instance, defended his decision not to write a preface to *Les Fleurs du mal* (which would have set out his views on aesthetics and, from there, on morality in art) and to rely instead on the intelligence of his readers, by pointing out that the price of the published volume was high. As he put it, 'That's a significant safeguard in itself: it is clear that I am not writing for the masses [*la foule*]' (Baudelaire 1930: 326). At two francs, the cost of *Les Fleurs du mal* was equivalent to about a day's wages for an ordinary worker, and it was twice the price of *Madame Bovary*, for instance. Likewise, part of Pauvert's defence in the Sade trial consisted in emphasizing that the low number of copies he had produced of Sade's works and their consequently high cost meant that they were not available to most people, a line of argument encapsulated in Bataille's remark to the judge that 'what prompted most people to buy the Pauvert edition of Sade's works could not, in view of the price that they paid, have been the type of unhealthy curiosity which you are worried about, but the curiosity of the scholar [*une curiosité d'érudits*]' (in Pauvert 1963: 58).

The use of the market as a mitigated form of censorship can also be more active. This is the case of pornographic films, where the government's approach seems to imply that life should not be made easy (though it should not be made impossible) for those whose publications, films, and so on are of questionable moral or artistic worth, and whose naked economic interests can therefore be perceived. Conversely, the government is prepared, as it was keen to point out in its report of 1987 to the Human Rights Committee, to subsidize those whose motives are less worldly and who may consequently be too fragile to survive the rigours of the free market: its aid to the theatre is 'very considerable' (in Article 19 1989: 7), and specifically 'in order to encourage freedom of expression' it offers reduced postal rates and tax concessions to newspapers (see Article 19 1989: 5).

In contemporary France government intervention into the market has also taken place at a more fundamental level in (not enormously successful) attempts to tackle the question of the concentration of media ownership. This tendency emerged strongly after the First World War, and in 1944 a new ordinance, modifying the law of 1881, sought to arrest and even reverse the trend by stipulating that the ownership structure of a newspaper should be transparent to the public, and that any one person could own only one paper. This ordinance was never enforced, however, and after a period of relative stability media ownership began once again to concentrate in the 1970s, above all into the hands of former Nazi-collaborator Robert Hersant, who, between 1971 and 1978, acquired *Paris-Normandie*, *Le Figaro*, *L'Aurora*, and *France-Soir* (see Stone 1992: 173–208). By 1983, according to Article 19 (1989: 17–18), only seven large cities in France enjoyed true competition in the local press. Gradual concentration of ownership has taken place in the realm of book publishing, too, such that by the end of 1987 three major groups—Hachette-Matra, the Compagnie Européenne de Publications, and the Presses de la Cité (themselves controlled by other major concerns)—accounted for 80 per cent of the turnover of French publishing. In the broadcasting media, meanwhile, it was decided to end the government monopoly, and the first two private television stations came on air in 1985.

The mid-1980s saw a frenzy of debates concerning the best way to regulate these various processes of concentration and privatization. I do not have the space here to go into details, but, to end this section, I wish to use the example of those debates to make some points of more general relevance. First, it is notable that there was relatively little concern about the concentration of ownership in book publishing. Secondly, left- and right-wing politicians took the question of ownership in other media very seriously, and, unsurprisingly, agreed that television and newspapers had a profound (though not necessarily legitimate) influence on the public's political opinions. To a large extent, as far as newspapers were concerned, the immediate issue for the Left was to limit the influence of Hersant (and of his right-wing papers), whereas for the Right it was to defend Hersant's (and their own) interests, but the debate could not be conducted in these personal terms. Thirdly, then, it should be noted that the notion which centred and depersonalized the debate was that of pluralism. The sense in which this term could be used proved broad, not only with regard to newspaper publishing but also in the realm of audio-visual media, where, as the government (at that point dominated by the right-wing RPR party) explained in its report to the human rights committee, priority was supposedly given even in the private sector 'to the requirement of pluralism over that of free competition', and where there was an independent regulatory body, the Commission Nationale de la Communication et des Libertés (whose independence was doubted by many) designed to ensure 'freedom of communication, equality of treatment, free competition and the pluralist interests (protection of children and shedding lustre on the French language) [*sic*]' (cited by Article 19 1989: 6). The RPR argued that, in the case of newspapers, pluralism was protected by the indissoluble link between freedom of expression and private enterprise, by the absence of State intervention, and by strong media groups able to compete in a tough international market. The constitutional council was not entirely convinced by the RPR's arguments, however, and ruled in July 1986 that pluralism (understood in this instance as a non-concentration of ownership) was a constitutional principle which no government could weaken.

Finally, then, it should be noted on one hand that even RPR politicians, when it suited them, acknowledged that pluralism did not necessarily develop automatically from a 'free market'; and, on the other hand, that the idea of 'pluralism', though it provided terms for the debate, did not provide consensus. In some cases this may have been because the term was wilfully misapplied, but in others there were clearly genuine differences of opinion about what the term meant and how whatever it meant could be achieved. What is important about all this for my purposes is not only that there was wide agreement that freedom of expression does not necessarily look after itself, but also that there was wide disagreement concerning the point at which one should locate the shift between laying the ground rules of that freedom, and exercising it or allowing it to be exercised: and it may be wrong to think that one can ever arrive at a definite point where such a shift simply takes place.

There are various points which I wish to retain from this section's examination of the history of freedom of expression in France, and which will underpin, and resurface in, my argument henceforth. First, it should be noted that the clear lines of the rhetoric of freedom of expression make it easy to forget the muddled historical background of Enlightenment thought and administrative ambivalence from which the right grew, and which shaped the way it was subsequently understood. Secondly, it is clear that censorship has always acted 'productively' in some respects, helping create—partly deliberately, partly in spite of itself—a consensus on issues surrounding what is socially acceptable, and what is interesting. Thirdly, as numerous examples have shown, censorship (even in the narrow sense of pre-censorship) has continued as a practice since 1789, and moreover, despite the compelling rhetoric of freedom of expression, has in many cases been widely accepted. Fourthly, the right to freedom of expression was conceived of, and developed conceptually as, a means of protecting the individual (or certain individuals) from the State. Fifthly, the right in itself has not necessarily increased the freedom of those whose access to the means of expression has been limited by social inequalities linked to wealth, gender, and so on. Finally, it is clear not only that freedom of expression does not necessarily look after itself, but also that the rhetoric of freedom of expression cannot always point the direction in which greatest freedom lies.

JUDGING LITERATURE

In modern France, as we have seen, there have been two major paradigms of governmental censorship. The first is designed to facilitate the smooth running of affairs of State, both internal and external, and manifests itself in sporadic attempts to make use of remaining broad powers of suppression. The second is concerned essentially with morality and *les mœurs,* and involves limited interventions restricting the public's readiness of access to various media. It emphasizes the need to protect children from corrupting influences (including those that would tarnish the lustre of their language), pays closer attention to the visual than to the verbal, and, in the case of books, is more often carried out as post-censorship than as pre-censorship. This section will be concerned primarily with this type of moral censorship, and with the problems of authority raised by post-censorship in this area (as against the types of pre-censorship with which I was primarily concerned in the previous section). By examining the trials provoked by *Madame Bovary* under the Second Empire and by various works by Sade in

1956, I hope to gain an understanding of the changes in the capabilities and in the types of responsibility imputed to fiction-writers and their fiction; and, relatedly, of the ways in which fictional writing and literary culture more generally responded to the attentions of the censor, from whose overt interventions, in twentieth-century France, fiction has been increasingly exempt.

'*L'Art sans règle*'

At the beginning of the nineteenth century books were generally expensive. Piracy still formed a considerable part of the book trade, however, and counterfeit Belgian editions were available up to six times more cheaply than their official French counterparts. Writers, meanwhile, were finding ways of adapting to the end of patronage. For many novelists this meant allowing their work to appear in instalments in periodicals which reached a wider audience than did books, such as the *Revue des deux mondes*, founded in 1828, and its rival the *Revue de Paris*, which was founded in 1836. Balzac's *La Vieille Fille* of 1836 was the first novel to be published originally in daily instalments. By 1840, at a time when many of the journals were becoming increasingly political, this form of lucrative prepublication prevailed, and led to closer links between the financial and political interests of writers, on the one hand, and the press and its growing audience, on the other. One outcome of this was the Riancey Amendment (see n. 8 above), but writers soon found ways around this: Nerval's *Les Faux Saulniers* ('The Salt Smugglers'), for example, which appeared from October to December of that year in *Le National*, and which was enough of an adventure story to have been republished in 1986 by Larousse as a *classique junior*, was made acceptable by its sketchy historical setting, only rarely evoked after the first few paragraphs.

This special attention to periodicals and the like clearly came into play in the case of Flaubert's trial, too, when many felt that *Madame Bovary* was being used as a pretext to attack the *Revue de Paris*, and when the worries of the revue's editors that they were being watched by the censor became self-fulfilling. Before publishing *Madame Bovary* (whose subtitle, incidentally, was '*Mœurs de Province*') they asked that a total of sixty-nine passages be suppressed or altered, but Flaubert, who considered censorship to be 'monstrous, worse than homicide' (in Pottier and Berthet 1992:

18), initially refused to make any changes to his text. When he later capitulated over the scene in which Emma and Léon remain enclosed in a shuttered coach for many hours, (presumably) having sex, he asked that a note be inserted indicating this piece of pre-censorship to his readers. This note doubtless drew the attention of potential censors by suggesting the missing passage was explicit in a way it is not, although it must also be said that a nineteenth-century reader would have considered it relatively unproblematic to expand the text beyond its written limits according to shared presumptions and conventions concerning the appropriate demands of a writer's self-censorship, which made such extrapolations effectively part of the text. As Cellard argues in his essay 'Le Vicaire et la rabouilleuse' (The Curate and the Black Sheep), in which he discusses allusions to sex in *La Comédie humaine*, 'to assert that "it" is not there because it has not been said (or written) explicitly [. . .] is to react as a post-1960 reader and not as a reader would have reacted in 1830' (in BPI 1987: 144). This particular nineteenth-century reading convention was no doubt reinforced by another, whereby readers tended to assume all opinions expressed or implied in a book were those of the author. The origins of such a convention could perhaps be traced back in one direction to the tradition of Bible study, and in another to the historical links between literature and a largely polemical press which offered readily understandable and specifiable opinions whose moral and political thrust was plain to any reader. So it was that in this period, Bécourt argues, 'writing in general was viewed in the same light as newspapers and found itself burdened with a presumption which it took a long time to shake off, the presumption that it was necessarily expressing a particular opinion for which it was to be held accountable' (1961: 80).

The kinds of responsibility imputed to authors were also, of course, a product of the history of censorship itself, and Flaubert's heightened sense of his own authority over his text was characteristic of a certain post-Enlightenment phase of that history. Flaubert's attitude is illuminated by Foucault's claim that the modern author was first conceived of as an individual property owner, a conception already to be found in Diderot's *Lettre historique et politique sur le commerce de la librairie* of 1763, for instance, and whose political implications altered as the *ancien régime*'s rhetoric of absolute authority and the related publishing monopoly crumbled. In this connection, it is striking that in 1790 Condorcet revived a pamphlet, *Fragments sur la liberté de la presse* of 1776, which, as Hesse notes,

had originally circulated as a radical indictment of the inquisitorial institutions of the Old Regime, now to serve as a conservative check on the flood of ideas unleashed by the collapse of those very institutions by proposing a law that would hold authors, publishers and printers legally accountable for their publications. [. . .] The first revolutionary attempt [unsuccessful, as it turned out] to give legal recognition to the author's claim on the text, then, was *not* a granting of freedom to the author, but the imposition of accountability and responsibility. (Hesse 1991: 106–7)

Flaubert's note indicating the absence of the coach scene was already provocative, but this provocation was redoubled when, in reaction to the *Revue de Paris*'s eventual suppression of various other passages without his permission, he put together a small anthology of other potentially provocative words and phrases from works which had already appeared in the journal, including work by one of its editors, Du Camp, and sent it to a journalist who duly published an article on the subject. In this moment of petulance Flaubert's approach to literature was one which he generally considered superficial, as we know from a letter he wrote to another of the *Revue*'s editors in which he remarked, 'You are attacking details, but it is the book as a whole which you need to take on. The element of brutality lies deep within it, not on its surface' (cited in BPI 1987: 161). However, it was an approach which, offering the hope of isolating the book's offensive elements, held an obvious appeal for those who wished to prosecute it.

These remarks also make it clear that Flaubert himself saw his book as one which the censors *ought* to find threatening, quite apart from the contingencies of its publication in the *Revue de Paris*. Various characteristics of the book itself, such as the mobility of its narrative voice or its ironic use of quotation, could be seen as ways in which an awareness of and antagonism to censorship and censorious reading practices were woven into the very fabric of the text, frustrating the censor's desire for non-fictional writing and for an identifiable, responsible subject behind it. Thanks to the way in which it was written as well as the way it was published, then, the work was doubly politicized in the context of the trial, on one level as an apparently amoral form of representation of a type promoted and brought into wide circulation by certain journals, and on another in relation to its author as a representative subject who failed in some way to show sufficient respect for his civic duties. To some extent the speeches of the prosecution and defence counsels, Pinard and Sénard, split on to these two levels, the former emphasizing that, in reading the book, one simply could not tell, in his words, 'what is in the author's conscience' (*ce que pense la conscience de l'auteur*) (in Flaubert 1971: 380), while the latter, before holding forth on the basically moral character of the story, stressed that Flaubert's father was a highly respected doctor and that Flaubert himself had put in a lot of good hard work to write the book. The failure of the two levels to coincide was clearly disconcerting to the judge, whose confusion was seen in the way he acquitted Flaubert only after concurring almost entirely, in his summing-up, with Pinard's arguments.

In other cases since 1831 a precedent had been followed which allowed a court to examine other works by an author, in order to establish the author's intentions—a strategy which again presupposed the identity it set out to discover—but this was not applicable in Flaubert's case, since *Madame Bovary* was his first major work. So it was that Flaubert, who had so carefully fragmented and dispersed himself in the body of his text, was reassembled by Sénard and identified as the respectable, predictable bourgeois individual to whom sound intentions could be attributed; and it was no doubt partly due to the success of this strategy that Flaubert, backed by his family connections, was acquitted. Conversely, Pinard adopted different tactics in this area in Baudelaire's trial, carefully separating the man (with his undoubted talents) from the work (with its pernicious effects), and also tapping into the popular image of the artist as someone who *was* inconsistent and who produced work which inevitably betrayed this.

The judge's confusion in the *Madame Bovary* trial was one sign of the developing crisis in the self-confidence of the censoring authorities with regard to the foundations of their own criteria of evaluation. Another aspect of this crisis was seen in Pinard's attempts to launch an attack on *Madame Bovary* on specifically aesthetic grounds, to back up his feeling that *proper* art would not display such indifference when faced with the kind of immorality to which Emma Bovary was prone. From this point of view the book's crime seems to have been realism, and Pinard concluded his speech thus:

[Christian] morality stigmatizes realist literature not because it portrays [*peint*] human passions—hatred, revenge, love, these are the things which make the world turn, and art must portray them—but when it portrays them unbridled and with no sense of moderation. Art without rules is no longer art: it is like a woman ready to take all her clothes off [*L'art sans règle n'est plus l'art; c'est comme une femme qui quitterait tout vêtement*].[10] Obliging art simply to respect the rules of public decency is not to enslave it but to honour it. It is only thanks to rules that one grows in stature. Those, gentlemen, are the principles which I hold, and they form a doctrine which I can defend in good conscience. (In Flaubert 1971: 381)

Furthermore, the judge agreed that unbounded replication of the world's vices would lead to 'a realism which would be the negation of beauty and goodness' (in Flaubert 1971: 428). In the Baudelaire trial, too, Pinard stigmatized Baudelaire's aim as being to cut through the 'artificial rules' of traditional art and, in Pinard's words, 'to portray everything, to lay everything bare' (*de tout peindre, de tout mettre à nu*) (in Baudelaire 1930: 331). From here, however, he went on, not to criticize Baudelaire's purported aims, nor to contest the aesthetic theory he had just described—a theory to whose ascendancy he was clearly quite sensitive, no doubt particularly after his defeat in the *Madame Bovary* trial—but to argue that it was not the judge's job to be a literary critic, and that all that mattered was the effect which Baudelaire's poems had or might have.

The fact that one critic of Baudelaire could attempt to vilify him by associating him with 'the bohemian realist press' (in Baudelaire 1930: 319) makes it clear that the idea of realism had a broader application at this point (when it was a relatively new and unstable term in literary criticism) than it does today, and that it was understood to signal a field of moral as well as aesthetic change and antagonism—though this signal was an ambiguous one, as the trials attest. Baudelaire was, unsurprisingly, horrified to be thought of as a realist, but the term had evidently taken on a general pejorative force for someone such as Pinard. What exactly Pinard found offensive about 'realism' is not always clear, however. In some

[10] Pinard's arguments, including this disconcerting analogy, are discussed again in my 'Conclusion: *Tout dire*'.

instances, such as Flaubert's description of the intertwining of Emma's and the Viscount's legs as they danced at the ball, the reasons why certain passages met with opposition are not hard to guess. Pinard quoted extensively from the book during the trial, drawing attention to the sensuousness of Flaubert's descriptions of adultery and even of Emma's extreme unction, descriptions which thereby offended, Pinard argued, both public morality and religious morality. To the latter charge Sénard was able to respond that Flaubert's descriptive enumeration of Emma's sensory organs and their sins was based on a religious text written by a priest in 1851: and clearly it was impossible for Pinard to refute this, though his feeling that Flaubert's text was somehow seductive (in a way the priest's was not) is one that many modern readers doubtless share.

In other instances, though, it is very difficult to understand today what was found objectionable about Flaubert's writing. For example, the *Revue* was not happy with the words 'a piece of veal cooked in the oven' (*un morceau de veau cuit au four*) in the following passage: 'To spare him expense, each week his mother sent him by the carrier a piece of veal cooked in the oven; and on this he lunched when he returned from the hospital in the morning, drumming his feet against the wall as he ate' (cited by Gribinski, in BPI 1987: 162; Flaubert 1950: 22): The *Revue*'s editors, like Pinard, made some attempt to justify their misgivings aesthetically, saying that the scenes of the agricultural show and club foot, for instance, were 'too long' and 'pointless' (*inutile*) (cited in BPI 1987: 166), but, as the word *inutile* might suggest, these aesthetic considerations were again more than just matters of taste and of what Flaubert explained to himself as the bourgeoisie's inherent antipathy to style. Fully to understand what made sixty-nine particular passages unacceptable to the *Revue* is an impossible task, but some insight into the basis of their objections is gained from Bennington's account of the way in which, until the nineteenth century, it was a novel's maxims which justified and controlled the novelistic illusion, whereas in the nineteenth century the illusionistic side tended to be privileged. The problem with the piece of veal, perhaps, was that it *made no sense*,[11] and that the profusion of such 'useless' details in *Madame Bovary* submerged any axiomatic truths

[11] Leclerc argues that the veal is one of a series of bovine images running through *Madame Bovary*. Even if this explains why Flaubert was unwilling to abandon this phrase, it does not explain why the editors of the *Revue* found it offensive.

which it might 'otherwise' have offered up. What Pinard found most frustrating was that he could perceive no stable standards within the novel by which to judge it, and in this respect he, with his comment on the inscrutability of 'the author's conscience', was a more subtle reader than Sénard, who contrived to summarize the work's message by saying it 'incited its readers to virtue through the horrors of vice' (in Flaubert 1971: 381)—though admittedly the former's remark was a complaint, and the latter's perhaps more strategic than sincere. If Sénard's purposes at this point were indeed strategic, however, his somewhat unsettling turn of phrase (in French, 'l'excitation à la vertu par l'horreur du vice') was perhaps a mistake, particularly in view of the sexual connotations of *excitation*. Pinard also argued that the novel gave no grounds for condemning Emma in the name of conjugal honour (given Charles's stupidity and lack of pride), nor in the name of public opinion (represented by Homais, 'a grotesque creature' (in Flaubert 1971: 380)), nor in the name of religion (represented by the equally grotesque Bournisien); and for this reason, he suggested, one had to go outside the novel in order to condemn it in the name of Christian morality.

Despite this conclusion, it is significant that Pinard allowed the possibility that moral standards might have been found *within* the novel, and this, along with his tendency to use visual images to describe the process of representation (a tendency he shared with Sénard, who talked of 'an altogether daguerrean accuracy' in Flaubert's descriptions (in Flaubert 1971: 387), and also with Sade, amongst others), implies an acceptance on some level of the realist premiss that art's task is to imitate reality as faithfully as possible. Behind this, in Pinard's case, lies a hope that the values he seeks to uphold will emerge as if of their own accord, and as if immanent in the world. He consequently also criticizes the book, seemingly in contradiction to his attack on realism, for its failure to respect its obligations towards reality, asking the court, 'Is it natural that a young girl should invent small sins [to confess], when we all know that for a child it is the smallest sins which are the most difficult to admit to?' (in Flaubert 1971: 368).

What smooths over this contradiction, and what is being invoked through the words 'natural' (*naturel*) and 'we all know that' (*on sait que*) is the idea of *vraisemblance* (plausibility, verisimilitude) whose standards overlie a world vision which passes for an unquestionable reality to the extent that the *vraisemblable* passes for the probable. It is also closely linked to the idea of *bienséance* ((literary) propriety), which the Robert dictionary defines as 'that which is acceptable, which conforms with the rule' (*ce qui convient, ce qui est conforme à la règle*)—the point of contact being the rule, which denotes both that which is normally done and that which is obligatory. The effect of Flaubert's irony is to prise the two apart, thereby undermining the basis of any assessment according to the criteria of *vraisemblance*, and the models for the comprehension of human behaviour which it provides and on which both realist narratives and legal proceedings rest. This split, in other words, coincides with that of the author from the work, to the extent that Flaubert's behaviour, in writing a book which seemed amoral to Pinard and the judge, appeared inconsistent with his status as a bourgeois. Similarly in the Sade trial, Maurice Garçon, the defence counsel for Pauvert, attempted to turn the same line of thought to his advantage: on one the hand, by arguing in his speech that the reputation for sadism of Sade as an individual was overblown, and tended (or so he implied) to distort the reception of his writing; and, on the other hand, by attempting to rehabilitate him as something of a revolutionary hero and a lover of freedom, in order to reflect some revolutionary glory on to his work.

The law under which *Madame Bovary* was prosecuted was that of 17 May 1819, which remained in force until 1881 and which aimed to suppress the exhibition, distribution, or sale of any printed matter which constituted an 'outrage à la morale publique et religieuse et aux bonnes mœurs'. Under the First Empire the legislation for the equivalent offence had made no mention of religion and emphasized the sale and display of the offensive material rather than its immorality *per se*, thus making the issue a secular one of *trouble social* (social disturbance). This development was reversed, however, under the Restoration, and at the time of Flaubert's trial in 1857, the law of 1819 was applied once again by *tribunaux correctionnels* (courts without juries), whereas for a time under Louis XVIII and again under Louis-Philippe it had been within the domain of the juries of the *cour d'assises*. The apparent advantage of a jury was that it encapsulated public opinion and so, on one interpretation, provided (pragmatically) a means of settling or circumventing vexed questions of precise legal definition and distinction, while, on another, more radical, interpretation, it was (as a representation of public opinion) the grounding instance of secular morality. The idea that everyone has equal moral authority, however, means that no one has moral authority in the sense in which it was once (or could once have been) understood, and the changes in the letter and application of the law in this area during the nineteenth century could be seen as indications of a crisis of moral authority faced by the society as a whole.

Though the apparent conflict between the judge's concluding remarks in the *Madame Bovary* trial and his verdict may be one sign of this crisis, it was doubtless experienced most consciously not by the judges but by the judged. Most of the writers who were tried during the nineteenth century (of whom there were twenty-four in all, the majority of them tried for offences to *les bonnes mœurs*) seemingly felt scant respect for the courts which tried them and for the justice they supposedly represented. A typical attitude was that of the Naturalist writer Desprez who, accused of *outrage aux bonnes mœurs* in 1884, remarked that the only jury with the competence and authority to judge him would be one composed entirely of 'major figures of contemporary literature' (cited by Leclerc 1991: 126). This, of course, was to miss the whole point of a jury; but, from Desprez's perspective, a jury was liable to miss the whole point of literature. With such attitudes, writers also had little interest in asserting in the public arena their own moral authority, preferring where possible to pull strings behind the scenes in order to escape punishment. Flaubert, for one, made good use of his family connections, which indubitably influenced the outcome of his trial, while Baudelaire (who was from a less privileged background) managed to get his fine reduced from 300 francs to 50 by writing to the Empress. In other cases, such as those of Barbey d'Aurevilly's *Les Diaboliques* in 1874 and of Maupassant's poem 'Une fille' in 1879, proceedings were quickly dismissed once some extra-judicial wangling had taken place. In d'Aurevilly's case this included the undertaking not to publish any more copies of the book, a promise he broke once the law of 1881 had been passed. D'Aurevilly in particular made it clear that what offended him was less the fact of being accused (of *outrage à la morale publique*) than the prospect of having to defend himself in the public gaze. To one of the high-placed friends whom he asked to pull some strings, for instance, he remarked, 'The idea of being sentenced does not bother me, but the idea of being paraded before a court makes me want to vomit' (cited by Hamelin 1956: 65). Flaubert's attitude was not dissimilar, and he expressed disgust at the idea of having to sit in a dock which at other times was occupied by 'pederasts' and thieves. It was perhaps for this reason that he hesitated for a long time to publish the proceedings of the trial, eventually allowing them to be appended to an edition of *Madame Bovary* in 1873.

Although the examples of d'Aurevilly, Flaubert, and even Baudelaire may suggest that the authority of the courts was being undermined primarily by continued autocratic privilege amongst certain classes and by the mentality it inspired more widely, the situation was more complicated than this, and the structure of fragmented moral authority more convoluted than this analysis would imply. It is notable, for instance, that, although d'Aurevilly was charged with moral offences, and although the ecclesiastical authorities disapproved of his work, and although it was seemingly the conservative press which alerted the authorities to *Les Diaboliques* in the first place, d'Aurevilly was himself very conservative, a practising Catholic who apparently saw the stories which made up *Les Diaboliques*—based on true stories (or, in one case, a folk tale) of people who had given into sin, in his terms—as profoundly moral and as an endorsement of Catholicism.[12] As in Flaubert's case, then, different aspects of the defendant's behaviour and background failed to converge, and this problem again became acute in relation to his artistic practice and its relation to morality. With greater conviction (or hypocrisy) than Flaubert, d'Aurevilly maintained that his writing was inherently moral, arguing (in the familiar terms of a metaphor of painting), 'powerful artists can portray everything [*les peintres puissants peuvent tout peindre*] and [. . .] their art is always quite moral when it is tragic and inspires horror of the things it depicts' (cited by Hamelin 1956: 61). Thus, although he spoke out elsewhere against the realist school, it was in

---

[12] Another instance of an ambiguous use of religious vocabulary, the *Enfer* of the Bibliothèque Nationale, was conceived of towards the end of the Second Empire, some time between 1867 and 1870, and put in place in 1874. The *Enfer* was a collection of books considered unsuitable for general consumption, set aside—not particularly systematically—mainly on the grounds of their obscenity. The last addition to the collection was made in 1972. Access to this collection was never very strictly controlled, and, given that it contained rare books which would have been quite difficult to obtain elsewhere, and that, importantly, it preserved books which many would have considered unworthy of preservation and would perhaps even have wished to see burnt, the passage into this particular 'hell' represented at once condemnation and salvation.

terms of a direct relation to the real that he defended his work—
though, again, he had to assume that the real world he described
was one in which evil never prospered.

Maupassant's case was somewhat different. He was not concerned with morality in any straightforward sense, and the journal
in which 'Une fille' had been published, the *Revue moderne et
naturaliste*, clearly saw itself as provocative, proclaiming its contributors to be united by their hatred of the conventional in art and
in literature. Maupassant declared himself ready to defend himself
'fanatically', but explained that this was not for his own sake—'I
couldn't give a damn about my civil rights', he remarked—but for
the sake of his poem (in Hamelin 1956: 92). It is unclear from this
what he considered his rights to be, but the implication is that, even
if the freedom of expression could have been considered relevant,
technically, his own feeling was that his poem was situated elsewhere, lacking any essential connection to the (political and moral)
realm in which such rights operated (as he put it in his introduction
to the Flaubert–Sand correspondence, 'the social order and literature have nothing in common' (1884, cited by Leclerc 1991: 35))
and lacking even a significant relationship to him himself. To
Flaubert, whose help he sought in defending 'Une fille', he expressed his attitude to morality in art in the remark, 'artistic morality is simply Beauty' (*la moralité artistique n'est que le Beau*) (cited
by Hamelin 1956: 93). This was self-consciously close to the attitude of Flaubert himself, who wrote, in his letter of support for
Maupassant 'What is beautiful is moral, that's all there is to say
[. . .] Poetry, like the sun, makes manure shine gold. It's just too bad
if some people cannot see it' (cited by Hamelin 1956: 97). Both of
them were seemingly most interested in Beauty, however, and perhaps secondarily in manure, and in morality after that, if at all; and
Flaubert no doubt felt confirmed in his belief that art and not moral
posturing provided the only way of rising above the manure when
he discovered in 1877 that Pinard was secretly an author of obscene
verse.

The fact that Maupassant turned to Flaubert is itself interesting
in terms of the structure of moral authority, quite apart from any
question of intellectual parentage. The idea of asking Flaubert for
help was suggested to Maupassant by his lawyer, who was convinced that a letter in support of Maupassant from Flaubert, published in the newspaper, would put an end to the affair. In writing

to Flaubert to make his request, Maupassant explained that Flaubert's support would be especially valuable in helping him to keep his post in a government ministry, since the case would take on a more general interest and his boss would not punish him, for fear of falling foul of the press. Flaubert himself, worried about irritating the judge in advance, was actually unconvinced by the idea, but he wrote the letter as requested and it was published in the *Gaulois* on 21 February 1880, under the title 'Gustave Flaubert and Literary Trials'. Perhaps coincidentally—Flaubert and Maupassant thought otherwise—that same day the public prosecutor decided to dismiss the case.

Compared with the authority of the friends in high places to whom d'Aurevilly and Flaubert turned, the type of authority invested in Flaubert's letter was a complicated matter. Though the charges against Maupassant concerned morality, Flaubert's opinion carried weight by virtue not of his moral but of his artistic standing. Furthermore, the authoritative weight of the letter he wrote depended on the fact that Flaubert had no *a priori* connection with the judicial system or even with the press, and that the letter was (or played at being) a private one, even though it could have an effect only by becoming public. Becoming public in the press meant that in some sense the letter became an expression of public opinion, though Flaubert's ready access to the press depended precisely on the fact that he was a somebody and not any old member of the public. His letter, in other words, pretended to express the point of view of a neutral, private individual (with a high literary reputation), and this lent it a kind of Olympian authority with respect to (supposedly) collective, public, moral commitments.

Sade *and* les mœurs

In the Sade trial, too, there was evidence of the tensions and contradictions seen in these nineteenth-century trials with regard to the relation of public opinion to morality, literature, and the realm of politics, and with regard to the role of the court in negotiating the difficulties to which these tensions gave rise. Pauvert's defence lawyer Garçon, for instance, placed great emphasis on the role of the jury in dealing with offences to *les bonnes mœurs*, referring to them on more than one occasion as the 'natural judges' in this area (e.g. in Pauvert 1963: 25). This emphasis must be understood partly in the context of his strategy of attacking the Commission du Livre, an extra-judicial body branded by Pauvert 'a secret society' (in Pauvert 1963: 136) which was established on 29 July 1939 under the *Décret-loi Daladier*, a statutory order which gave the government renewed power to deal with offences to *les bonnes mœurs*. The Commission was designed as a means of giving a privileged level of protection to books (as opposed to periodicals, etc.), its opinion a prerequisite for any governmental prosecution. In the Sade case, Garçon attempted to convince the court that the whole prosecution was ill-founded due to the laxity of the Commission's operation, arguing that this made it unjust that its opinions were so influential, and added—rather surprisingly, at least from a tactical point of view—that these opinions were, moreover, approximately thirty years out of date because the commission was made up of late-middle-aged men who had been set in their ways since the age of 20 and who, in his words, 'arrogantly crush anything new in the name of their supposed experience, which in fact is nothing more than the disheartening bluster of men who have reached a mature age and no longer open their minds to new ideas' (in Pauvert 1963: 32–3).[13] All this he contrasted with the extreme efficacy (and relative youthfulness) of juries, and he drew the following lesson from history:

for one hundred and fifty years, except for the two interruptions from 1822 to 1830 and from 1851 to 1871, juries were the sole arbiters of social mores [*les mœurs*] and no one would dare claim, I imagine, that as a result French literature sank into pornography or that moral depravity [*la dépravation des mœurs*] was encouraged. Juries condemned that which was truly an affront to their moral conscience and this did not mean that the country fell into licentious ways [*la licence*]. (In Pauvert 1963: 26)

Though at moments the way in which Garçon presented this argument suggested that he was hoping to achieve an acquittal for Pauvert merely on the basis of a technicality (that is to say, the failure of the Commission to fulfil its decreed role), the positions he adopted fitted into a wider framework. He insisted on the idea of juries as the *natural* judges of moral issues, a use of the term connected to Pinard's 'Is it natural that a young girl should invent

[13] Though Garçon initially spoke of the commissioners' being 'thirty years out of date', he was haggled down to fifteen years by the judge, who complained, 'you are making my colleagues old before their time, by saying they are older than they really are'. Garçon retorted that even fifteen years was a lot, 'when you think of how quickly moral standards [*les mœurs*] often evolve' (in Pauvert 1963: 32–4).

small sins?' in that it tapped into the same discourse in which moral values were presented as ultimately inherent in the world and its inhabitants; and he also referred explicitly to 'a sort of natural law' (in Pauvert 1963: 19) which meant that certain acts were almost universally regarded as immoral. This view clearly acted as an alternative, or a counterbalance, to the moral position which allies traditional Christian doctrine according to which humans are fundamentally immoral, with a conservative political position which perceives in the process of social change the erosion of a generalized Christian morality which has been built up and inculcated in the masses over the centuries in order to protect them from themselves. The presiding judge, for instance, referred to the offending passages of Sade as destroying 'what remains of social morality' (in Pauvert 1963: 58). In the same vein Bécourt, in his book *Livres condamnés, livres interdits* of 1961, quotes approvingly the opinion of a *tribunal correctionnel* in Orange which defined the role of such courts in 1950 as

to slow down a process of moral evolution [*une évolution des mœurs*] which they judge to be damaging to a higher moral code whose time-honoured rules have slowly solidified into positive laws and are reiterated in current legislation out of a concern to react against the debauched habits which are no longer shocking to the majority of our contemporaries. (Cited by Bécourt 1961: 112)

Accepting that morality changes is difficult, however, especially for those whose task it is to give moral judgements legal backing. In this respect, the fate of *Les Fleurs du mal* after 1857 is illuminating. The six poems originally judged to constitute an offence to public morality, religion, and *les bonnes mœurs* remained subject to a ban until 1949, by which time the censors' hand was forced since the book in uncensored form was already one of the most widely disseminated works of French literature. Consequently, as Leclerc suggests, the decision of 1949 to lift the ban arguably aimed to rehabilitate the law more than the poems. Various editions of the banned poems had been readily available since as early as 1864, and in 1925 the Baudelaire Society asked for the original verdict to be revised. The law held that it could not be revised unless new facts came to light, and did not accept the argument that changes in Baudelaire's reputation and in reading practices constituted such facts. The change eventually came when a virtually tailor-made legal text was introduced which allowed verdicts on literary works to be revised after a minimum of twenty years. This text seemingly accepted the principle that reading practices and morality could alter, and that extra-legal opinion on this matter could show the law the way forward (though the revised sentence of 1949 made it clear that there was still a legal limit to the liberties allowed to artists); but, Leclerc points out (1991: 278), the new decision avoided an acknowledgement that its own bases were relative and changeable by couching its annulment of the original sentence in terms which implied that the judge had simply made a mistake in 1857.

In the context of the Sade trial, any overt emphasis on the idea of moral progress would in any case have been difficult to present persuasively, given the age and nature of Sade's writing, so it is unsurprising that Garçon offset his ideas about the mutability of moral values against references to the naturalness of those values. Near the beginning of his speech, he explained *les mœurs* in the following terms:

Les mœurs generally means our natural or acquired habits regarding the practice of good and evil from the point of view of our conscience or of natural law. It is an imprecise notion which evolves continuously and which can be understood only in relation to the general climate of opinion. *Les mœurs* derive from what the majority thinks at a particular moment in time, and the latter's state of mind varies incessantly. (In Pauvert 1963: 17)

Despite the apparent openness of this definition, however, his use of the word 'evolution', and of words and phrases such as 'authoritarian', 'suppression' (*étouffement*), and 'abuses of power' in his account of censorship under earlier (especially pre-revolutionary) regimes (in Pauvert 1963: 16–19), made it fairly clear that to support censorship was indeed to oppose progress. Similarly Bataille in his testimony stressed that Sade lived in a society where, in his words, 'injustice still reigned' (in Pauvert 1963: 55). This whole line of argument was reinforced and given a literary emphasis by the implicit threat that from some vantage-point in the future a decision against Pauvert would appear as ludicrous as did already the 'incredible trials' of the mid-nineteenth century or the '*attardés* [people who are behind the times and/or mentally retarded] who now seem completely ridiculous' (in Pauvert 1963: 25, 29) who wished to brand Zola a pornographer a few decades later.

However eloquent Garçon may have been on the shortcomings of the Commission and on the injustice of earlier regimes' systems of censorship, there was clearly a need for him also to suggest some positive reasons why Sade's work should be published in its entirety. This need was exacerbated by his decision not to adopt the line of argument that freedom of expression was an absolute right (he favoured the aura of moderation created by such statements as, 'while freedom is profoundly imprescriptible, it must not degenerate into excessive licence' (in Pauvert 1963: 19)), and by his statement that *les mœurs* were defined by the opinion of the majority and that laws were 'the expression of the will of the majority' (in Pauvert 1963: 19), when in fact the majority of French people would probably not have considered it desirable, or even acceptable, that a book such as *Les Cent-vingt Journées de Sodome* be published. His answer to this was to stress the idea that, in his words, 'the Book is the noble vehicle of thought which is the medium of intellectual exchange' (in Pauvert 1963: 27)—and that books therefore merited a special degree of tolerance,[14] and to insist on the usefulness of Sade's writing for the work of an academic élite. There was extensive agreement amongst the participants in the trial that such an élite could read Sade safely, a consensus perhaps determined by the very structure of authority in such a situation where it was deemed appropriate for those involved (including, fundamentally, the members of the Commission du Livre) to have read books which they might then decide others should not be permitted to read.[15] Garçon, for example, referred to Sade's

[14] This notion is one that was embodied not only in the Commission du Livre but also in the important law of 2 August 1882 to which Garçon referred, and which, as he explained, made judicial control of books a matter for juries at a moment when that of all other printed material was returned to a regime of summary jurisdiction, after the law of 1881 had placed all printed material deemed offensive to *les bonnes mœurs* under the Cour d'Assises.

[15] Conversely, much was made of the fact that Pauvert had publicized two of the offending volumes in a non-academic, non-exclusive magazine called *Le Crapouillot*, which specialized somewhat (though this was not made explicit in the trial) in debates connected with sex, and whose tone was typically fairly irreverent. An anecdote told by Pauvert (and recounted, fittingly enough, in *Le Crapouillot*) shows clearly the split in the minds of the Commission members between themselves and the mass Other: 'one day, at my friends' house, I saw an elderly academic, a member of the Commission, who came up to me and said to me confidingly, "I hope that we will soon have some more books from you, Monsieur Pauvert, because at the Commission after we've judged them, we draw lots for them. The thing is that they are so nice [*beaux*] that everyone wants copies of them, so we put our names in a hat

œuvre as 'a literary and psychological document of the first order which is indispensable for certain workers' (and the choice of the word 'workers' (*travailleurs*)—rather than 'scholars' or 'intellectuals', say—is reminiscent of Sénard's insistence on the hard (which is to say, real) work behind *Madame Bovary*); the judge conceded that Sade's writing might not have any effect on 'cultured minds, or 'trained minds' (in Pauvert 1963: 57); and the prosecuting counsel acknowledged in his speech that books such as Sade's might be useful or even necessary to 'a few specialists who are particularly open and well-informed—scholars (*savants*), in other words' (in Pauvert 1963: 81).

The reasons behind the exemption of *savants* from certain moral considerations were not left entirely unfocused. Bataille, for example, when asked by the judge if he did not think that the effect of Sade's work was likely to be harmful, asserted: 'reading it cannot be harmful since from the very beginning we are dealing with documents analogous to medico-legal documents' (in Pauvert 1963: 57).[16] The latter emphasis, as part of a general attempt by the defence to argue that Sade's work was of scientific as well as literary and philosophical importance, was an insistent one throughout the trial.[17] Science in general, psychology, psychiatry, pathology, psychopathology and also psychoanalysis, in addition to medicine, were all invoked at least once (see Pauvert 1963: 46, 57, 81, 82, 93, 94, 104, 109, 112, 113, 114, 123). Garçon talked of the need to

and it's pot luck . . ."' (cited in *Crapouillot* 1963: 21). This commissioner apparently thought that to confide in Pauvert on this issue was a means of bonding with him, which suggests that the consensus to which I referred above was strong enough both to preclude his having any sense of hypocrisy, and to prevent him from having any sense of Pauvert's own perception of the importance of his publications.

[16] Here and elsewhere, the extent to which all Sade's defendants gave the court what (they thought) it wanted, rather than what they themselves thought, should not be underestimated. Pauvert himself, looking back on the trial, wrote that all the arguments put forward by the defence had always seemed to him to be fundamentally irrelevant (Pauvert 1981: p. xvi).

[17] It should be noted that the French terms *science* and *scientifique* have a wider range of applications than their cognates in modern English. The Robert dictionary, for example, offers a list of 'sciences and activities of a scientific nature' which includes law, onomastics and psychoanalysis (amongst other things) alongside the natural and physical sciences. The example of psychoanalysis shows, however, that the label *scientifique* can operate on several levels: most broadly, simply as a mark of intellectual seriousness, but also as a means of appropriating some of the prestige of hard science, at the same time challenging the privileged status of the latter and also working in some cases to undermine the distinction between science and non-science.

recognize Sade's work as 'a systematic examination of forms of depravity', describing Sade as 'a boring clinician who makes no attempt to win over the reader' (*un clinicien ennuyeux, ne cherchant point à séduire*) (in Pauvert 1963: 111), and complained that the unavailability of Sade's texts obliged those interested in him to rely on his commentators, which was, he suggested, 'contrary to all scientific principles' (in Pauvert 1963: 113). The aim of all this—though not necessarily a fully conscious or co-ordinated one—was presumably to recuperate a place for Sade in the discourse of progress, within which science is firmly inscribed, and so to exempt it from the demands of morality.

The appeal to science was a popular one amongst nineteenth-century Naturalist writers, too, several of whom were put on trial. Desprez and Bonnetain, for instance, the authors of two novels dealing with the perils of masturbation (*Autour d'un clocher* and *Charlot s'amuse*, respectively), defended themselves in court in 1884 (successfully, in Bonnetain's case) by insisting that their writing was based on scrupulous scientific observation. Similarly, Dubut de Laforest, in defending his novel *Le Gaga* in court in 1886, said that the story, of a highly respectable man arrested for indecency in a public urinal, was a true one; and he attempted to pre-empt the implicit criticism that he had written one of *ces livres qu'on ne lit que d'une main* ('books one reads with only one hand', a phrase used by Rousseau) by stressing that his spare hand had a legitimate (and legitimizing) occupation elsewhere. In his words, 'it was with a scientific manual in my hand that I described the successive phases of the moral and physical degradation of the Comte de Mauval' (cited by Leclerc 1991: 408). It is difficult for the modern reader not to regard this use of science as a thinly veiled pretext for prurient moralizing, and the prurient moralizing in turn perhaps as a distortion of a more straightforward interest in sex, but there is actually no reason to assume that the defendants themselves did not believe in their defence, especially given that 'science' of this period in some instances covered terrain similar to that of these Naturalist novels and did not necessarily distinguish itself from them by greater theoretical rigour. On the subject of masturbation, Tissot's *L'Onanisme, dissertation sur les maladies produites par la masturbation* of 1758, which claimed that to lose one ounce of seminal fluid was more debilitating than to lose forty ounces of blood, was still cited as an authority in the late nineteenth century (see Kendrick 1987: 88–90); and Bonnetain was doubtless telling the truth when he said that numerous doctors, as well as writers, had congratulated him on his work. Nevertheless, there was a tension (not necessarily consciously felt) between such novelists' claims to be scientific and their belief that their writing had specifically literary qualities, or between their supposed scientific detachment and the emotive, moralizing vocabulary in which they described their observations. Bonnetain thus claimed he had created 'a useful work whose scientific morality and whose attention to form redeem its more daring moments' (cited by Leclerc 1991: 400), thereby trying to justify his subject-matter by insisting that his story was at once close to reality and distanced from it by its literariness.

Given the emotional and sexual pull which a literary text can exert, however, the idea that literariness automatically opens up a space of moral distance is problematic. One indication of this in the Sade trial was the uneasy status of the occasional literary–aesthetic judgements which surfaced in the course of the speeches, and which the men of letters chosen as defence witnesses—Paulhan, Bataille, Breton, and Cocteau—seemed ideally placed to make. Though they were willing to proclaim the importance of Sade as a precursor of other important writers, however, none of them chose to disagree with a standard dismissal of Sade's writing *per se*, which was (and is) that it is boring. Indeed, this claim was accepted explicitly not only by the judge and the prosecuting counsel, but also by Garçon and Cocteau, Cocteau adding that Sade's style was weak. What was not explicit, though, was the higher relevance of this tediousness to the judicial proceedings, since it was always mentioned in such a way as to suggest that it was, *a priori*, irrelevant. On one level, saying Sade was boring was, it seems, a means of making it clear that the speaker's overall assessment of his importance was an entirely rational one, undistorted by sexual excitement or sexual repression. On another level, it was perhaps a means of saving the sacred space of Great Literature from profanation by sadism, a manifestation of the persistent liberal belief (or hope, or feeling) that artistic and moral elevation are inseparably linked. Thus Garçon mentioned as an example of the merits of juries their capacity to make the important distinction between 'that which constituted an affront and that which, though somewhat risqué, was an honour to literature' (in Pauvert 1963: 29), and Pauvert himself was cornered into stating that, 'despite its obscenity, Sade's work is important' (Pauvert 1963: 45), as if obscenity were not an integral part of the importance he attributed to Sade.

For the prosecution and the judge, then, Sade's tediousness was invoked to make it easier to exclude him disinterestedly from the protected realm of literature, while for the men of letters it was a sign that his importance was not *merely* literary, and that they were not being duped by his artistry into accepting the unacceptable. There was a shared anxiety, however, that Sade threatened them, as individuals and as representatives of the law or of literature, with a sort of moral contamination; and this anxiety was ultimately inseparable from that which provided grounds for prosecution in the first place. All this helps explain why Pauvert's defence was initially unsuccessful, and why the judge concluded that, 'despite its literary value, the nature of Sade's work does indeed represent an affront to public decency' (*un caractère outrageant pour les mœurs*) (in Pauvert 1963: 132). Although subsequently the appeal court looked more favourably on his case, greatly alleviating the penalty to be imposed on Pauvert (effectively, Pauvert felt, his sentence had been suspended), it reiterated explicitly the first court's assumption that only hard science (in this instance, medical) provided automatic grounds for moral exemption (in Pauvert 1963: supplement pp. v–vi).

The other aspect of the privileged status accorded to science, apart from its link with 'progress', is that it is regarded as able to provide an unchallengeable sanction for a moral position if it can provide it with an amoral, material anchorage. This is seen in the currency given to the idea of the genetic risks of incestuous breeding, for instance, or in the enormous efforts made to establish (or less often, refute) links between pornography and 'real-world' violence. In a sense, this may show how censorship, though fuelled by motives which are ingrained and may be to a greater or lesser extent unformulated, irrational, and unconscious, has always sought to justify itself by reference to some external, codifiable set of values. Scientists now fulfil a role analogous to that of earlier Churchmen, whereby a privileged socio-moral positioning, and a privileged relationship to a form of knowledge accepted as universal place them outside the mundane orbit of the 'layman' within which moral corruption takes place. Perceiving historical continuity in this dynamic should not, however, obscure the fact that the nature of the authority invested in the justification is not historically constant. The authority of a religious censor derived from his position *within* the moral code, such that he could not only speak its language well enough to generate new applications, but also came effectively to embody that code, whereas that of a scientist derives from his or her (supposed) position *outside* such a code and ability to approach with indifference the issues it presents.

In post-revolutionary, secular France, most people have had to find legitimacy for their moral opinions somewhere between these two positions. Tensions of the type to which this can give rise help explain the attempts made in both the *Madame Bovary* and Sade trials to displace moral criteria into other values, such as specifically literary considerations. These tensions were no doubt experienced especially keenly in the former case, at a time when the sense that the authority of the Church had been usurped was perhaps stronger, and when science was not so well placed to answer the positivistic desire to find ultimate guarantees for morality in the natural world. The urge towards a moral discourse which concealed its religious origins behind the rhetoric of legal neutrality and objectivity found expression in the series of laws and their modifications introduced under the Third Republic in 1871, 1875, 1881, 1882, 1898, and 1908, all of which dropped any reference to 'la morale religieuse' and relied on the notion of *bonnes mœurs* (adding in some instances that of obscenity), a fact that was alluded to by the appeal court in the Sade trial. The law-makers emphasized the need to protect *la pudeur publique* (an expression close to the English 'public decency'), which helped avoid some of the difficulties of defining *les bonnes mœurs* and moved the accent on to seemingly more immediate questions of the acceptability of incursions into the public space (or, in later legislation, into the private space via direct mailing and so on).

The transition from the first type of authority (that of universal religious morality) to the second (that of a scientistic secularism) was eased by those publishers of obscene books who justified their publications in conventional moral terms (as cautionary tales, for example), or who, in ways I have discussed, inscribed them in the discourse of natural science or medicine as case histories of aberrations with which the public should be acquainted, the better to avoid such horrors themselves. Furthermore, the argument was often used that only those who were themselves corrupt could inflate delicate allusions into gross obscenity, a strategy designed to play on the moral insecurities of those who wished to suppress the obscene. All of these arguments, as will be seen at the beginning of Chapter 3, were very popular throughout the nineteenth century (and into the twentieth) with publishers of Sade.

The vision of human nature on which all such arguments were premised assumed that sexuality was essentially a threatening and antisocial force. Its contagious properties were taken to be particularly pronounced amongst members of the working class (even though most pornography of the period, for example, was destined for the bourgeoisie, if only because of its cost), a social stratum whose lack of civilization in the narrow sense was confused with a lack of civilization in the broad sense—that is to say, a failure to overcome primeval urges. Symptomatic of the fears to which this vision gave rise, and of the way in which religious values continued to be displaced and transmuted into new contexts, was the strong anti-abortion and anti-contraception groundswell which came to a head in the early twentieth century. Supporters of this movement justified their position less in terms of Catholicism than of anti-Malthusianism, and used a rhetoric dating from the end of the previous century which promoted and conflated physical and moral hygiene. At this time legal action was frequently taken against small advertisements and the like which, though couched in non-obscene euphemism, provided publicity for prostitutes or for abortionists (the latter's work described as 'an infallible remedy for the cessation of menstruation', for instance (cited by Stora-Lamarre 1990: 140)). The number of trials of obscene publications, accused of 'feminizing' the nation, leapt from fourteen in the period 1881–1910 to 165 in the four years preceding the First World War, and a law aimed specifically against 'anticonceptional and abortive propaganda' was finally passed on 31 July 1920, at a time when great international congresses of moral leagues were organized at which, according to Stora-Lamarre (1990: 148), 'every speech stressed the idea of civilized nations threatened with decadence by the emergence of sexual immorality'.

After the Second World War, worries of this sort gradually became less prominent, though they did not disappear. Though the *Décret-loi Daladier*, for instance, under which Pauvert was prosecuted, included the offence of *outrage aux bonnes mœurs* in a section entitled 'Protection de la race', even the prosecuting counsel in Pauvert's trial, Maynier, hesitated to base his argument on the claim that books constituting an *outrage aux bonnes mœurs* were necessarily threatening to society (let alone to the French 'race'). Maynier explained to the court that they did not need to distinguish between 'obscenity, i.e. something crudely sensuous' and 'excessive licence [*la licence*], i.e. something which, without appealing particularly to the senses, aims to destroy certain moral principles', and that all that had to be decided was if the books merited 'the respect of decent French people' (*l'estime des bonnes gens de France*) (in Pauvert 1963: 80). This argument seems to have formed the basis of Pauvert's initial conviction, but in the Court of Appeal *outrage aux bonnes mœurs* was presented as something to be conceived of pragmatically, in terms of a book's impact, rather than dogmatically, in terms of a moral code. This impact, it was implicitly recognized, was something not easily measured by the court. It is notable that the issue of freedom of expression was invoked categorically by the appeal judge (which it had not been in the original trial), who concluded that 'criminal law [*la loi pénale*] is not designed to sanction a moral code [*la loi morale*] but to suppress breaches of morality only in so far as they are liable to provoke social disturbances' (in Pauvert 1963: p. iv of supplement).

PORNOGRAPHY

I suggested at the end of the first section of this chapter that the most widespread contemporary interpretation of the freedom of expression, whose historical emergence I continued to trace in the second section, tends to see in that right a means of protecting the individual from the State. From these first two sections it can be seen that this interpretation of the freedom of expression draws on a number of interconnected assumptions. First, it is assumed that freedom of expression is basically a given in a modern democratic society, or at least a readily attainable goal towards which steady progress is being made; secondly, that individuals in such a society are basically autonomous and capable of independent judgement (an exception being children, who are susceptible to corrupting influences, which are more likely to be visual than verbal); thirdly, that individuals inhabit an essentially private domain which must be kept separate from areas of public concern; fourthly, that 'expression' should be considered separate from action, with the exception of various types of defamation; and, fifthly, that on occasions when juridical post-censorship is called for (as opposed to the pre-censorship necessitated by areas of State secrecy), the most appropriate level on which to enact it is financial, since this poses the least threat to the fundamental right of freedom of expression.

As I tried to show in the last section, the status of literature in relation to this freedom is ambiguous. If freedom of literary expression has increased, on balance, since the Revolution, this is perhaps best explained not by the idea that the criteria of censorship have been forgotten or abandoned, but by the idea that they have lost their grip on literature. It is no longer clear, in other words (or better: it has been increasingly felt, or recognized, that it is unclear), how one can evaluate literature morally, and what kind of responsibility can be imputed to it. In contrast to the eighteenth century, when there was a wide presumption that novels, in particular, tended to have bad effects, there seems now to be a wide presumption that the effects of literature in general are good. The one major exception to this, perhaps, is pornographic literature (a phrase some would wish to see as a contradiction in terms), but the Pauvert trial marked a turning-point after which not only did the idea of a literary text's being *contraire aux bonnes mœurs* in any active sense become increasingly implausible, but it also was increasingly widely believed that to act against literature on this basis represented an unacceptable compromise of the freedom of expression.

The idea that the freedom of expression is a right whose main function is to protect the individual from the State is, however, a misleading one in certain respects in the case of modern France. First, as I showed in the first section, there is a fairly broad consensus with regard to the press and broadcasting that governmental action can be beneficial to that freedom. Secondly, it should be remembered that the government does exercise a limited but systematic type of censorship against pornography in forms other than literature (films, especially, and also magazines), and this action is widely held to be acceptable. These two types of intervention are often regarded as exceptions which do not compromise the basic individual-versus-State paradigm (which is to say their problematic relation to that paradigm is often simply disregarded), but a pointed and highly visible challenge to that paradigm has emerged in recent years in a certain current of British and American feminism, where the idea of State intervention in favour of pluralism and the idea of censoring pornography have been incorporated into a different understanding of the freedom of expression, as part of an attack on pornography.

The current British and American situations regarding pornography are different from that of France in significant respects, not least in that the theory with which I am concerned, primarily that set out by Catherine MacKinnon in her books *Feminism Unmodified* and *Only Words*, has had no appreciable impact in France and has no French equivalent. Particularly in the States, the arguments of pro-censorship feminists and their *ad hoc* alignments with conservatives on the issue of censorship have cast doubts on the usual liberal understanding of the history of moral censorship as a gradual shedding of conservative, moralistic hang-ups, an understanding which, as I indicated in the second section of this chapter, has been a powerful current in French thought, too. I now propose to turn to these feminist arguments, which though addressed in part to issues specific to the United States and/or Britain, provide a useful means of questioning French attitudes towards freedom of expression and the place of pornography within it.

A Lack of Restraint

For MacKinnon, equality of the sexes is a fundamental right (or goal) in modern secular democracy which is yet to be achieved. On her account, the pursuit of that goal is actively hampered by pornography, which is protected by an abstract version of the right to freedom of expression which divorces it from any political aims. Pornography,[18] for MacKinnon, is not just a metaphor for op-

---

[18] The legal definition of pornography proposed by MacKinnon, which was framed in collaboration with Andrea Dworkin, states that, 'Pornography is the graphic sexually explicit subordination of women, whether in pictures or in words, that also includes one or more of the following: (i) women are presented dehumanized as sexual objects, things or commodities; or (ii) women are presented as sexual objects who enjoy pain or humiliation; or (iii), women are presented as sexual objects who experience sexual pleasure in being raped; or (iv) women are presented as sexual objects tied up or cut up or mutilated or bruised or physically hurt; or (v) women are presented in postures of sexual submission, servility or display; or (vi) women's body parts—including but not limited to vaginas, breasts and buttocks—

pression but is itself a practice of sex inequality, not only because the very conditions of its production in the case of the cinema, photography, and live shows are sometimes coercive, but also because it works to encode male dominance as a central matrix through which to make sense of experience, particularly sexual experience, and as an inevitable result of the biological difference of the sexes. In her words,

Pornography turns sex inequality into sexuality and turns male dominance into the sex difference. Put another way, pornography makes inequality into sex, which makes it enjoyable, and into gender, which makes it seem natural. By packaging the resulting product as pictures and words, pornography turns gendered and sexualized inequality into 'speech', which has made it a right. Thus does pornography, cloaked as the essence of nature and the index of freedom, turn the inequality between women and men into those twin icons of male supremacy, sex and speech, and a practice of sex discrimination into a legal entitlement. (MacKinnon 1987: 3)

Within this dynamic, sex discrimination is not an aberration from a basically just system but is itself systemic, and those who bear the brunt of this—women—are not really 'free' to express their opposition to it, MacKinnon argues. As she puts it, 'freedom before equality, freedom before justice, will only further liberate the power of the powerful and will never free what is most in need of expression' (1987: 15). Furthermore, the inequality which pornography enforces and reinforces is hard to perceive, and still harder to redress, since it is intimately linked to pleasure. This link distinguishes it from the literatures of other inequalities (although racism, for instance, frequently expresses and supports itself through specifically racial sexual stereotyping).

Even from this brief summary one can see how MacKinnon's analysis is built on different foundations from the conventional liberal approach to pornography, and how her initial contention

are exhibited, such that women are reduced to those parts; or (vii) women are presented as whores by nature; or (viii) women are presented being penetrated by objects or animals; or (ix) women are presented in scenarios of degradation, injury, torture, shown as filthy or inferior, bleeding, bruised or hurt in a context that makes these conditions sexual.' This definition can be expanded to include 'the use of men, children or transsexuals in the place of women', MacKinnon says (1987: 262), but it is clear that she is concerned almost exclusively with heterosexual pornography involving *women* in a position of subordination. She has nothing to say, for instance, about gay pornography. It is also clear that she is more concerned with 'pictures' than with 'words'. These are issues to which I return later in this section.

that a culture of freedom remains an unattained goal in modern democratic societies leads inevitably to the destruction of the various other presuppositions on which the liberal position is built. One such is the notion of the autonomy of individuals, since she holds that our thoughts and behaviour are determined, partially but fundamentally, by the society in which we live—both at the level of our individual personality, and at the level of our insertion into socially defined collectivities. Individuals may not be free to act as such, in other words, if they are prejudged as members of a group which is constructed *as* a group, and as inferior, within a certain hegemonic formation to which they are marginal.[19]

In this respect, then, the challenge posed by MacKinnon is directed, as Post has argued, against a certain brand of individualism, and is particularly hard to accept for those who wish to believe in the capacity of every individual to transcend his or her 'background'. Post places the feminist critique of pornography in the context of three different possible approaches to the law, of which the individualist strand which rejects the feminist position is only one, the others being what he terms respectively pluralist and assimilationist approaches. According to his definition, 'Assimilationist law strives toward social uniformity by imposing the values of a dominant cultural group; pluralist law safeguards diversity by enabling competing groups to maintain their distinct perspectives; individualist law rejects group values altogether in favour of the autonomous choices of individuals' (Post 1988: 305). These three types of law are not, of course, sharply distinct or mutually exclusive in all situations. Both pluralism and individualism base themselves on certain underlying assimilationist values, for example. In the case of obscenity, an individualist approach may seek to impose certain norms of interpersonal respect, but can by definition support these only by reference to a very narrow set of assimilationist values which all individuals are assumed to share.

---

[19] The fact that certain women, in this instance, may escape their definition as inherently subordinate does not contradict this: the feminist question is not whether any particular woman can escape women's place, but whether society is constructed in such a way that women collectively cannot. MacKinnon points out that 'to show that an observation or experience is not the same for all women proves only that it is not biological, not that it is not gendered' (1987: 56). She backs this up by drawing an analogy between sexism and racism, arguing that the fact that a few of the rich people in the States are coloured, or that many of the poor are white, does not mean that the widespread poverty of coloured people has nothing to do with white racism.

This approach, in Post's words, 'enforces a constitutional symmetry between speaker and audience: it allows the law to redress audience outrage only when that outrage stems from characteristics potentially shared by all individuals, rather than from characteristics that are constitutive of particular social or religious groups' (1988: 323). Pluralist law, on the other hand, presupposes stronger assimilationist values, which enable it to identify groups deserving of legal protection and to lay down the norms of respect to which different groups must submit. It is this conception of the law which lies behind a MacKinnon-type perspective, from which women are identified as a group deserving of protection, and a group which is harmed collectively by the pornography to which individualist law gives everyone the right.

On another level, MacKinnon's argument challenges the distinction between the public and the private on which free-speech debates so often turn, in that sexuality, which is often located near the heart of definitions of privacy, is considered to be inherently social and is tied both to pornography and to broader political forces which cut across the line dividing the private from the public. An understanding of the private as a sphere of choice completely impermeable to external intervention is thus revealed to be untenable. MacKinnon writes that,

> To confront the fact that we have no privacy is to confront the intimate degradation of women as the public order.
> In this light, a right to privacy looks like an injury got up as a gift. Freedom from public intervention coexists uneasily with any right that requires social preconditions to be meaningfully delivered. (1987: 100)

What is being suggested here is that the State may act as a source of greater liberty (and may be obliged to do so) in the face of a 'free market of ideas' which is indeed a market and which does less than nothing to redress social inequalities. It is from this perspective that in the first section I emphasized the significance of governmental moves to limit the process of concentration of media ownership, since whatever the politicians' explicit motives (and however limited the measures taken), such action implies a recognition at some level that the structure of the market is not necessarily propitious to the flourishing of freedom of expression in any meaningful sense.

In order for such an intervention to be effective, however, it should be made in full cognizance of the values that are at stake: the kind of ambiguous, half-hearted measures against pornography taken at present are, in MacKinnon's analysis, counter-productive, since they reinforce the conventional liberal belief that the State is hostile to speech and to sex, thereby making pornography seem liberatingly transgressive, and sending much of the left scuttling to its support, for fear of being tainted with what Kappeler, another anti-pornography feminist, terms 'Mary Whitehouse-ism'. On another level this means that pornography passes for the type of unorthodox 'expression' (or, at least, is seen to be effectively in-separable from it) that laws enshrining freedom of expression were originally designed to protect, when in fact, MacKinnon and Kappeler argue, it is complicitous with and a part of the broad orthodoxy of sex inequality. The law at present, in other words, does anything but delegitimize pornography, and it is its legitimacy which feminists such as MacKinnon, Kappeler, and Huston (who publishes in France) aim to destroy.[20]

Another point made by Kappeler is that if one shifts one's atten-tion from obscenity to sex inequality, and therefore identifies the pornographic not with a variable quantity of sex but with the systematic objectification of women, then any firm distinction be-tween popular and high culture (of a type often used to distinguish pornography from 'erotica', for instance) is compromised from the start, since such objectification 'is a common place of art and literature as well as of conventional pornography' (1986: 103). From this perspective, circulation figures and degrees of mediation are not a crucial issue, since what is being scrutinized is the very system or structure which produces the whole spectrum of por-nography, with its varying degrees of offensiveness. In Kappeler's words, 'In terms of the structure of representation, the distinction between one spectator or reader and a whole "mass" audience of viewers is irrelevant. The essential positions of author and spec-tator—the subject positions in the representation—and the objectified "role" of the victim, are all present' (1986: 32). To consume pornography, according to Kappeler, is to insert oneself into a structure of representation in which the position of the viewer or reader is a dominant one, and to view or to read it is itself an act of domination.

[20] Kappeler and Huston, unlike MacKinnon, do not believe that the law offers a potential means of achieving this. I return to this question at the end of this section.

In this perspective representations of all types must be taken seriously in relation to us all as individuals in process, exposed to and traversed by such representations, and individuals should not be considered discrete, fully self-conscious units who, when exposed to pornography (or anything else), simply do or do not translate its mental impact into the separate realm of actions: pornographic fantasy may be a part of sexual reality, and, to the extent that pornography is sexual, sexuality is pornographic. The assumption behind the use in law of the phrase *contraire aux bonnes mœurs* is that *les bonnes mœurs* are the societal norm, but that people can be induced to depart from them under certain pernicious influences. Again, this conception gives no purchase on a political reality of which pornographic representations are a pervasive feature, and judgements based upon this conception from a supposedly objective standpoint cannot discern harm that is systemic rather that an aberration. It is, then, inappropriate to assimilate human behaviour in this sphere to clear-cut models of cause and effect, or to try to entrap pornography within a crudely causal conception of harm and disruption which, as was seen at the end of the second section of this chapter, is the principal potential objection to immoral or obscene material in the modern, secular legal system.

Attempts to link pornography and violence (understood as private speech and public action, respectively) in sociological experiments and in statistical surveys are fundamentally problematic for this reason. A further problem is that researchers' presuppositions are liable to exert an illegitimate influence on the character of their experiments and the conclusions they draw from their results, and such results as have been produced suggesting a correlation remain controversial and have generally been held to be too inconclusive for legal purposes. These links are widely believed to exist, nevertheless, and some research—in Itzin's *Pornography: Women, Violence and Civil Liberties* of 1993, for instance—would seem to support this view.

It could be argued, though, that the recourse to purportedly neutral data to support what are primarily political/ethical positions already betrays a failure fully to assume responsibility for those positions as such. In this respect, at least, it is reminiscent of crude attempts by nineteenth-century moralists to justify their values scientifically with reference to the 'case histories' of those—

usually female and/or working class—who had been destroyed by inappropriate reading.[21] This kind of argument did not die out at the turn of the century: Pauvert, for instance, was once given a talking-to by a policeman, who informed him that, by publishing Sade, he was 'ruining our young people' (*en train de pourrir la jeunesse*), and who asked him, 'Do you realize that people who are mentally deficient will read this and will then go and chop children to bits?' (cited by Kajman 1990: 22). In Pauvert's trial one of the witnesses, Jean Paulhan, gave this causal model an original twist when he answered the judge's challenge as to whether he denied that Sade's philosophy was dangerous by saying, 'It is dangerous. I knew a girl who went into a convent after she had read Sade's works, and it was because she had read them' (in Pauvert 1963: 49). The appeal judge's remarks which I quoted at the end of the second section show that he held only evidence of this causal type to be legally admissible, though its anecdotal nature (and the kinds of unpredictability pointed up in Paulhan's remark) also make it legally suspect.

What I want to emphasize is that all such approaches, and the limited categories of instrumentality which they recognize, are unable to respond to the critical understanding of pornography proposed by MacKinnon-type feminism. What they cannot consider is whether pornography *itself* is violent, whether its production and consumption are themselves acts of male supremacy, and whether it encourages violent sex. Efforts to brand the latter an oxymoron are also misguided: as MacKinnon says (1987: 6), 'Violence is sex when it is practised as sex' (and also, of course, violence can be sexual even when practised as violence). Relatedly, many liberal critics attempt to criticize pornography by arguing that it is basically a lie which distorts the truth of human sexuality and eroticism, but this argument is hard to uphold in the case of soft pornography (which may not count as pornography under MacKinnon's definition) or when confronted by women as well as men willing to participate even in violent sex scenes, or violent sex. In one sense

[21] A book of 1883 by Eugène de Budé entitled *Du danger des mauvais livres*, for instance, told the following story: 'A young man, a skilled watch-maker, whose behaviour was exemplary till the age of 18, had the misfortune to come across some reading matter guaranteed to inflame his passions and as a result of this [*ses mauvaises lectures*] he suddenly lapsed into a state of idiocy and his parents had to put him in a lunatic asylum, where he lives to this day' (cited by Stora-Lamarre 1990: 67).

this criticism is nevertheless accurate: the dynamics of pornography as described by MacKinnon, which turn sex inequality into sexuality and reduce women to object bodies, mean it tends inevitably to claim universality for itself (in the form of human nature), a claim made credible by the broader context of sexism, since sexism—like any other politics of prejudice—assumes certain real or imagined traits in certain individuals to be representative of the entire group which the prejudice works to subordinate. But the fact that there are people who enjoy being humiliated, or that people do not necessarily object to being treated as objects, means that such criticisms are limited. As in the case of Pinard's attempts to discount aspects of *Madame Bovary* as *invraisemblable*, what is at stake is not primarily a problem of realism and its claims to truth, but the social reality which is its starting-point and in whose construction it participates.

Pornographic Experience

In many respects, MacKinnon's approach to pornography and to its censorship provides a dynamic alternative to the traditional liberal approach, in the United States or in France. Her position, in summary of the account of it that I have given, consists of and rests on a series of interconnected arguments and strategies. She refuses the assumption that the 'right' to equality of the sexes is a social reality; she displaces the emphasis away from individuals and towards collectivities; she refuses the idea that women 'have' freedom of expression to the same degree as men; and she argues that pornography is itself a practice of sex inequality. In the course of these arguments, various related dualisms on which the liberal approach is built come under attack: that of the individual versus the collective, that of the public versus the private, that of 'speech' versus action, that of fantasy versus reality, and that of the personal versus the political. The first three of the arguments (as I have just set them out) seem to me to be persuasive, and to represent a gain in understanding over a traditional liberal approach. At this point I want to look a little more closely at the fourth argument, that which represents pornography as a practice of sex inequality. That argument is in a sense MacKinnon's own starting-point, and so far I have given a broadly sympathetic account of it. I shall now argue (as have various feminist critics of MacKinnon) that it raises certain problems and is in need of certain refinements.

MacKinnon defines pornography as being 'not fantasy or simulation or catharsis but sexual reality: the level of reality on which sex itself largely operates' (1987: 149). Her strategic aims here may be understandable, in that she is attempting to challenge the assumption that pornography inhabits the realm of 'fantasy' and that this is entirely separate from 'reality' (or that it inhabits the realm of 'speech' and that this realm is entirely separate from that of action); but her description is a misleading one, in that it simply inverts the oppositions she wishes to challenge. In fact, the experience of pornography surely does involve fantasy and simulation, if not catharsis (an idea to which I will return), and these are part of sexual reality.

MacKinnon links these thoughts on sexual representation to the nature of female sexuality, writing:

> Pornography participates in its audience's eroticism because it creates an accessible sexual object, the possession and consumption of which *is* male sexuality, to be consumed and possessed as which *is* female sexuality. In this sense, sex in life is no less mediated than it is in art. Men *have sex* with their *image* of a woman. [. . .] It is not that life and art imitate each other; in sexuality, they are each other. (1987: 150)

Again, the momentum of her own polemic seems to carry her past her target. Sex in life is indeed 'mediated', but this does not mean that, in sexuality, 'life and art [. . .] are each other'. MacKinnon ends up talking as if the mediation of sexuality were inherently wrong: the sentence 'Men *have sex* with their *image* of a woman', for instance, is intended to be critical, but men and women cannot avoid having an image (some sort of image) of their sexual partner. A distinction is being elided here between *representation* as a mental process (the way in which we represent reality to ourselves) and *representations* or images as exterior objects which enter into the mental process. MacKinnon's basic point is that, for men, this process is likely to be invaded by or shaped by pornography, and to this extent is likely to be implicated in images of (and in the reality of) sex inequality, and perhaps also (though this is a different argument) that the reality of certain images can work to constrict the reality of our own experiences.[22] She expresses herself in such a

---

[22] This latter point is made by Barthes in *La Chambre claire* when, describing a display of sado-masochist pornography, he writes: 'you will not find vice, but only its *tableaux vivants* [. . .]; it is as if the anonymous individual (never an actor) who gets himself tied up and beaten conceives of his pleasure [*son plaisir*] only if this pleasure joins the stereotyped (worn-out) image of the sado-masochist: pleasure [*la*

way, however, as to suggest that her objection is to any image at all, writing as if there were a natural sexuality prior to its mediations. At the same time, she is at pains to establish that sexuality simply *is* pornographic, and is lived as such. This seems to leave little space in which that sexuality could be reshaped.

As various writers have argued (see, for instance, Cornell, Huston, Phillips, Segal, and L. Williams), there is, then, a sense in which a pro-censorship argument such as that of MacKinnon accepts fundamental terms of the pornographic discourse on women and on sexuality which it intends to delegitimize. When MacKinnon states that female sexuality consists in being possessed and consumed as an accessible sexual object, she is making it clear that women who desire men should feel guilty, and that their sexual pleasure, as so often in pornography, is something to be confessed rather than freely admitted. (She is also assuming, incidentally, that to be a 'sexual object' is always and necessarily to be dehumanized, an idea challenged by Feminists Against Censorship (1991: 60)). Relatedly, there is a danger that MacKinnon's world comes to resemble that of pornography in being populated by male masters and by female slaves whose sexuality is a fact to be known and defined from the position of the male masters. MacKinnon's point is, of course, that we live in a (the) world of pornography, which serves to undermine rigid distinctions between fantasy and reality, say, or art and life, or high and low culture; but it depends too greatly on a vision which allows no room for manœuvre within the monolithic world she describes. The sexuality and gender relations which MacKinnon delineates are presented as a cultural construct, but there is a risk that, in her account, it is one so profoundly embedded that there is no effective means of distinguishing it from Nature.

It is in this respect, most importantly, that MacKinnon's vision is apparently complicitous with pornography. In places, at least, she ends up saying that pornography tells us the truth about sexuality and gender and so about ourselves, and there is a danger, as Merck suggests, that she has thereby 'elevated the pornographic sign to the

jouissance] passes through the image: this is the great transformation. Such a reversal inevitably raises an ethical question: not that the image is immoral, irreligious, or diabolical (as some declared it when photography started), but because, when generalized, it completely de-realizes the human world of conflicts and desires, under cover of illustrating it' (1980: 182; 1982: 118).

epistemic status it might wish to claim' (Merck 1991: 59). Sontag seems to run the same danger when she discusses pornography as a type of knowledge (in 'The Pornographic Imagination'), and Linda Williams does, too, when she asserts that 'explicitness helps us to see things how they are' (1989: 277). The problem with all this is that it suggests that sexuality and gender exist in a fixed, general-ized, visible form in the world, and that pornography simply reflects or reveals them, when in fact—as other aspects of MacKinnon's argument suggest—pornography is a part of that world (not least in that it is a business which seeks to expand its market). Its relationship to sex and to gender is dialectical and mobile, however much its own logic compels it to arrest that dialectic and to claim that all it is doing is 'showing' sex, 'showing' gendered individuals doing 'what comes naturally'.

In the light of this, one can see that MacKinnon has good reason to reject the idea that pornography is cathartic, for, just as the sexual scenarios which pornography depicts are not simply there in the world waiting to be depicted, but are actively constructed and framed, the sexual feelings that the reader or viewer ex-periences are generated (at least in part) by that pornography, and not merely released by it. Pornography is not an uncluttered passageway through which the reader or viewer passes from an established external sexual reality to an established internal sexual reality, for the two realities are neither so established nor so distinct, and the relationship of pornography (which is also real) to both of them is complex. Furthermore, as Cowie points out ('Pornography and Fantasy' in Segal and McIntosh 1991: 132–52), pornography may be desired for its own pleasures and is not merely or always secondary to a 'real', 'physical' pleasure exterior to it.

As I have already argued, one can see the strategic appeal of establishing a Kappeler-style theory of representation which cuts across generic distinctions and which subverts oppositions such as that of high and low art, or of art and reality; but it is unfortu-nate if the strategy encourages complete insensitivity to the differ-ences to which these crude distinctions and oppositions point. MacKinnon's arguments supposedly apply equally to pornography whether it is 'in pictures or in words', but theoretical priority is tacitly given to pictures (meaning photographs, films, and videos). The reason for this is partly, no doubt, that visual pornography is the more common type, but partly, I would suggest, that the element of ontological realism in visual pornography (and relatedly, the economic conditions of its production) make it easier for MacKinnon to make the claim—which, I have argued, is also the claim of such pornography—that one is dealing with the Real Thing. In important senses, of course, it *is* real, since the pornographic enactment of sexual pleasure will almost invariably involve some degree of sexual pleasure—at least for the male participants. The 'harder' the representation, the truer this is: hard pornography is the least allusive and the most detached, vouching for its own reality in the cinema by including 'come shots' (also known as 'money shots') and by dispensing with the aesthetic and intellectual gloss of softer appoaches. Even in such cases, however, one is dealing with reality only in a mediated way, and MacKinnon ultimately does not help her argument by invoking too often the real abuse of women in the making of pornography, both in her description of instances of violence and in generalizations such as 'pornography has to be done to women to be made' (1994: 27). This strategy, another instance of what I referred to earlier as the recourse to purportedly neutral data, is problematic here in that the violence to which she rightly objects is supposedly illegal already; and, though it would be naïve to suggest that present law against such violence is fully effective, it would surely be equally naïve to assume that additional, overlapping law would improve the situation. Furthermore, the extent to which her argument becomes dependent on this strategy is the extent to which it renders itself incapable of addressing 'literary' pornography, which her definition was intended to include. MacKinnon rightly objects to the way pornography is treated as words even when it is pictures (1994: 8); by the same token, it is misleading to treat it as pictures when it is words, or as something indistinguishable from reality when it is pictures. The type of mediation involved in different instances has to be taken into account if one is to give an adequate account of any 'message' the pornography may convey.

For MacKinnon, pornography's message (more insidious than a message in real 'speech') is essentially that of sex inequality, and it is illuminating to see where this analysis leaves her with regard to gay pornography involving only male participants. In one sense, it could be argued that pornography of that sort is not pornography at all in MacKinnon's terms, and it is certainly not the pornography she cares about; but the legal definition she proposes does state that men can be used in the place of women, and examples of gay pornography can certainly be found where men are 'presented as sexual objects who enjoy pain', for instance. The sexual–political stakes in such a case are quite different from those when a woman is involved, however: the man in the representation is less likely to be taken as a representative of men collectively, and beyond that, it is not clear that men collectively can be 'subordinated'. Indeed, the idea of an object which enjoys pain is harder to accept, easier to perceive as the contradiction it ought to be (at least when applied from without, as it were), in the case of a representation which is not reinforced by the contradictory subordinating discourses which would be activated by and can coexist in an otherwise identical representation of a woman. If, on the other hand, the man in this example is black, then the situation is clearly rather different, and it becomes apparent that it is precisely to the extent that the actors in a pornographic scenario are *not* interchangeable that MacKinnon's theory is relevant, and can be applied to any non-hegemonic social group.

There is, of course, no doubt that MacKinnon is aware of the asymmetry between men and women—it is the basis of her theory, and the reference to men in her legal text may well have been nothing more than a strategic attempt to make her definition more acceptable constitutionally. It is also true that the oppression that gay men suffer as gay men is only exceptionally at the hands of the people who are exposed to 'gay' pornography, whereas women's oppression is far more likely to be at the hands of those who have been exposed to 'straight' pornography. This does not alter the fact, however, that in gay pornography, too, individuals may be objectified and brutalized, and the pleasure of the reader or viewer may be composed partly of the pleasure of domination (and, again, racial factors, for instance, may play a role in this). To distinguish the case of gay pornography from that of heterosexual porno-graphy, in the way MacKinnon might wish to, one needs to recog-nize (amongst other things) that one is dealing with political contingencies of reception, and that, while these can be seen to inform the representation and to be inscribed within it, a working distinction nevertheless needs to be maintained between the representation and the way in which it is received. Conditions of reception affect what the message of a particular piece of pornography is, in effect, and how it changes.[23]

Though to distinguish representation and reception is not to claim that they can be completely separated, then, the value of MacKinnon's challenge to an opposition such as this (or the related oppositions of fantasy and reality, or art and life) is compromised, as I have already suggested, if she refuses to recognize that their component terms have a useful application. It is true that rape and rape fantasy, say, are connected to one another, and that they can be viewed as points on a given spectrum of sexual response, and that rape fantasy is a part of rape for a rapist: but these things should not be rendered theoretically indistinguishable. MacKinnon tends to talk about the experience of pornography as if the porno-graphic image were simply incorporated into the reader's or viewer's life, and as if it were ultimately the reader's body which determined what he or she made of it: according to *Only Words*, for instance, pornography's message is 'addressed directly to the penis' (1994: 15). This view lends insufficient autonomy to the realm of fantasy, and again denies sexuality any mobility. Sexual arousal, as Cowie has pointed out, is 'not merely a bodily affair but first and foremost a psychical relation' (in Segal and McIntosh 1991: 135); the ways in which one can identify with or imagine oneself into the pornographic scenario, consciously or uncon-sciously, are not fixed by one's body, nor even by one's 'sexuality', in the (questionable) sense of one's characteristic sexual activity (and, indeed, it is to the extent that such fantasy is real, though not 'bodily', and is mobile, that the idea of 'characteristic activity' carried out by the 'body' becomes problematic).

The way in which one imagines oneself into the pornographic scenario is shaped not only by factors external to the text or image, but also by the text or image itself, of course. As I have already indicated, MacKinnon's theory is somewhat insensitive to the

---

[23] Another distinction which would be useful here is one made by Hunter, Saunders, and Williamson in their treatment of pornography and obscenity law in England and the United States, a distinction MacKinnon fails to make between a 'legal–governmental' argument concerned with discrimination, and a 'philosoph-ical–aesthetic' argument concerned with objectification. In their words, 'there is clearly a danger that the important attempt to construct the harm of pornography as an infringement of civil rights may be swamped by aesthetically conceived rights and harms (the right not to have one's being objectified and misrepresented) whose limitlessness puts them beyond legal claim and redress' (Hunter, Saunders, and Williamson 1993: 235).

varying amounts of leeway which different representations and different types of representation allow.[24] Having said this, I think it should be emphasized that it is easy, particularly within a certain poststructuralist consensus, to underestimate the power of the constraints upon one's interpretation of an image or a text. These constraints are both internal and external to the representation, and MacKinnon rightly stresses that the interior and the exterior of the text form a continuum in important respects. A woman reading a pornographic text, for instance, may create (with more or less difficulty, depending on the text) a psychic space in which she is able to slip in fantasy between different subject positions, but there is another level on which she cannot simply ignore or reverse subject positions which are established in the text and outside it as gendered and unequal. Critics who stress the unruliness and mobility of fantasy tend to regard fantasy as the individual's means of fleeing and/or resisting harsh realities such as gender inequality, but it is not the case that those fantasies surface from, or are played out in, an area utterly outside those realities. The mobility of the subject is not inherently subversive: after all, it allows women to be sexist with regard to other women, for instance. Fantasy and sexual pleasure, as MacKinnon indicates, do not exonerate the fantasizer and pleasure-taker from these sexual politics, and fantasy and pleasure may themselves, therefore, be politically charged. As Foucault notes (1976: 207), we should not believe that, in saying yes to sex, we are saying no to power.

I want to make some final remarks about the significance for the notion and practice of censorship of the arguments I have set out in this last section. MacKinnon's theory of pornography can in large part be applied to the French context, I have suggested, to provide a persuasive challenge to the version of freedom of expression whose historical origins and historical weight I examined in the first two sections of this chapter. I have argued that her claim that pornography is a practice of sex inequality needs certain refinements, but with these in mind it seems to me that one can indeed argue that pornography, on MacKinnon's woman-centred definition, is inseparable from the practice of sex inequality, and in that

---

[24] It could be argued in MacKinnon's defence on this point that pornography which allows significant leeway in its interpretation is again not pornography at all in her terms.

sense is itself one such practice. MacKinnon herself proceeds from this to argue that one should be able to, and should, combat pornography with censorship, and it is to this latter argument which I will now turn.

MacKinnon, I have argued, tends to accept pornography's claim that it tells us the truth about the world of sexual relations. She believes, in other words, that our world (the world of societies including the United States, Britain, and France) is a pornographic one; but this claim makes sense, and has political force, only in so far as one keeps alive the *distinction* between the world and pornography. In a passage I quoted earlier, MacKinnon writes, 'pornography makes inequality into sex, which makes it enjoyable, and into gender, which makes it seem natural. By packaging the resulting product as pictures and words, pornography turns gendered and sexualized inequality into "speech", which has made it a right' (1987: 3). The trouble with this is that it implies that pornography exists first as a quasi-natural phenomenon in the world, and is then offered up to us in words and images which are nothing more than a 'package' for this pornographic substance. Pornography both helps produce and is produced by a lived reality, but it consists in a set of representations, and takes its place in the tradition of such representations, as well as in a socio-economic nexus.

Pornography *is* 'speech', a form of expression, a discourse, and is not just 'cloaking' itself as such in order to be considered a right, as MacKinnon's formulation implies and as she argues more explicitly in *Only Words*. The question of sex inequality is indeed apposite to the right to freedom of expression, but it does not occupy the entire space of that right, thereby ruling pornography out of court. In the case of pornography, in other words, freedom of expression is compromised from two directions: by censorship, on the one hand, and by sex inequality on the other. To put it another way, censorship in this instance compromises the freedom of expression, but non-censorship does, too. The *right* to freedom of expression cannot resolve such conflicts, which exist within the right, and which, as I argued in examining the relation of the rhetoric of *liberté d'expression* to the political and social context in which it was declared, are what makes the right both necessary and insufficient. When MacKinnon objects to 'freedom before equality', she is right that freedom of expression could only truly be achieved, absolutely achieved, once absolute equality was achieved, and right that this in turn means that the freedom of expression is conceived in and shot through with politics and its inequalities, rather than hovering above them; but freedom of expression cannot be purified of all conflict, and her insight does not determine which way one jumps when faced with one of those inequalities.

In any particular case, one needs to consider firstly the history of pornographic representations and censorship in order to understand where one is jumping from and what the options actually are with regard to pornography. In France, this history shows that pornography is and always has been subject to censorship in one form or another, so the type of measures proposed by MacKinnon would not really represent a new *sort* of compromise to the right of freedom of expression. Furthermore, it seems to be true that legal tolerance of pornography has increased in the last century, and that, in the same period, pornography has become more widespread and less socially unacceptable (though in the United States and England, again far more than in France, feminism itself has to some extent undermined this acceptability). This may seem to suggest that MacKinnon is right to turn to the law as a means of delegitimizing pornography, but counter-evidence to her theory is provided by the fact that, in the same period, sex inequality has decreased. Although it is obviously correct that the law is one factor shaping what is considered acceptable in a society, it does seem from French history—the case of *Les Fleurs du mal*, for instance— that changes in acceptability in the area of *les bonnes mœurs* originate elsewhere. This analysis is supported on another level by Linda Williams's claim that pornography in the United States has itself begun to respond to the increased unacceptability of sex inequality, becoming less pornographic in MacKinnon's terms.[25] It must also be recognized that extensive repressive measures of the type MacKinnon seemingly favours have not been very successful,

[25] According to statistics Linda Williams cites, the depiction of rape, for instance, in pornographic films, has decreased, so that, while it constituted 33% of sex acts in the most popular films between 1976 and 1979, it constituted 7% in those between 1980 and 1985. These statistics (see Linda Williams 1989: 292) regard the United States rather than France, and I do not know for certain that the same trend could be observed in France. According to Faligot and Kaufer, foreign films have come to dominate the French pornographic film market since 1975 (see Faligot and Kaufer 1987: 145), so it seems likely that many of the most popular films in France and in the United States from 1976 to 1985 were the same. Faligot's and Kaufer's own perception is that the 'hardness' of films has increased in this period, but they are not specifically concerned with the issue of sex inequality.

historically. On one level, their lack of success is simply empirical, in the sense that banned publications—such as *Justine*—have never been completely unobtainable, and to make them unobtainable has become increasingly difficult as printing technology has become more widely available. On the other hand, if it had not been for the censors, *Justine* would probably have been read by many more people in the nineteenth and early twentieth centuries.

I would suggest, though, that if it had not been for the same censorship which previously meant that few people could read *Justine*, it would almost certainly have been read by far fewer in the latter part of this century. It would also have been read differently. The lack of success of censorship with regard to sexual material is not just a problem of logistics, but, on a more fundamental level, is an inevitability in that it produces what I am terming a circle of censorship, a process by which structural complicities between the censoring agency and the censored material make them mutually perpetuating. To talk of the gradual de-censorship of pornography simply as a falling away of restraints (or, conversely, to see the throwing-up of barriers as a means of containing it) is, in important respects, to accept not only the language of the censor but also that of the pornographer, for whom there is a pre-given sexual reality which one simply 'packages', and, behind that, pre-given sexual urges which simply are or are not given expression. Sade's *Les Cent-vingt Journées de Sodome* is arguably the most extreme example of this, in that the fiction of cataloguing pre-existent perversions persists even when he is describing 'the' perversion which consists of turning a girl into a firework rocket, for instance. Sade's work shows us too how this sexual reality tends to be viewed by both pornographer and censor as the reality of all reality, the fundamental reality which the artifices of superficial, social reality disguise: and what guarantees that it is fundamental, by a circular logic, is the fact that it is sexual, and is experienced as such. This circular logic means that the idea that one is breaking through superficial, social restraints and towards reality becomes sexualized itself, and (in dialectic with pornography) acts as a fundamental component of the pleasure pornography offers. This, too, we can see in Sade's work, for example in the Duc de Blangis's declaration in *Les Cent-vingt Journées de Sodome*, 'it is evil alone, not the object in itself, which gives us an erection' (OC xiii. 164; 1987: 384). Laws against pornography, then, caught up in this circle, are part of what makes it sexual, part of what makes it pornographic, and part of what makes it popular.

The fact that pornography thrives on its sense of its own prohibition does not necessarily mean that prohibitions of all sorts and on all levels should be abandoned, however, and to think otherwise is again to accept pornography's own claim of the priority of sexual 'reality' over the social medium in which it is played out. Having said this, it clearly *is* true that exterior restraints have fallen away from pornography since around the time of the Pauvert trial, and this has been part—an ambiguous part—of a process of 'sexual liberation' which has indeed seen sexual freedom increase. What I want to emphasize is that this process has not simply led towards a *tabula rasa* of natural, unmediated, uncensored sexuality. On the one hand, sex has been politicized in such a way that it has become possible to talk about and fight for certain sexual freedoms, while, on the other hand, this politicization of sex may itself have been (and be) oppressive, and may have served to perpetuate and disguise sex inequalities. Freedom in this area, as I have tried to show, is not just a matter of a lack of restraint.

PART TWO

Metaphors of Censorship

2. Freud: The Return of the Political

∾❧∽

A recurrent feature of the discourses of censorship (particularly moral censorship) that I discussed in Chapter 1 was the notion implicit in them that, if carried out with complete efficiency and good faith, censorship might render itself unnecessary. According to this notion censorship is an ambiguous supplement to self-censorship, understood simultaneously to provide standards for its object group and to provide an external reinforcement of standards which the individuals in that group ought already to recognize spontaneously as their own. In the case of the *Index*, for instance, these standards were those of Christian morality, while in the case of post-revolutionary censorship, Republican values supposedly guaranteed and were guaranteed by freedom of expression, only 'abuses' of which (literary or otherwise) could bring it into conflict with other rights and standards. By the same logic, post-revolutionary censorship constantly presented itself in terms of temporary, emergency measures which would be unnecessary once the status quo had been 're'-stabilized; and, similarly, the arguments of a pro-censorship feminist such as MacKinnon often suggest that emergency measures to repress pornography are necessary, even if they infringe other people's rights in some respect, until a stable basis of sexual equality has been reached. Conversely, if the historical moment at which the notion of a supplementary, self-abolishing censorship was at its weakest was the end of the *ancien régime*, this was perhaps because, as I argued in the first section of Chapter 1, the system of censorship at that time had a built-in awareness of a split between the public or social and the private or individual, and of the fact that this was a period of transition in which that which was censored in the present was potentially the orthodoxy of the future.

Even in periods when the implicit model of the 'supplement' was powerful, however, it was not necessarily true that proponents of censorship genuinely believed that the projected moment when censorship would be unnecessary would ever arrive. In the case of the *Index*, for example, it was no doubt thought that the ubiquity of sin would mean that this moment was infinitely deferred. More-over, the imagined chronology of which that moment was the endpoint was fissured along lines of social division, so that, while the censor himself spoke as if from a plateau of complete stability, the end moment at which internal and external values coincided perfectly, his need to speak was dictated by the fact that others—above all the 'masses'—were permanently 'backward' and socially unstable, their development arrested at an earlier point on this time-scale.

These notions of the complementarity and mutual sup-plementarity of censorship and self-censorship, and of the direc-tions from which the social values represented by censorship were potentially threatened, came to the fore in a new way in the work of Freud, whose model of censorship[1] I examine in this chapter. Freud himself obviously worked at a certain distance from the French context with which I have been concerned so far, and I do not want to appear to be slipping surreptitiously from one to the other. Freud's conception of censorship, as I will be showing, was marked in distinctive ways by his own milieu, and historical infor-mation specific to that milieu will be cited where necessary. In the present context, Freud's models are not only of theoretical interest, but above all, for my purposes, are of historical importance for their influence on the notion of censorship in twentieth-century France, an influence traced in Chapter 3, where this Freudian material and my French subject-matter are intended to reconverge. It should be noted, however, that the impact of some of the events and phenomena which I discussed earlier—the French Revolution, for instance, or the *Index*, or indeed a certain discourse of freedom of expression—was evidently not limited to France. Furthermore, the notion of supplementary censorship which I have drawn from French history was sufficiently apparent in Germanic culture that Marx discussed it in *The Holy Family* of 1844, attacking the idea that, as he summarized it, 'the writer's fight against the censor is not a fight of "man against man"', that 'the censor is nothing but *my own tact personified* for me by the solicitous police', and that 'the struggle of the writer with the censor is only seemingly, only in the

---

[1] The German word *Zensur* can mean a school report or mark, but otherwise has the same meanings as its English and French cognates. Freud uses the term primarily in these latter, shared senses, so there is no serious loss as it crosses linguistic borders.

eyes of wicked sensuousness, anything else than the *inner* struggle of the writer *with himself*' (Marx and Engels 1975: iv. 83). Freud's theory, it will be seen, has affinities with the point of view which Marx is criticizing; but it was also new in important respects, and redefined the way in which censorship was thought of subsequently.[2]

It is partly in order to retain a sense that censorship and self-censorship are separable, and that censorship can still be the work of police or others representing an external force which is less than solicitous, that my chapters concerning Freud and French literary culture influenced by him, grouped under the heading 'Metaphors of Censorship', are separated from the first part of this book. Freudian psychoanalysis is being given no particular theoretical privilege here, and on one level Freudian censorship is simply the first of the 'metaphors of censorship' (I explain in the first section of this chapter what I understand by 'metaphor') with which I am concerned. On another level, though, Freud's concept is of interest in that it came to establish a certain theoretical priority for itself in French literary culture and to function as the grounding gesture behind the other metaphors of censorship I will be discussing in Chapter 3, a gesture whereby censorship was displaced away from politics in its narrow sense and towards other dimensions such as the psychic and the artistic. This movement was initially meta-phorical, but censorship found itself reliteralized in new positions from which the boundaries of its original literality appeared less secure.

My aim throughout Part Two is to follow this movement, and to explore different ways in which censorship can be understood, while remaining attentive to what is being left behind as one drifts metaphorically from one domain to another, or what is being submerged when apparently solid conceptual ground emerges in one place just as, in another place, what seemed solid becomes immersed in the metaphorical flow. Certain metaphors of censor-ship materialize and seem substantial, I will argue, only if the sort of historical and material complexities of censorship which I exam-ined in Chapter 1 are ignored, or given insufficient weight. If, on the

---

[2] It is notable in this connection that the term self-censorship, which now seems an almost self-evident concept, came into English only in about 1950, according to the *OED*. The first use recorded by the Robert dictionary of the French equivalent, *autocensure*, occurred in 1960.

other hand, legal-historical, psychoanalytic, and literary discourses on censorship are woven together with sufficient sensitivity to the insights each can provide, then the 'metaphors' of censorship may, I hope, lead to a new understanding of the whole area that falls within the circle of censorship, understood in the broad sense towards which they carry us.

THE SEDUCTION OF AN ANALOGY

In *An Outline of Psychoanalysis*, Freud sums up the epistemology of psychoanalysis in the following words:

we infer a number of processes which are in themselves 'unknowable' and interpolate them in those that are conscious to us. And if, for instance, we say: 'At this point an unconscious memory intervened,' what we mean is: 'At this point something occurred of which we are totally unable to form a conception, but which, if it had entered our consciousness, could only have been described in such and such a way'. (1940; *Standard Edition SE* xxiii. 197)

The problem, of course, is that there is never only one way in which such an occurrence can be described, and no possible means of description which carries no ideological baggage. In Freud's case certain favourite images, such as those of and surrounding censorship, occur time after time, and move fluidly between the metaphorical and the literal in a way which makes them all the more compelling. Freud's own explanation of how such images are chosen, in his essay 'Constructions in Analysis', is that he is not one to resist 'the seduction of an analogy',[3] and that the charms of a seductive analogy are not completely superficial, but owe their power to the element of repressed historical truth which they contain (1937; *SE* xxiii. 268, 269).

Before considering in more detail what makes the particular analogy or metaphor of censorship seductive to Freud, to what extent it is appropriate to the 'historical truth' of his subject-matter, and what problems it presents as a psychoanalytic concept, I propose to look a little more closely at the question of how we are to

[3] Freud uses the term *Analogie* with a broad range of applications for which modern English would tend to use the term 'metaphor', and the two terms can be treated as synonymous in the present context.

understand 'censorship' in contexts where it seems to be non-literal. To this end, I will now turn briefly to some theories of metaphor which help elucidate the status of the concept/metaphor of censorship in Freud's theory.[4]

'Metaphor', on its most widespread interpretation, means a word which is applied to an object or action which it does not literally denote, in order to indicate some sort of affinity or resemblance. Thus Laplanche and Pontalis, for instance, in the course of their definition of censorship in *Vocabulaire de la Psychanalyse*, remark: 'It should be noted that, wherever this term is employed, its literal sense is always present: those passages within an articulate discourse that are deemed unacceptable are suppressed, and this suppression is revealed by blanks or alterations' (Laplanche and Pontalis 1967: 63; 1988: 66). The underlying assumption here is that Freud is using the term in a primarily metaphorical way, whose meaning is separate from, but in some way illuminated by, its original, literal meaning. This conceptual separation is indeed frequently taken as the sign of a successful metaphor, in that success is seen to lie in the bringing together of two terms that are normally considered *dis*similar. On this model, it is unsurprising that the jolt that an unexpected but somehow apposite metaphor can bring is missing from Freud's attempts to discuss psychic censorship metaphorically in terms of political censorship.

The criterion of dissimilarity cannot usefully be applied to many perfectly 'successful' metaphors, however, and it should be noted that there are in any case apposite types and degrees of dissimilarity which are themselves subject to social determinations. Even apparently 'natural' metaphors such as 'eagle-eyed' are in fact dependent on culturally specific connotations for their effect, such that 'metaphor in all societies will have a "normative" and reinforcing aspect, as well as an "exploratory" one' (Hawkes 1972: 91). In many cases, then, the interpretation of a metaphor presupposes a certain unstated unifying viewpoint, and serves to promote what Cooper terms the 'cultivation of intimacy' (1986: 40). In this perspective, one can see how metaphors may be in part the product of a

---

[4] I am not primarily concerned, I should emphasize, with Freud's own understanding of analogy/metaphor, but with the way in which his metaphors function. The theory on which I draw is consequently chosen on the basis of its usefulness in approaching this question, irrespective of its relation to any theories with which Freud himself may have been acquainted.

consensus which metaphor itself helps to cultivate and reinforce, such that, when Freud considers the social psychology of crowds, for instance, he follows the middle class's (and the censor's) historical tendency to view the masses as a phylogenetically underdeveloped horde, a tendency which is both a cause and an effect of common metaphors of 'barbarism' and the like—which are furthermore liable to be rendered self-fulfilling to the extent that these attitudes solidify into policies of 'crowd control' and so on.

It is clear at this point that one needs to distinguish between metaphor in its schoolroom definition, too restricted even to cover all rhetorical and poetic usages, according to which two 'subjects' are explicitly linked, and metaphor in its expanded sense, designating a broad range of instances where a single subject is not to be understood in its conventional, literal sense. (Confusingly the latter definition may itself be seen as metaphorical in its own terms, which explains some of the difficulties which arise when it is asked whether language in general can usefully be described as metaphorical.) Culler points out that the expanded sense of metaphor is now a commonplace as 'a figure for figurality' (Culler 1981: 6), or even as a deliberate signal of a writer's awareness that language does not consist merely of logically proper nouns. Such a broad categorization may ultimately be self-defeating, however. If one follows the usual argument in favour of a distended sense, which tends to hinge on metaphor's purported cognitive function— namely, the idea that, if thinking of an object, event, or whatever involves thinking of it *as* something, then all language is metaphorical—then the figurative/literal distinction is completely undone. Furthermore, metaphor is in this way valorized at the expense of the notion of truth. As Culler argues, commenting on Nietzsche's famous characterization of truth as 'a moving army of metaphors, metonymies and anthropomorphisms' (Nietzsche 1976: 46): 'The line of argument that gives metaphor cognitive respectability ends by abolishing cognitive respectability. In general one might observe that any attempt to ground trope or figure in truth always contains the possibility of reducing truth to trope' (Culler 1981: 15).

One solution to the problem of metaphor's definition which retains the insights afforded by the expanded application while avoiding its paradoxes, is that urged by Cooper, who uses metaphor in its classic sense to designate a distinguishable (if pervasive) figure of speech, alongside a more general notion of metaphorical speech or writing. Such a distinction may be understood by analogy with the difference between executing a particular dance and dancing, or between producing symbols and acting symbolically: in each case, individual instances are part of and merge into the general category, without exhausting its scope. A statement which is intended to be literal may be interpreted metaphorically, after all. In the case of Freud's 'censorship', it can be agreed for the moment that it is metaphorical, even if it is unclear if it should be considered *a* metaphor in any narrower sense.

Uncertainties of this type over the extent of the term's application, and the related difficulties in attributing to metaphor a broad cognitive function, undermine the view of metaphor apparently espoused by Laplanche and Pontalis in the quotation cited above. This view is known as the 'interactive' one, and is summarized as follows in Max Black's essay 'More about Metaphor':

> the two subjects 'interact' in the following ways: (*a*) the presence of the primary subject incites the hearer to select some of the secondary subject's properties; and (*b*) invites him to construct a parallel implication-complex that can fit the primary subject; and (*c*) reciprocally induces parallel changes in the secondary subject. (Black 1979: 29)

The implication of Black's definition is that metaphor, in so far as it 'induces changes', promotes mental work and so depends in some way upon novelty for its success. This argument is shown to be too narrow by Davidson's observation that, 'In its context a word once taken for a metaphor remains a metaphor on the hundredth hearing, while a word may easily be appreciated in a new literal role on a first encounter. What we call the element of novelty or surprise in a metaphor is a built-in aesthetic feature we can experience again and again' (Davidson 1980: 244). When a metaphor dies, on the other hand, one seeks no similarity to the original meaning. There is no element of cognitive enrichment of the type suggested by Black, no oscillation or disparity between the figurative meaning of the living metaphor and the literal meaning of the dead. If one operates Cooper's distinction of metaphor and the metaphorical, however, one can answer the apparent need to differentiate between dead metaphor and the literal, for the metaphorical may be so conventional as to appear 'dead' (that is, literal) until revived by its position in an unusual context. Cooper's own example is that a phrase like 'he sifted the evidence', which is not novel and whose metaphorical qualities are likely to pass unnoticed, is capable of coming alive if placed in a sentence such as 'he sifted the evidence through the fine sieve of his mind' (Cooper 1986: 130). It is this capacity which distinguishes metaphors from polysemous literal expressions.

Death amongst metaphors is not, then, necessarily caused by old age, but may be no more than a symptom of their relation to an established system of metaphorical language capable of engendering new expressions which, though new, are scarcely novel. This point is made at length (and in slightly different terms) in Lakoff's and Johnson's *Metaphors We Live By*, a prime example of theirs being our habit of discussing arguments in a vocabulary of attack, defence, victory, and so on derived from warfare. In this perspective, one could see Freud in his use of 'censorship' as having invented a dead metaphor, a term which may at times be read literally (as when it is used to explain other phenomena) but which elsewhere reveals itself as metaphor. If this is the case, its dual role is made possible partly by its derivation from a metaphorical system which already underpins the text and is sufficiently established to have died—that is, sufficiently established to give birth to readily acceptable metaphorical usages for terms derived from the 'parent' domain.

The system in question here both constitutes and is an expression of a vision of the psyche as a site of forceful territorial conflict, and manifests itself in a great number of Freud's key terms. The derivation of many of these is self-evident, as in the case of *Abwehr* ('defence') and *Konflikt*, but in others it is less so, especially in an English translation which fails to retrace the original German's metaphorical threads—for example *Besetzung* ('cathexis', but literally occupation (of land)) or *Drang* ('pressure', but in German connoting also a drive to expansion)—and others again, such as *Widerstand* ('resistance') or *Unterdrückung* ('suppression'), have a place in this model once one is aware of it. It is in accordance with this metaphorical system that Freud's illustrations of his model of censorship most frequently involve the passage of information across some sort of border, on which the censor or censoring agency is positioned.

This claim that Freud's theory is being given shape by an underlying metaphorical matrix needs, however, to be qualified. First, it should be noted that several different models are to be found in

Freud's work, and that quite different metaphorical networks have been uncovered by commentators such as Bowie (1987) and Lichtman (1982), who dwell on his use of archaeological and hydraulic metaphors respectively. Secondly, stress on the metaphorical qualities of the conflictual model is liable to obscure the extent to which it is grounded in the literalities of psychological and sociological analysis in Freud's day. It is interesting from this point of view to compare Freud's metaphors of censorship with those of Pinard, the prosecuting counsel in both the *Madame Bovary* trial and the *Fleurs du mal* trial of 1857, who described the judge as 'a sentry who must protect the border' (*une sentinelle qui ne doit pas laisser passer la frontière*) (in Baudelaire 1930: 331) and book printers as 'advance sentries: if they allow an offence [*le délit*] to pass, it is as if they had allowed the enemy to pass' (in Flaubert 1971: 379). For Pinard, the idea of the sentry was certainly metaphorical, but that of the frontier (the limit) was less so, and that of the enemy for a man such as him, a Christian with a strong sense of moral embattlement, was almost certainly not.

In Freud's case, the 'naturalness' of the metaphor of censorship is seemingly a product not only of the reality-based interconnections *within* the metaphorical system of which it is a part, but also of the external, two-directional interconnections between the two poles of the metaphorical movement, which is to say between that which is ('metaphorically') censored in the psyche and that which is literally eliminated by censors in the outside world. The two 'poles' are inscribed not on a line but in a circle, in other words, and to look for a point at which the switch from the literal to the metaphorical is made—and, more particularly, to look for the point at which it would have been made in another culture, at a different point in history—is to misunderstand the status of the metaphorical usages of 'censorship' in Freud's work.

Having said this, Freud's metaphorical language remains open to question as such. Though there is no home medium into which metaphor can be translated and though, as Kuhn points out in his discussion of 'Metaphor in Science' (in Ortony 1979: 409–19), certain metaphors may be constitutive of the theories they express rather than merely exegetical, it is nevertheless possible and productive to draw out Freud's metaphoricity, and to gain some sense of the factors which made the metaphor of censorship seductive to him, which is to say the broader social, political, linguistic context of which it was a part. At least as far as censorship is concerned, Freud was perhaps right that metaphors may contain an element of repressed historical truth; and the entanglement of Freud's metaphorical censorship with literality can be taken both literally as a sign, I will argue in the next section, of what is really at stake in psychic censorship, and beyond that, as Chapter 3 will show, as a metaphor of the ways in which any discourse which purports to operate purely on a 'metaphorical' or literary level is inevitably tugged at by other interconnected discourses with their own claims to truth.

THE FREUDIAN CIRCLE

Though as a young man Freud was a member of the Nationalist *Leseverein der deutschen Studenten Wiens* ('The Vienna Reading Club for German Students') and was active on the student political scene, as he grew older he developed something of an aversion to politics. This aversion was not just a personal matter, but a product of social changes towards the end of the nineteenth century which saw the liberal middle ground of Viennese politics, on which Freud found himself or would have found himself, submerged, threatened on one side by the rising tide of Socialism but more importantly overwhelmed by supporters of the anti-Semitic Christian Social party, which obtained a majority in Vienna in 1895. These events and their impact on Freud have been documented elsewhere (see Schorske 1981, McGrath 1986, and Beller 1989) and cannot be repeated here in any more detail, so at this stage I want to make just two basic observations as a starting-point for my argument that the shifts and instabilities in Freud's use of the term 'censorship' are signs of his reluctance (itself a form of censorship, I will be suggesting) to acknowledge and unpack the baggage which the term brings with it, and that some sense of the social and political contexts from which it is drawn make the notion a more useful one.

First, the political situation in Vienna at the time Freud started to develop his theory of psychoanalysis was a particularly repressive and threatening one for a liberal middle-class Jew, and one in which a political voice was hard to find. In a sense, then, especially in view of Freud's earlier political activity, there is circumstantial evidence that his work may have provided an oblique means of engaging with politics, which reinforces the evidence that the text itself provides to this effect. It is in this light that one should read the Latin epigraph on the title-page of *The Interpretation of Dreams*, which reads 'Flectere si nequeo superos, Acheronta movebo' (If I cannot bend the higher powers, I shall stir up hell). Drawn from the *Aeneid*, this quotation is 'intended to picture the efforts of the repressed instinctual impulses' (1900; *SE* v. 608), according to a footnote in the body of the text. Schorske suggests that Freud was probably familiar with this phrase not only as a line from the *Aeneid* but also as the epigraph to Lassalle's *The Italian War and the Task of Prussia* of 1859, a work whose political sympathies, according to Schorske, were close to those of Freud (see Schorske 1981: 200–1). Even if Schorske were wrong, it would be difficult not to interpret Freud's allusion as a political one, a signal of a more or less conscious wish that the political scene from which he had been excluded should feel shock waves as he conjured up anarchic energies from the unconscious.

The second, related observation I want to make about Freud's political background is that, because of political repression in Vienna, Freud had first-hand experience of censorship. At the height of the political crisis of 1897, Freud's daily paper, the *Neue Freie Presse*, was twice withheld, and partial censorship was commonplace. As McGrath explains, 'Long experience of living with censorship in the theater and the press had taught all educated Viennese to read between the lines in search of a writer's true meaning. Likewise, an author learned to veil his message so as to elude the censor but still to reach his audience' (1986: 247). One of my aims in this section is to show that, reading between the lines of Freud's own text, one finds politics. Further information about Viennese politics will be brought to bear where necessary to substantiate this claim and to elucidate the ways in which the notion of censorship is best understood, but my concern beyond this is the way in which Freud's political self-censorship—his censorship of politics within his theory and within his self, under the influence of political censorship without—skews his theory. The Freudian theory of censorship, I will be arguing, remains skewed, both in Freud's own work and in that of the French writers to whom that theory was an inspiration, and whose conception of censorship I will be examining in Chapter 3.

Reading Blanks

It is in *The Interpretation of Dreams* of 1900 that the term censorship is used most extensively and systematically by Freud. It first appears in a passage in which dream distortion[5] is likened to 'the political writer who has disagreeable truths to tell to those in authority' and who must consequently 'soften and distort the expression of his opinion'. Freud provides an example:

For instance, he [the political writer] may describe a dispute between two Mandarins in the Middle Kingdom, when the people he really has in mind are officials in his own country. The stricter the censorship, the more far-reaching will be the disguise and the more ingenious too may be the means employed for putting the reader on the scent of the true meaning. (1900; *SE* iv. 142)

This image makes explicit the way in which the values of an external authority are internalized: taken literally, Freud's story of the political writer shows how this may be a conscious decision, but as a metaphor it is designed to indicate that even the unconscious responds to these values, being furthermore responsive to the conscious agency's ability to see through them as an imposition of censorship. This is a good instance of the uncertainties of regarding Freudian censorship as a metaphor, or as 'a social parallel to this internal event in the mind' (1900; *SE* iv. 141), since the two strands of thought are not so much parallel as woven together. These uncertainties are compounded by the fact that what Freud terms a 'disguise' is the kind of practice frequently referred to nowadays as 'self-censorship'. Similarly in the 1916 text on 'The Censorship of Dreams' (*SE* xv. 136–48), Freud recognizes that 'censorship' may resemble the waking practice of circumlocution, or again may operate through a 'displacement of accent', a process about which he remarks, 'I know of no parallel in the operations of the press censorship' (1916; *SE* xv. 140, 139). Although he does not ex-

---

[5] Distortion is Freud's general term for the effect of dreamwork, a process which transforms latent ideas or representations into a dream whose manifest content makes little manifest sense. Freud sees four basic factors in dreamwork: namely, condensation, which means that a single element of a dream-representation may have a place in several chains of associations; displacement, which means that the relative psychic importance of different elements is redistributed and so obscured; considerations of (visual) representability; and secondary elaboration, which gives the dream a patina of coherence (and which is not to be seen as chronologically separate from other dreamwork).

plicitly draw the implication that psychic and internal censorship may form part of a continuum, the fact that Freud expects parallels to pre-exist his writing—that is to say, to have a substantial reality—makes it easier to comprehend why the boundary between what is illustration and what is illustrated is hazy. Furthermore, the claim of Freudian censorship to literality within the theory is given weight by the solidity it frequently has as a psychoanalytic concept, such that it has an explicative power: on the basis of the metaphor of the 'political writer', it would seem that dream distortion is created (and so explained) by 'the' censorship.

A further implication of this metaphor is that the form a dream takes is in one sense irrelevant, in that the thought the dream expresses exists, on this model, before and independently of its particular verbal expression. Freud is contradictory on this matter, however. The unconscious has acquired some positive connotations at this point by being linked to creativity: and the censorship seemingly acts not only as the reason for, and precondition of, this creativity, but also as its agent, founding the movements of displacement and condensation and also secondary elaboration, which is more obviously creative (in a narrower sense). The latter process means that the dream is always already a positive negotiation with rational thought and with intelligibility (where displacement and condensation mean it is also a negative negotiation), though the dream's ends—like those of the work of art—may be elsewhere. The idea that the dream language is potentially transparent does not fit with this latter version of censorship and of the dream-work, and it is to be contrasted with a footnote from later in *The Interpretation of Dreams*, where Freud writes, 'At bottom, dreams are nothing other than a particular *form* of thinking. [. . .] It is the dreamwork that creates the form, and it alone is the essence of dreaming—the explanation of its peculiar nature' (1900; *SE* v. 506–7 n.). On this latter account, Weber suggests in *The Legend of Freud*, the dream is an *Entstellung* (the word translated as 'distortion') as *opposed* to a *Darstellung* (the usual German word for 'representation'), and is not 'the representation of one (self-identical) set of thoughts by another' (1982: 66).

Freud's inconsistency on the issue of how readily a dream can be understood emerges again in *The Interpretation of Dreams* in a footnote added in 1919 where he sets out to justify his choice of terminology by citing a dream which he interprets as a vindication of the analogy of censorship. The dream, recorded by Frau Dr H. von Hug-Hellmuth from another woman's recollection, consists of a trip to a military hospital during wartime, where the dreamer offers to perform *Liebesdienste*, a term meaning unremunerated services but which can also be construed to refer to sexual favours. The soldiers at the hospital understand her offer to be a sexual one, although in her recollection of the dream the word *Liebesdienste* itself never actually occurs, being replaced by a mumble. Freud notes that, 'In this example the dream distortion adopted the same methods as the postal censorship for expunging passages which were objectionable to it. The postal censorship makes such passages unreadable by blacking them out; the dream censorship replaced them by an incomprehensible mumble' (1900; *SE* iv. 142–3 n.). The 'postal censorship' which Freud has in mind here is of the crudest, most obvious type, closely akin to that which Freud referred to in 1897 in a letter to Fliess where he wrote: 'Have you ever seen a foreign newspaper which has passed the Russian censorship at the frontier? Words, whole clauses and sentences are blacked out so that what is left becomes unintelligible. A *Russian censorship* of this kind comes about in psychoses and produces the apparently meaningless deliria' (*SE* i. 273). Though it is unclear how close a parallel this self-conscious metaphor, used again in *The Interpretation of Dreams* (1900; *SE* v. 529), is supposed to be, another reference to censorship from this period in the essay *Further Remarks on the Neuropsychoses of Defence* implies that the idea that the process has a verbal aspect is supposed to be a literal truth. In the *Further Remarks* Freud asserts that, in the course of paranoia, the 'censorship of the words involving the self-reproach' becomes weakened until, finally, 'the defence fails altogether and the original self-reproach, the actual term of abuse, from which the subject was trying to spare himself, returns in its unaltered form' (1896; *SE* iii. 183).

In the case of the *Liebesdienste* dream, however, the parallel with postal censorship is flawed for two reasons. First, a feature of dream-censorship as Freud explains it is that it covers its traces through the process of secondary elaboration. Secondly, and more importantly, the dream incident hinges on the fact that the mumble *is* comprehensible, both within the dream and without, and merely replaces the offending word. This bears little relation to the methods or results of an extreme postal censorship which blacks out whole phrases, since the dream is still readable. A conception of censorship as something defensive or destructive, derived from a certain political context, persists in tension with Freud's dream-based 'creative' notion.

In 'The Censorship of Dreams' (on which the footnote of 1919 is based) Freud again uses the analogy of blanks in the newspaper, about which he remarks: 'In these empty places there was something that displeased the higher censorship authorities and for that reason it was removed—a pity, you feel, since no doubt it was the most interesting thing in the paper—the "best bit"' (1916; *SE* xv. 139). This image is notable for highlighting the perverse way in which complicity is established between the censor and the recipient of censored material (intrapsychically too, perhaps) over which aspects of the material are considered important and 'interesting': how, in other words, a circle of censorship binds them together. This is the same process I discussed in the last section of Chapter 1 in relation to pornography, and the circles of censorship with which we are most familiar now are indeed those encompassing sexual material. Such a circle underpinned the gameshow *Blankety-Blank*, for instance, and also lay behind Maurice Lemaître's special edition of the *Lettrisme* journal entitled 'Le Boudoir de la philosophie' which was published in 1965. In it he explained that for several years he had wanted to record a version of *La Philosophie dans le boudoir* from which all the 'philosophy' had been removed, leaving only a 'lesson in erotic technique' (1965: p. i). He was confident this would have been a commercial success, but abandoned the idea because of the threat of censorship. He notes that the effect of such censorship is perverse, however: as he explains it, 'prohibitions [*les interdits*] have always been defied, for creators make light of repressive measures. The latter—and this is only seemingly a paradox—eventually even become sites of exquisite torment [*des 'gênes exquises'*], thanks to which works emerge which defy and ridicule idiotic laws all the more violently' (Lemaître 1965: p. i). To prove his point, the rest of this issue of the revue is given over to a version of *La Philosophie dans le boudoir* from which all the rude words have been removed and replaced variously with nonsense words, unrelated words and phrases lifted from other sources, unrelated drawings, and instructions for unrelated sounds, silences, and gestures. This gives rise to passages such as,

Véronique should lie in your arms; while I takraze her, I will bardore her oglu with the superb tip of Albert's héhé and he, in order to conserve his aou-aou, will take care not to burze.

Que Véronique se couche dans tes bras; pendant que je la takraze, je bardore son oglu avec la superbe tête du héhé d'Albert, qui pour ménager son aou-aou aura soin de ne pas burzer.

(Lemaître 1965: 31; adapted from Sade, *La Philosophie dans le boudoir*, OC iii. 471–2)

Though in the case of Lemaître's text part of the effect derives from our knowledge of the obscene Sadian original, there is no equivalent original, it should be noted, in the case of *Blankety-Blank*— or indeed of the *Madame Bovary* coach scene, to return to an earlier example. In the latter cases, it is the circle alone—a shared assumption that sexual images and vocabulary are censorable and 'censored'—which achieves the effect.

Johnson, addressing issues related to these in her book on Baudelaire, cites the American equivalent of *Blankety-Blank* in support of her contention that, 'It is doubtless *because* sexuality is censored or blanked out [*raturée*] that every blank [*rature*] tends to become a sign of sexuality' (Johnson 1979: 198 n.). A statement such as this, though resonant alongside the examples I have given, should not disguise the fact that *ratures* or blanks are not *always* signs of sexuality, nor are they always taken as such. Blanks in newspapers such as those with which Freud was acquainted pointed not towards sex but towards politics, after all. If Johnson's remark nevertheless seems plausible as a universal claim, at least at first sight, then this is partly, ironically, as a result of Freud's own influential thinking on these matters, since Freudian theory gave a new weight to the idea that that which was censored was 'the most interesting thing', and that this 'thing' was fundamentally and invariably sexual.

The Return of the Personal

When Freud writes later in 'The Censorship of Dreams' that 'When you reject something that is disagreeable to you, what you are doing is *repeating* the mechanism of constructing dreams rather than understanding it and surmounting it' (1916; *SE* xv. 145–6), he is circumscribing his own circle of censorship, instituting the disagreeable—that which he and his patients consider the censored, the taboo—as an index of comprehension and of truth. The fact that this circle came to turn around the sexual in the work of Freud (and of those he influenced) is partly the result, I want to argue, of processes of censorship which meant that political blanks within Freud's own text were covered over. This censorship may have started as an objective, external threat in Freud's society, but its effects are apparent internally to his work, too, in the tensions and silences left by the self-censorship to which Freud felt obliged to resort in his writing.

To support this argument it is easiest to start with an example of one such silence, imposed from without, where political material was excised from Freud's text.[6] In May 1898 Freud sent Fliess the manuscript of *The Interpretation of Dreams*, asking him to criticize it and also to point out any parts of the text which he thought should be cut to avoid possible embarrassment. Fliess answered that Freud should leave out one important and elaborate dream account. On 9 June Freud sent Fliess a reply, in which he wrote:

I must acknowledge that I need your critical advice because in this case I myself have lost the modesty which an author must have. So the dream is damned. But now that the sentence has been imposed I must shed a tear for it and confess that I am sorry and that I can hope to find no better substitute. You must know—a beautiful dream and no indiscretions—they don't go together. (Cited by McGrath 1986: 259–60)

Freud thus submitted to the 'sentence' of censorship imposed by Fliess, and though we do not know exactly what the original account contained, McGrath follows Max Schur in arguing that its exclusion was motivated by its political theme. Furthermore, as McGrath shows, the various dreams which replaced it all expressed attacks on authority, but in each case Freud, like his hypothetical 'political writer', 'honoured the need for censorship either by disguising the individuals involved or by obscuring the true point of his criticism' (McGrath 1986: 306).

Freud's behaviour on this issue is to be compared with the following passage from the essay 'On Beginning the Treatment' (1913; *SE* xii. 121–44), in which he makes it clear that, in order for psychoanalysis to work, censorship cannot be honoured, and, in-

---

[6] My account of this episode is drawn from McGrath (1986: 259–306).

deed, must be actively overcome. He is discussing the 'fundamental rule' of analysis, the rule which states that the analysand must say everything that comes into his or her head, irrespective of how seemingly 'irrelevant', 'unpleasant', 'embarrassing', or 'intimate'[7] it may be:

> It is indispensable, and also advantageous, to lay down the rule in the first stages of the treatment. Later, under the dominance of the resistances, obedience to it weakens, and there comes a time in every analysis when the patient disregards it. We must remember from our own self-analysis how irresistible the temptation is to yield to these pretexts put forward by critical judgement for rejecting certain ideas. How small is the effect of such agreements as one makes with the patient in laying down the fundamental rule is regularly demonstrated when something intimate about a third person comes up in his mind for the first time. He knows that he is supposed to say everything, but he turns discretion about other people into a new obstacle. 'Must I really say everything? I thought that only applied to things that concern myself.' It is naturally impossible to carry out analysis if the patient's relations with other people and his thoughts about them are excluded. *Pour faire une omelette il faut casser des œufs.* [. . .] It is very remarkable how the whole task becomes impossible if a reservation is allowed at any single place. (1913; *SE* xii. 135)

On Freud's own terms, then, his acceptance of the political censorship for which Fliess was the channel was crucially misguided. Freud's theory works on the basis, as we have seen, that when he arrives at the censored, he has arrived at the truth, and it is on that basis that he is attentive to the seemingly irrelevant, the unpleasant, the embarrassing, and the intimate—categories of subject which the analysand is reluctant to broach. What is missing from this list, in the way Freud uses it, is the political. Freud censored the censorship to which he himself submitted, and though in practice this may have been necessary, in theory it was inexcusable.

My point here is not so much to see Freud hoist with his own petard, as to provide an instance of the way in which censorship may mark a text and a theory, and to suggest that this particular theory may benefit from having a political dimension restored to it. Having said this, it is also true that Freud's own use of the notion of censorship allows politics a potential place in his theory, albeit in somewhat covert form. Dreams attacking authority, of the type

---

[7] These adjectives are used in 'On Beginning the Treatment' and/or in 'Freud's Psycho-Analytic Procedure' of 1904 (*SE* vii. 247–54).

alluded to by McGrath, provide one channel for this, as in the case of Freud's own 'dream of the uncle with the yellow beard', the dream to which the *Liebesdienste* dream I discussed earlier is a footnote. On close examination it reveals a particularly complex interplay of the personal and the political, and of the literal and the metaphorical.

The main thrust of the dream is summarized by Freud as follows: 'My friend R. was my uncle.—I had a great feeling of affection for him' (1900; *SE* iv. 137). The uncle in question was a criminal, so to substitute R. for him is interpreted as a way of denigrating R., while the feeling of affection is (the mark of) the dreamwork's distortion, since it dissimulates this effect of denigration. In other words, there is a defence against the affective charge of the wish: Freud suggests further that, 'The politeness I practise every day is to a large extent dissimulation of this kind' (1900; *SE* iv. 142). He then draws further parallels both from Goethe and with the 'political writer' discussed above. Again, these parallels are not as close as Freud wishes to suggest: the whole point of the political writer's task is that the affective charge remains basically the same through the formal change from officials to Mandarins, whereas it is precisely the affect which is distorted by censorship in Freud's dream.

From his initial interpretation, Freud concludes that 'dreams are given their shape in individual human beings by the operation of two psychical forces' then goes on to assert that 'one of these forces constructs the wish which is expressed by the dream, while the other exercises a censorship upon this dream-wish and, by the use of that censorship, forcibly brings about a distortion in the expression of that wish' (1900; *SE* iv. 144). Using this model, Freud then spots another 'complete analogy' in politics to explain the extraordinary affection which he felt for R. in the dream:

Let us imagine a society in which a struggle is in process between a ruler who is jealous of his power and an alert public opinion. The people are in revolt against an unpopular official and demand his dismissal. But the autocrat, to show that he need take no heed of the popular wish, chooses that moment for bestowing a high distinction upon the official, though there is no other reason for doing so. In just the same way my second agency, which commands the approaches to consciousness, distinguished my friend R. by a display of excessive affection simply because the wishes belonging to the first system, for particular reasons of their own on which they were intent at the moment, chose to condemn him as a simpleton. (1900; *SE* iv. 144–5)

Again, the analogy is in fact less than complete. The second agency and its censorship are stigmatized by association with the autocrat, and indeed their effects render the dreams 'hypocritical', a word used in a note of 1911 (*SE* iv. 145) which implies a particularly strong personification of the censorship as a conscious moral agent. Here, censorship represents a crude, external intervention rather different from the self-censorship of the political writer. Conversely, the unconscious wish is connoted positively by association with the people and its alert opinion. The problem with this is that, whereas the autocrat's action is a wanton display of power, that of the second agency is an attempt to counterbalance the unwarranted condemnation of R. as a simpleton by the first agency.

Of course, the image of the autocrat is nevertheless suggestive of the way in which the censoring agency may often be fickle and seemingly vicious in its operations, but the fact that the analogy can be 'literalized' against Freud's intentions is a sign of ambiguities in the values the censorship represents. In this case, Freud's unusually high regard for 'alert public opinion' is a clue to the existence of underlying tensions in which Freud is himself implicated. It is far more common, as I indicated in the first section of this chapter, for Freud to equate the unconscious with the masses on the basis of an image of the latter as irrational and threatening, an image he attempts to rationalize by collapsing together phylogeny and ontogeny. Thus in his essay *The Unconscious*, for example, he says that, 'The contents of the Ucs.[8] may be compared with an aboriginal population [*Urbevölkerung*] in the mind' (1915; *SE* xiv. 195), and in a later work states that the mind is 'to be compared with a modern State in which a mob, eager for enjoyment and destruction, has to be held down forcibly by a prudent superior class' (1932; *SE* xxii. 221). An image such as the latter, in particular, is exactly what one might expect to find illustrating the notion of censorship—this sort of conception of the relationship of the

---

[8] The abbreviations *Ucs.–Pcs.–Cs.* stand for the Unconscious, the Preconscious, and the Conscious, the three levels in Freud's first topography of the psyche. Part of the purpose of these abbreviated forms is to suggest that 'Unconscious' and 'Conscious' are being used in a technical sense distinct from, though closely related to, their everyday adjectival meanings.

masses to their masters was a commonplace of the discourses of censorship of the type I examined in Chapter 1, after all—but it is not what one finds in this instance, where the masses' habitual connotation is reversed.

This reversal can be explained, I would suggest, by the fact that the analogy as a whole is closely related to the real situation which Freud recounted in the preamble to the dream, and that this affects the balance of his sympathies. The preamble explains how he was recommended for a position as a 'professor extraordinarius' but feels he is unlikely to receive the post, since two friends (one of whom was R.) had been similarly recommended in the past, only to be passed over subsequently. He then reveals that it seems the reason for their ultimate rejection was 'denominational consider-ations' (1900; *SE* iv. 137)—that is to say, anti-Semitism. This revelation explains his dreamwish to denigrate his friend, for if he can believe R. to have a flawed character, he can discount his being Jewish as the reason for his rejection, and his own prospects are unimpaired.

In fact anti-Semitism was indeed to impair Freud's prospects: according to Schorske, the normal wait for a professorship in the medical faculty was eight years, but Freud waited seventeen, and was finally given an associate professorship at the age of 45. Even at this point his success carried a certain moral cost, since, against his long-standing principles (though not against Viennese custom of the time), Freud used personal connections to advance his cause. In a letter to Fliess of 1922, Freud spoke of his decision in terms of the triumph of his 'zest for life' over his 'zest for martyrdom', and explained, 'One must look somewhere for one's salvation, and the salvation I chose was the title of professor' (cited by Schorske 1981: 203).

Though this decision was taken after many years of frustration, even early on in his career Freud was very conscious of the diffi-culties he would face and the types of censorship to which he would have to submit. His very first use of the term 'censorship' in print, in the *Studies on Hysteria* of 1895, is notable in this respect. Discussing the fact that some of his patients could not be hypnot-ized, he notes that, 'by means of my psychical work I had to overcome a psychical force in the patients which was opposed to the pathogenic ideas becoming conscious (being remembered)' (1895; *SE* ii. 268), and goes on to say that,

From all this there arose, as it were automatically, the thought of *defence*. It has indeed been generally admitted by psychologists that the acceptance of a new idea (acceptance in the sense of believing or of recognizing as real) is dependent on the nature and trend of the ideas already united in the ego, and they have invented special technical names for this process of censorship to which the new arrival must submit. (1895; *SE* ii. 269)

Little attention is drawn, then, to the word 'censorship' itself, which is used in an almost commonsensical tone in contrast to the 'special technical terms' employed by other psychologists, but Freud's model here, as McGrath points out (1986: 169), is not primarily modern censorship but the role of the Roman censor in drawing up lists of those to be admitted to the Senate, where admission depended on the appropriateness of the 'new arrival' to the existing membership. There are evident parallels with Freud's own hopes of advancement, and it would seem that this model of censorship remained in Freud's mind even when his model was seemingly a different one, exerting a pull towards his personal history and its embroilment with politics.

In his account of his dream Freud's first explicit reference to 'denominational considerations' is made in such a way as to suggest that they are less than essential to his story, but it becomes clear that they are actually at its crux when he explains how one of the friends in question challenged an official at the Ministry to deny that anti-Semitism was at the root of their rejection. As Freud recalls:

The reply had been that, in view of the present state of feeling, it was no doubt true that, for the moment, His Excellency was not in a position, etc. etc. 'At least I know where I am now,' my friend had concluded. It was not news to me, though it was bound to strengthen my feeling of resignation; for the same denominational considerations applied to my own case. (1900; *SE* iv. 137)

Here public opinion plays a rather different role from the one it has in the case of the autocrat, but that of the 'unpopular official' is not dissimilar. In each case what is offensive about him is his position in relation to an illegitimate authority—that of the tyrannical ruler, or that of a prejudiced public.

In the real-life case, however, as the mocking tone adopted by Freud in reporting the official's response indicates ('His Excellency was not in a position, etc. etc.'), the distinction between the masses and the official is negligible, since both subscribe (by default or more actively) to the anti-Semitism which permeates their society. Not only is this incident the *meaning* of the dream, in the sense that it is Freud's frustrations which ground it and which the dream seeks to relieve, but tellingly it also provides a closer model for the type of psychic censorship he set out to describe: the same wish or affect, which is irrational and a derivative solely of socially conditioned responses (namely, the denigration of R. arising from Freud's ambition/the rejection of Jewish academics arising from anti-Semitism), persists through the different strata of the mind/society—Freud can remember his dream, after all—but the upper agency (the conscious/official) is sufficiently sensitive to the demands of rationality and decorum to deny its/his own part in it. Thus Freud conceals his anger and states that he is not ambitious: the official acts politely in his encounter with Freud's friend and shifts responsibility for anti-Semitism elsewhere. Censorship is operating on several levels and in several ways here, and if these parallels are hard to sketch and to follow, it is not because the two instances are too far apart but rather because they tend constantly to collapse together, 'literal' and 'metaphorical' censorship seemingly flowing together as the barriers between them dissolve to allow Freud's personal and political experience to leak back into his theory.

Depths of Censorship

The type of self-censorship Freud operated in concealing his anger and ambition, and in underplaying the significance of 'denominational considerations' in his career, represented an attempt not only to avoid objectively contentious, potentially censorable issues, but also to rid his theory of those personal elements which pointed to historically variable social and political factors. His project was, on one level, to understand the essence of humanity, which he hoped to extract from its particular manifestations. His vision of the unconscious as an *Urbevölkerung* (a word used for 'natives', aboriginal inhabitants, etc.), of dreaming as 'regression to the dreamer's earliest condition' (both phylogenetically and ontogenetically (1900; *SE* v. 548)), and of the murky processes of primal repression (*Urverdrängung*) are indications of this, and help explain the positive connotations attached to the idea of the unconscious in places, as it is seen as more profound and more vital than the mere 'chance circumstances' to which consciousness and censorship must respond. Another indication is his constant appeal to the supposedly timeless truths of mythology and literature. In *The Interpretation of Dreams*, for instance, in support of his discovery in children of generalized patterns of love and hatred for their parents, Freud refers to the myth of Oedipus for the first time, writing:

> This discovery is confirmed by a legend that has come down to us from classical antiquity: a legend whose profound and universal power to move can only be understood if the hypothesis I have put forward in regard to the psychology of children has an equally universal validity [. . .] His [Oedipus'] destiny moves us only because it might have been ours— because the oracle laid the same curse upon us before our birth as upon him. [. . .] Like Oedipus, we live in ignorance of these wishes, repugnant to morality, which have been forced upon us by Nature, and after their revelation we may all of us well seek to close our eyes to the scenes of our childhood. (1900; *SE* iv. 261–3)

The kind of 'confirmation' which a legend can provide for a theory is dubious, however, and the very idea that it can provide such confirmation, along with the ideas that the legend's appeal is 'universal', that our 'destiny' is 'the same' as that of Oedipus, and that it is imposed on us by 'Nature', are the attitudes of a particular society—attitudes which accord special privilege to classical civilization, and which, also privileging Nature and the Universal, fail to recognize themselves as such, as attitudes.

Freud, in talking about the legend's 'profound' power, implies that he is dealing here with the deepest recesses of the psyche. The question of how deeply sited are the censored wishes and the censoring agency is a vexed one, however. It is not clear, for instance, what the nature is of the revelation to which he refers, such that it could, until the moment Freud wrote this, occur only in allusive form in legend, in Sophocles' version of that legend, and in a more repressed form in *Hamlet*. This problem arises again in connection with his remarks on the frequency with which his patients dreamed of killing their parents. Again, his interpretation is based on the manifest content of the dream, the justification for this being that the repressed murderous wish entirely eludes censorship. Certain 'special factors' supposedly make this possible, most notably the fact that 'there is no wish that seems more remote from us than this one: "we couldn't even *dream*"—so we believe—of wishing such a thing. For this reason the dream-censorship is not armed to meet such a monstrosity' (1900; *SE* iv. 266). This explanation is highly problematic, however. First, we are not supposed to know, without Freud, that all our dreams are wishes. Secondly, Freud literalizes the figurative expression 'we couldn't even dream' in such a way as to miss its point—which is that its use for emphasis depends precisely on the fact that we all dream of doing things we would not dream of doing. Thirdly, the conception of the route to consciousness as the site of a conflict between opposed forces is extended metaphorically into the allusion to the censorship's armaments, whose power and range seem to have been definitively fixed. Only a very static concept of psychic censorship would suggest that, once forewarned of these terrible wishes by Sophocles, Shakespeare, or Freud, it is not forearmed; and if it is not, it is not clear why we had to wait for Freud to make them explicit.

Freud was not unaware of the problems of determining the 'depth' of censorship and how responsive it was supposed to be to changeable social factors, and it was partly in an attempt to resolve these issues that he worked towards the concept of an ideal ego. In the 1914 essay 'On Narcissism: An Introduction' (*SE* xiv. 67–102) he attributes functions previously attributed to the censorship to the ideal ego, using 'watchman', which he used in *The Interpretation of Dreams* (1900) as a metaphor for the censorship (see *SE* v. 567–8), as a metaphor for the conscience, and then 'censoring agency' (the latter in inverted commas (*SE* xiv. 96)) as a further synonym. He even claims that censorship was never conceived of as a special power, but designated one side of the repressive trends governing the ego, the side turned towards the dream-thoughts. When in the *Introductory Lectures on Psycho-Analysis* he revises these arguments, however, it is clear that it is conceived of more broadly than this, for he writes: 'We know the self-observing agency as the ego-censor, the conscience [. . .] When in delusions of observation it becomes split up, it reveals to us its origin from the influences of parents, educators and social environment—from an identification with some of these model figures' (1917; *SE* xvi. 429).

One source of these equivocations is that the relationship of the conscience and its censorship to consciousness is unclear. In *The Unconscious* (1915; *SE* xiv. 161–215) Freud suggests that the *Pcs.* has 'taken over' from the *Ucs.* in regulating access to consciousness (in the active sense) and motility, and that it is therefore the *Pcs.* which must 'set up a censorship or several censorships' (1915; *SE* xiv. 187), but this sits uneasily alongside the comment: 'A very great part of this preconscious originates in the unconscious, has the character of its derivatives, and is subjected to a censorship before it can become conscious. Another part of the *Pcs.* is capable of becoming conscious without any censorship' (1915; *SE* xiv. 191). This latter description demands a model in which there are *two* censorships situated at different points on the path to consciousness, whose different relations to the ideal ego are hard to imagine. Freud sums up:

The *Ucs.* is turned back on the frontier of the *Pcs.* by the censorship, but derivatives of the *Ucs.* can circumvent this censorship, achieve a high degree of organization and reach a certain intensity of cathexis in the *Pcs.* When, however, this intensity is exceeded and they try to force themselves into consciousness, they are recognized as derivations of the *Ucs.* and are repressed afresh at the new frontier of the censorship, between the *Pcs.* and the *Cs.* Thus the first of these censorships is exercised against the *Ucs.* itself, and the second against its *Pcs.* derivatives. One might suppose that in the course of individual development the censorship had taken a step forward. (1915; *SE* xiv. 193)

By this stage the model is becoming increasingly unwieldy, demanding an unduly spatial conceptualization to make the hypothesis at all workable. Already in *The Interpretation of Dreams* Freud had stressed that one should resist the urge to conceive of the mental apparatus spatially (1900; e.g. *SE* v. 165), but it is impossible not to when the account given of it depends heavily on metaphors such as the 'frontier of the censorship'. He is still more explicit about these difficulties in the *Introductory Lectures*, where he writes:

I hope you do not take the term [censorship] too anthropomorphically, and do not picture the 'censor of dreams' as a severe little manikin or a spirit living in a closet in the brain and there discharging his office; but I hope too that you do not take the term in too 'localizing' a sense, and do not think of a 'brain-centre', from which a censoring influence of this kind issues, an influence which would be brought to an end if the centre were damaged or removed. For the time being it is nothing more than a serviceable term for describing a dynamic relation. The word does not prevent our asking by what purposes [or trends: *Tendenzen*] this influence is exercised and against what purposes it is directed. (1916; *SE* xv. 140)

This is an ambiguous gesture, however, for Freud is recording the resonances inevitably produced by the term in any reader's mind, and which doubtless contribute to its air of being 'serviceable'. The image sticks, but Freud is unclear about its precise position in his theory, so that—contrary to Lacan's claim that 'Freud never confuses *Widerstand* [resistance] with censorship' (1978: 159; 1988b: 130)—phrases such as 'the resistance of the censorship' and 'the censorship of the resistance' are used interchangeably, and Freud acknowledges on one occasion, in *The Interpretation of Dreams* (1900), that the agency is something whose existence he cannot explain (see *SE* v. 606 n.).

It was these problems which drove Freud, by his own account, to distance himself in the works after *The Interpretation of Dreams* from censorship as a psychic concept in its own right, though he never completely abandoned it. When in the *Introductory Lectures* he uses the mixed metaphor of a 'watchman' who 'acts as a censor' between two rooms (1917; *SE* xvi. 295), he goes so far as to characterize his conception as a crude one, but notes it is 'convenient'. He then proceeds to state that, 'It is the same watchman whom we get to know as resistance when we try to lift the repression by means of the analytic treatment' but adds that he knows that these ideas are not only crude but also 'incorrect' and that he has 'something better to take their place' (1917; *SE* xvi. 296).

What counts as something better, though not specified in that essay, is presumably the superego, a concept introduced in *The Ego and the Id* of 1923 and whose functions include the censorship of dreams. The superego is understood to avoid the problem of locating censorship along the *Ucs.-Pcs.-Cs.* axis, since one of its distinguishing features is that it may operate, unlike a more general conception of moral conscience, at any of these levels. It should be noted, however, that the original topography persists alongside that of the id, ego, and superego, and that although Freud attempts on occasion to trace their relation (e.g. 1940; *SE* xxiii. 162), it remains far from clear. It is on these grounds that Freud's notion of censorship is criticized by Sartre in *L'Être et le néant*, where Sartre argues that the agency of psychic censorship must know what it is censoring and know that it is doing so, and that it cannot therefore be truly unconscious. Sartre's objections are summed up in his question, 'in a word, how could the censor discern the impulses needing to be repressed without being conscious of discerning them? How can we conceive of a knowledge which is ignorant of itself?' (Sartre 1943: 91; 1969: 52–3). He concludes that the notion of censorship provides an alibi for *mauvaise foi*, and though one may be resistant to Sartre's own agenda here, which is to prove the complete translucidity of consciousness, these criticisms are indisputably damaging to the notion of a profound unconscious whose most antisocial products are (unconsciously) censored.

In the dream of the uncle with the yellow beard, where Freud's model was arguably at its most successful (though not always in the manner Freud intended), the different 'layers' of consciousness were closely interconnected, and those which were less readily accessible did not originate in a timeless unconscious but had been forced away from full consciousness under specific social pressures. Even Freud's first use of the term 'censorship', where his model was seemingly the Roman senate, implied a conception of the psyche which potentially incorporated such social pressures at a funda-mental level, but Freud failed to pursue its implications systemati-cally. When Freud asserts in this early work that in therapy, 'the acceptance of a new idea (acceptance in the sense of believing or of recognizing as real) is dependent on the nature and trend of the ideas already united in the ego' (1895; *SE* ii. 269), the word 'new' disguises an ambiguity on this issue, since, although the idea is new in that it is introduced verbally into the analysis at a certain mo-ment, the necessity of so doing is apparently dictated by the fact that, not conscious and/or not remembered, it is nevertheless al-ready present, with a meaning and affective charge determined in some way by the society in which the patient lives.[9] Freud, however, glossed over social factors of this type, emphasizing instead the importance of antisocial—and indeed asocial—sexual impulses, whose origins he located deep within the individual.

Freud's notion of a harsh superego and his increasing preoccu-pation in his later works with the theme of ubiquitous guilt were part of a wider pessimism concerning the impossibility of quelling these impulses in a satisfactory way. For the later Freud, the experi-ence of guilt is thus a product of the tension between the ego and

---

[9] This is to be compared with Lacan's point that censored material can remain very much alive and active under censorship, in the same way that, in his words, 'the amnesia of repression is one of the most lively forms of memory' (1966: 261; 1977: 52).

the unrealizable demands of the superego, and this is an inevitable result of the socialization of the infant. Freud explains, for example, that even punishment dreams are fulfilments of wishes, expressing the wishes not of the 'instinctual impulses' but of 'the critical, censoring and punishing agency in the mind' (1933; *SE* xxii. 27). As so often, Freud's attitude is ambivalent: writing on the same subject in the *Introductory Lectures*, he states that 'punishment is also the fulfilment of a wish—of the wish of the other, censoring person' (1916; *SE* xv. 219), a strange formulation which sits un-easily alongside his remark a little earlier that 'we [. . .] are on the side of the censorship' (1916; *SE* xv. 217). Quite who 'we' refers to here is intriguing: again, censorship's everyday connotations are generating tension, between one version of the theory in which censorship functions as the necessary condition of successful socialization or even of a reliable grasp on reality, and another in which censorship's negative connotations re-emerge when Freud implies that censorship is a clumsy and repressive intervention which comes between the analyst and the id, the latter effectively colluding with the analyst in that it tries to elude censorship and to give its (potentially antisocial) impulses clear, conscious representation.

What is crucial for the later Freud in both models of punishment dreams, however, is the presupposition that, as in the case of dreams deriving from the Oedipus complex, the dreamwork (which was earlier seen as the work of censorship) is avoided. In this way, if this is the point at which interpretation stops, the feeling of guilt and the problems which help create it are essentialized as a con-dition of civilization which transcends its specific forms. Freud's undue emphasis on the universal individual, conceived of as prior to any particular historical society, leads him to search for psychic material which is inherently censorable—whence the capacity he lends the Oedipus myth to terminate any interpretative chain, and whence his explanation in *The Ego and the Id* of how certain manifestly immoral dreams are permissible to the censorship simply because 'they do not tell the truth' (1923; *SE* xix. 131). Neither psychic nor external censorship has any inherent relationship with truth, however, and what may link it to truth are contingent factors of convention and power, which shape the 'specific unconsciousnesses', as MacCabe puts it (1981: 213), which Freud is reluctant to theorize.

In summary, it can be seen that Freud's model of psychic censorship is highly suggestive, and is fraught with difficulties. These difficulties are connected initially with its metaphoricity, since, although in places the term seemingly is designed to be nothing more than analogical and provisional, in others it functions as a concept in its own right in a semantic field where there are no 'literal' alternatives. This ambivalence is compounded not only by the substantive interconnections between the 'interior' world which the metaphor is supposed to illuminate and the 'exterior' world from which it is drawn, but also by the ways in which Freud's metaphorical illustrations reveal inconsistencies and ambiguities when they try to apply unmodified models of exterior censorship to the individual psyche. Freudian censorship is, in other words, both too far from its political origins, in that it frequently fails to locate the psyche within politics (in a broad sense), and too close to them in that it does not provide an adequate account of ways in which the dynamics of self-censorship are importantly different from those of other-censorship, nor of the ways in which the separate but interconnected and overlapping demands of interior and exterior censorship are negotiated within any one individual.

'Censored' material as Freud pictured it was predominantly sexual, and in general was held to offer a potential threat to social order. The metaphors of censorship which proved seductive to Freud, however, tended to draw in non-sexual social and political material and potentially offered an alternative model of the nature of unconscious material and its origins, a model more attentive to historical specificities. The way that the concept of censorship became largely subsumed under the neologism 'super-ego' could be seen, I have suggested, as Freud's flight from the difficulties he had encountered on two interconnected levels: first (as he himself indicated) in grappling with an excessively spatial model of censorship, according to which censorship was exercised predominantly against a profound pre-social unconscious; and, secondly, in trying to define censorship against the flow of its primary, political meaning. In Chapter 3 I will examine how Freudian censorship was subsequently revitalized and reinserted into a politicized discourse in French literary culture, without these difficulties ever having been truly overcome.

3. Counter-Censorship

⁂

Under the subheading 'La Censure, l'invention' in his book on Sade, Roland Barthes makes the following statement: 'The most profound type of subversion (counter-censorship) does not, then, necessarily consist in saying what shocks public opinion, the law, or the police, but in inventing a discourse that is paradoxical (pure of any *doxa*): *invention* (and not provocation) is a revolutionary act' (Barthes 1971: 130; 1977c: 126). My aim in this chapter is to analyse the discourse of 'counter-censorship' in twentieth-century French literary culture, of which Barthes's remark is an exemplary instance, and to argue that this discourse grew out of the intersection and overlap of the discourses which turn around the two broad notions of censorship I examined in Chapters 1 and 2, the legal-historical and the psychoanalytic.

Sade has almost invariably been located at the centre of the discourse of counter-censorship, which in turn has had a profound effect on the status of Sade's work and how it is read. Of course, not all twentieth-century French critics (and fans) of Sade have been equally influenced by Freud and not all could be situated firmly in the tradition with which I am concerned. Other factors (Romanticism, for instance) have clearly come into play, too, and are outside my scope here. I should emphasize, then, that my aim is not to give a comprehensive account of the French reception of Sade, but to show that it is exemplary in certain respects with regard to the discourse of counter-censorship; and it is as an example, and in these respects, that it is discussed.

I will concentrate on two distinctive points where the intersection of legal-historical and psychoanalytic discourses on censorship was at its most lively and influential. The first of these points is represented by the work of Breton and the Surrealists, in whose work an unequivocally positive discourse on Sade was inaugurated and Sade's singularity began to be regarded as a positive rather than a negative attribute; and in whose work Sade is most evidently and most explicitly placed at the intersection I have located. I look closely at the Surrealists' understanding of Freud in relation to these issues, in particular from 1921 to 1932, a vital period in the Surrealists' development which was bounded by two events, the Barrès trial and the Aragon affair (which I will recount in due course), in which the Surrealists were forced to articulate their relationship to the authority of the censor and its implications for artistic practice. The inadequacies of the Surrealists' use of Freud, of Sade, and of an idealist notion of freedom surface particularly, I will argue, in their attitudes towards sexuality, which they believed to be unconventional but which revealed significant complicities with deep-rooted reactionary conventions.[1]

Secondly, I come to the work of Barthes and the *Tel Quel* group. Like the Surrealists, they sought to explore the subversive potential of creative writing, their notion of subversion situated at the intersection of the psychoanalytic and political discourses on censorship, but not bound by their most orthodox interpretations; and, like the Surrealists, they were forced to focus their ideas about these matters when one of their associates was singled out by the censor.

In addition to examining these two points in isolation, I also attempt briefly to situate them in a broader literary-historical context. I do this first by giving, through an analysis of the ways in which Sade's texts were presented by their editors and prefacers from the time of their first publication until the early twentieth century, some sense of how Sade was perceived prior to the twentieth century and before Freud's ideas (or French appropriations of them) came into play; and secondly, after my more detailed look at Surrealism, by giving a brief account of the fate of Sade's works between the Second World War (by which time the Surrealists were past the prime of their influence) and the arrival of the *Tel Quel* group on the literary scene. This broader context will indicate the ways in which the reception of Sade's work was always shaped by the censorship to which it was subject, and conversely will make it clear that the Surrealists and the *Tel Quel* group had a notable

---

[1] The Surrealists' readiness to deal openly with issues of sexuality was unconventional in their day, and for this they should be given credit. At the Congrès International pour la Défense de la Culture of 1935, for instance, the Surrealists were denied a platform essentially because they were considered perverts (Breton 1972a: 256; 1969c: 244 n.), and, as Breton points out, it should not be forgotten that, when the Surrealists were young, Baudelaire was still officially considered 'a corruptor of youth' (Breton 1969b: 98). My concern here, however, is that the theory behind the Surrealists' sexual openness was flawed, and that its results were consequently conventional in damaging ways, and it is on these grounds that I will criticize them.

impact on the ways in which censorship, and through it Sade's work, were perceived.

My analysis of the Surrealists' and their predecessors' reception of Sade rests on various assumptions, the most basic of which is that my reader has some familiarity with Sade's work. I do not intend, consequently, to provide any exegesis of his different works nor samples of his writing styles in them. Though I seek to justify other of my assumptions in the course of my argument where necessary, there are a few preliminary points I wish to make here.

First, along with most preface writers of the nineteenth century, I assume that the historical figure Sade was guilty of most of the crimes of which he was accused, and also that his role in the Revolution was neither a particularly significant nor a particularly glorious one. While Sade's fans have tended to suggest that accounts of his sexual crimes were exaggerated to justify his imprisonment, and that his aristocratic family played down his commitment to the Revolution, it is clear that opposite pressures also existed, such as the difficulty (in terms of credibility, embarrassment, and procedural know-how) for prostitutes, children, or working-class women to accuse an aristocrat of sexual crimes against them. There were also obvious advantages after the Revolution in exaggerating one's Revolutionary fervour. We know from Sade's letters that he loved the king, for instance, that he had mixed feelings about the post-revolutionary Constitution, and that he believed in the value or even necessity of the nobility, and although his fiction frequently finds space for the discussion of liberal and radical political ideas, the contradictory framework within which they are generally placed makes it impossible to make his opinions, even as expressed in his fiction, into any clear-cut model of political progressiveness.

Secondly, I assume that the argument that Sade's work has positive scientific value cannot be taken seriously, even though as late as 1962 Breton, for instance, was still referring to Sade's invaluable contribution to biology (in Breton 1965: 388). This argument is evidently undercut by the work's particularities as fiction (an issue to which I will return). I also assume that the idea of literary value (introduced into commentary on Sade either as a positive attribute of his work, or as something his writing's monotony suggests it lacks) does not exempt literature from ethical considerations.

Thirdly, I assume (and will seek to prove) that it is an error—though one consistent with a certain individualist rhetoric of freedom of expression—to see the history of censorship to which Sade's works have been subjected, and the commonplace repugnance at their obscenity which lies behind that censorship, as a reason in itself for endorsing them, or for presuming they work against the reactionary ideologies they supposedly transgress, especially—and this is my main concern—in the area of sexuality.

At this stage I should indicate that this latter idea seems to me to be flawed on at least three levels. First, it is flawed in that it views transgression as an action which breaks and so works to eliminate a limit, when in Sade it is evident that it is a gesture which can be endlessly repeated (and narrated), and which is pleasurable as transgression precisely in so far as the limit remains in place. As Bataille puts it in *L'Érotisme*, 'transgression is not the negation of the taboo but goes beyond it and completes it' (1987: 66; 1986: 63). It is a mistake, consequently, to view Sadian transgression as a release of the body from its social fetters:[2] Sadian pleasure, as I suggested at the end of Chapter 1, is itself a *social* phenomenon.

The second level on which the idea of Sade's work as transgressive (in a positive sense) is flawed is in its assumption that the society which condemns him is homogeneously and monolithically reactionary, and that conflict with that society is therefore necessarily potentially liberating. Examples abound of the ways in which Sade's own writing generates or is complicitous with sexism and misogyny, which are themselves profoundly reactionary: the vagina is frequently treated as something repugnant, the right of women to sexual pleasure is confused with their supposed obligation to make themselves unconditionally sexually available to men, there is a particular aversion, as Mary Jacobus has argued, to the mother and to the internal, reproductive body (as opposed to 'sexuality' as an exterior system of signs), and, more generally, women are frequently dehumanized, subordinated, and treated as objects. Much of Sade's work is, then, pornographic, according to the definition of pornography offered by MacKinnon.

---

[2] This is a mistake to which Bataille too is prone, incidentally, despite his awareness of transgression's complex relation to social prohibitions. Consequently he is not immune to crude mind/body dualisms, writing, for instance, that one should think 'like a cock would think if it had the chance to demand that its own needs be fulfilled' (1970b: 85).

On a third level, it is a mistake to think that, in the supposedly monolithic society against which the counter-censors react, Sade's work is unambiguously condemned rather than subjected to the conflicting forces I discussed in the final section of Chapter 1, whereby pornography is on one level marginalized but on another considered close to the core of human nature.

Conflicting forces exist within the work, too, of course. It may be true, for instance, as Angela Carter argues in *The Sadian Woman*, that Sade's separation of sex from reproduction and his awareness of female sexual pleasure was (and is) in some respects progressive. Indeed, several writers have held Juliette up as some sort of proto-type of the sexually liberated woman—Pauvert,[3] for instance, writes in his *Anthologie des lectures érotiques* that he is proud that his first major publishing venture was the publication of 'a text [*Juliette*] entirely devoted to a female character. And what a woman she is!' (1981: 85)—but this gesture presents certain prob-lems. The types of sexual pleasure into which Juliette is 'liberated' are not obviously a model which real women would want to, or could, emulate, given the levels of violence involved and given that the language in which her experiences are described is frequently gendered as male (Sade's use of *décharger* (meaning to ejaculate), for instance, is striking to the modern reader). There is also the complex question of the position of the reader and the author in relation to the text, and the nature of *their* sexual pleasure, as discussed by Kappeler. Finally, even internally to the text, it is not clear how liberated Juliette is, for all her sexual activity. Jane Gallop has argued that Juliette's desires depend entirely on men's desires (1981: 57), and Nancy Miller has suggested that this is true also on the level of the book's framing narrative, in that Juliette's freedom is mediated by a higher, male authority in the form of Noirceuil, who tells her, 'I want you to be a woman and a slave to me and my friends; a despot to everyone else.' Juliette has already signalled that she accepts this framework ('As a woman I know my

[3] Pauvert, both through his publishing and through his writing, is an eminent counter-censor, with links to both the Surrealists and *Tel Quel*. In his *Anthologie des lectures érotiques* of 1981 he stated glibly that 'The MLF [Women's Liberation Movement], a misogynistic movement, is interested only in prohibitions' (Pauvert 1981: p. xviii), that the United States, in which this movement had its origins, was a 'country in which women are dominant', and claimed (and this is a claim which I will contest later in this section) that women's emancipation had been advanced by the Surrealists above all others (p. xliv).

place, and know that dependency is my lot' (both OC viii. 201; 1991: 207)), and Miller comments, 'The supremacy of the couple is maintained, and within that couple, the male prerogative supported by power in the world' (1975: 416).

I will end this introduction by quoting from an article entitled 'Une Lecture de femme' (A Woman's Reading), written by Catherine Claude. It appeared in 1972, three years before the first of the other feminist readings I have just cited (Miller's '*Juliette* and the Posterity of Prosperity' appeared in 1975), and, unlike them, it was written in France, where it appeared in a special Sade number of a journal called *Europe* whose editorial board included the Surrealists Aragon, Triolet, and Éluard. Claude begins her article thus:

I am sure that other writers in this issue will point out the 'revolutionary' character of Sade's work, when it attacks a dominant ideology which in his time and even in ours censors the sexual [*le fait sexuel*]. It is a commonplace that the sexual is part of, and plays a decisive role in, human reality; and violently proclaiming its existence, its influence, and its power to transgress the types of censorship [*les censures*] to which it is subject is indisputably a way of attacking this ideology at an important and heavily fortified point, in that it attacks its idealism and its hypocrisy. (1972: 64)

Only after this does she get on to her own thesis, which is that Sade remains 'on the same ground as this ideology' (*sur le terrain même de cette idéologie*) (1972: 65) with regard to the relationship between men and women. What is notable about this for my present purposes is not only that she begins by talking about the censorship of the 'fait sexuel' and about the transgressive power of Sade's writing with regard to this censorship, but also, more importantly, that she seemingly feels obliged to do so and to concede that her own criticism, whose tone in places is almost apologetic, is only of secondary importance. Indeed, she goes so far as to describe her reading as partisan, and to suggest that it may constitute 'a refusal to read properly' (*un refus de lire vraiment*) (1972: 70).

My purpose in the coming chapters, I should reiterate, is not to provide my own reading of Sade, nor to survey at greater length the feminist criticism to which I have alluded, but to offer an indication of the way in which certain French readings of Sade in the twentieth century grew strong on notions of counter-censorship, and to criticize those notions both with regard to Sade and in more general terms. The article by Claude gives some indication of the strength of those notions and of the readings of Sade which they spawned, readings which could marginalize other, more critical readings as 'un refus de lire vraiment'.[4] A voice such as Claude's has been hard to hear, and is to be compared with the confident tones of eminent counter-censors such as the Surrealists or *Tel Quel*. The notion of counter-censorship cannot fully 'account' for the Surrealist and *Tel Quel* readings and their influence, of course, but I will attempt to show that it was a crucial factor in what I will henceforth refer to as the Sade myth, the whole complex of ideas which has come to turn around Sade in modern France. It is a myth not only in the sense that it emerged from an indistinct mixture of fact and fiction but also, I will argue, in that it is a mystification which acts as an impediment to understanding psychic, artistic, and political freedom and the relation between them.

SADE AND SURREALISM

Introducing Sade

Prefaces to Sade's work throughout the nineteenth and early twentieth centuries, in a succession of editions which were mostly clandestine, all displayed an awareness of the work's marginality and all attempted to negotiate on some level the texts' (and the author's) relation to the law. Metaphorically, at least, Sade was always on trial, and it is typical that the preface to an 1878 edition of Sade's *Idée sur les romans*, for instance, should begin with the sentence, 'This is not a plea on Sade's behalf, since I would sooner act as his prosecutor than in his defence' (*Nous ne ferons pas ici un plaidoyer en faveur de Sade dont nous serions plus volontiers l'accusateur que l'avocat*) (Uzanne 1878: p. ix). Any approach to Sade and to his work inevitably passed via the censure and censorship to which they were subject, taking the preface writer and the reader outside the legal and moral boundaries delimiting and defining French society. The responsibility of any responsible citizen breaking a path into this off-territory was to justify his action

---

[4] Sade does come in for criticism in Bruckner's and Finkielkraut's *Le Nouveau Désordre amoureux* of 1977 in the course of their attack on the sexism of pornography. In my view, however, these authors greatly overestimate the impact of French feminism on the cult of Sade.

(invariably *his*, of course), distancing himself sufficiently from the man and his work to relocate himself within those boundaries, and to signpost the dangers that lay ahead; and, until the early twentieth century, this was exactly what most publishers of Sade attempted to do.

Publishers' prefaces cannot tell us how Sade was read, of course, but they can give us some sense of the impact of censorship upon the reception of Sade's work and can tell us in what terms it was possible to arrive at a positive assessment of a figure and of a series of novels whose rapidly established reputation depended on their ignoring or actively infringing many of the criteria on which a positive assessment of a literary text might normally have been based. Most of the prefaces protested their own *a priori* disapproval of Sade, in fact, and a few were even unrelentingly negative. This latter approach was clearly a self-defeating one, however, when the first task of the preface writer was to defend the texts despite their illegality and to justify their publication in the face of opprobrium, so most writers attempted to articulate their reaction to Sade in such a way as to suggest that they shared the censor's concerns and that the publication of Sade was compatible with them, contrary to first impressions. Appeals to a radical *liberté d'expression* were consequently avoided, in general, but the idea was present in negative, as it were, through a recognition of its common-sense limits and through an attention to areas where possible applications of the right to freedom of expression were not altogether clear. Unsurprisingly, then, many of the prefaces' arguments occupy similar terrain to the debates over freedom of expression discussed in Chapter 1, alluding to the impressionability of youth, women, and the lower classes (balanced in these prefaces by an emphasis on the (purportedly) small number of copies being produced), insisting on the division of 'expression' from action (though in ambiguous ways, as I will argue) and relatedly on the autonomy of art, asserting hopefully that moral and aesthetic values tend to coincide, appealing to the notion of historical progress in morality and, perhaps most importantly, suggesting that Sade's work had scientific interest and value which exempted it from moral considerations.

Sade had to be introduced to the reader precisely because on another level he was someone who needed no introduction. Even the early editions published under Sade's aegis sometimes situated themselves in relation to the law: the title-page of the 1795 edition of *Aline et Valcour*, for instance, states it was 'Written in the Bastille one year before the French Revolution', implying, amongst other things,[5] that revolutionary freedom and the book's publication had common roots in the rubble of the Bastille and of the archaic, unjust system of justice it represented; and the title-page of the 1797 edition of *La Nouvelle Justine* bears the couplet (drawn from Petronius) 'On n'est point criminel pour faire la peinture | Des bizarres penchans qu'inspire la nature' (Portraying the strange penchants that nature inspires does not make you a criminal). Part of the trouble, however, was that Sade himself was a criminal for other reasons, anyway. Most preface writers consequently felt obliged to deal with Sade's life, providing some biographical information and articulating its relationship to his work. In an essay of 1837 entitled 'La Vérité sur les deux procès criminels du Marquis de Sade', for instance, which formed part of an introduction to the 1870 edition of *Zoloé et ses deux acolytes*,[6] Paul Jacob commented, 'if the books did not exist, endlessly reproduced in secret by men whose greed is perhaps even more reprehensible than the calculated corruption which created those books, I would definitely attempt to defend the Marquis de Sade against the blind and unjust aspects of the sometimes exaggerated accusations which sully his name' (1870: p. lxxvi). Unsurprisingly, however, Jacob's own account is not without its biographical inaccuracies and exaggerations, such as his claim that in the Marseilles incident, 'two girls died as a result of their frenzy of immodesty [*leurs fureurs impudiques*]' (1870: p. xcviii);[7] and, despite his suggestion that corruption is in the eye of the beholder, he is also given to extravagant estimations of the books' impact on the reader—for

[5] Most important amongst these is the implication—made explicit in footnotes to the text of *Aline et Valcour* for readers who have not drawn it in the course of their reading, and often repeated by Sade's admirers—that Sade displayed a gift of prophecy in this book. As Louis Perceau noted in 1930, however, *Aline et Valcour* was adapted and updated after the Revolution.

[6] It has since been established that this work is not by Sade, but this was not known at the time.

[7] In 1772 on a visit to Marseilles Sade organized an orgy involving himself, his valet, and four young women. Two of these women fell ill afterwards, purportedly poisoned by pastilles intended as aphrodisiacs given to them by Sade. They recovered fairly quickly, and, though the episode undoubtedly had its unpleasant aspects, it became somewhat exaggerated in the hearsay accounts of it which rapidly gained wide currency.

example, in his reference to 'the terrifying contagion which these poisonous books spread every day amongst our young people [*la jeunesse*]' (1870: p. lxxvi).

Jacob's commentary is typical in other respects too, and, though it seeks to strike a tone of reasoned moderation, tinged with repugnance, it contains strands from many arguments (some contradictory) which are developed into bolder claims elsewhere. Fundamental to all of these is the feeling that Sade is a special case. Both his life and his work are considered extraordinary, remote, and even inaccessible from the everyday in various ways, and this provides a formidable impetus to make something of them which locates them back within the terms of common sense. Both his life and his work are considered open to interpretation. Jacob, like others, implies both the need to consider Sade and his writing separately, and the impossibility of doing so, an ambiguity which resurfaces elsewhere time and again as Sade's fiction is read as autobiography while his life is fictionalized and mythologized. When, for example, Anatole France writes in 1881 of Sade's fiancée, 'she was a beautiful, pious, cold young lady' and notes that her sister (with whom Sade had an affair), 'who had a less upright mind, had more charms to offer' (1881: 9), there seems to be an inextricable (and unacknowledged) interplay between biographical facts, cultural stereotypes, and the fictional characters of Justine and Juliette.

Later commentators with a greater (or more overt) enthusiasm for Sade also tended to interpret his biography to suit their own positions, often playing down Sade's sadism in order to divide his life and his fiction more neatly. Louis Perceau, for instance, in a preface written in 1923 (and used, under the pseudonym Helpey, in a 1948 edition of *La Philosophie dans le boudoir*), states glibly 'it is easy to reconstruct what happened' (1948: 17) then goes on to give an account of the Rose Keller incident in which it is assumed that Keller was mentally retarded.[8]

Another influential interpretation of the relation between Sade's life and work is the idea that Sade was made a monster by the society in which he lived and from which for much of his life he was excluded. Jacob, for instance, writes:

---

[8] In April 1768 Sade took Rose Keller, a young widow who was begging in Paris, to his retreat in Arceuil, where he whipped her and from where she then fled. By her account he also tied her up, threatened to kill her, cut her, and poured hot wax into her wounds.

originally, this unfortunate man was not the incredibly wicked monster as which he is now represented, and [. . .] he became such a creature as he grew older only in order to avenge himself on the society he held responsible for his suffering. There are two clearly demarcated periods in the Marquis de Sade's life: one is part of the history of the most appalling sicknesses of spirit; the latter is the consequence of the former; each, to different degrees, provides a satire on the prejudices, rules, and laws of civilized nature. (1837: p. lxxvi)

His need to sound tentative makes his meaning a little obscure, but on one level this seems to be a comment on the fact that Sade, in accordance with aristocratic custom, did not have a free choice about whom he should marry. This is something Jacob and others see as very important to Sade's later development: according to this line of argument, all Sade's bitterness (and beyond that, his perversion) is traced back to this fundamental frustration, made to seem all the more pressing if his biography is rearranged to allow his love for the younger Montreuil to predate his marriage to the older one. On a more general level, when Jacob speaks of 'the history of morals in his age' (*l'histoire des mœurs de son temps*), this can be interpreted as a statement to the effect that Sade was a man of his time, less atypical than we might think. Taken in this sense it finds an echo in an edition of *Aline et Valcour* of 1883, whose foreword terms it 'a reflection of its age' (Anon. 1883: p. vi) and explains, 'this agitated period generated literature in its image, full of crimes and orgies' (1883: p. v), or in an 1884 edition of *Justine* which presents the story as a sign of 'the extraordinary mental ferment on the eve of the Revolution' (Liseux 1884: 7). Scientistic evidence, too, is marshalled in some prefaces to support the contention that Sade was not so extraordinary—Perceau, for example, stating in 1923 that both human and animal coitus are accompanied by 'violent acts carried out by the male', that females of all species enjoy this, and that sadism is not a perversion so much as an indication of 'an excessive sensitivity of the genital organs, as in nymphomania' (1948: 32).

If it is Sade's books which make it ultimately impossible for Jacob to consider Sade's life (other than his book-writing) on its own merits, this impossibility stems from the sickness which he believes they spread, namely 'hideous sicknesses of the soul'. One sees the same idea at work in Jules Janin's warning of 1839, 'Believe me, whoever you are, stay away from these books. As for those who might read them for pleasure, they do not read them at all:

they are in prison or in Charenton [an asylum]' (from an article in the *Revue de Paris*, quoted by Jacob 1870: p. xxiv). Similarly Uzanne remarks:

the despicable works by this man who dreamt of murder have thankfully been put on the index and prosecuted as an affront to natural standards of decency [*atteinte aux bonnes mœurs naturelles*], and the revolting creations which carry his signature will bear for all time the mark of ignominy. We must lock away the poison, contain the epidemic, and build a pyre of those inflammatory books which destroy forever a heart's purity [*condamner au feu [. . .] les livres incendiaires qui anéantissent pour toujours la virginité du cœur*]. (1878: p. vi)

As usual, certain groups of people (such as 'la jeunesse') are considered to be at greater risk than others. This idea persists in Perceau's essay of 1923—'it goes without saying', he says, that teenagers, adults with 'weak minds', and so on should not read them (1948: 40)—although, rejecting the idea of contagion or even incitation in the case of fully mature adults, he argues that the contradictions in Sade's theory are easy to spot, and that adults, at least, do not simply imitate what they read.

It is tempting for the modern reader to treat Janin's idea of contagion as a metaphor, but this probably leads to a misapprehension of what appeared to someone like him or Jacob to be at stake. When Janin says that those who might enjoy reading Sade are already social outcasts, kept locked up in prison or in mental asylums, or when Jacob quotes an opinion on *Aline et Valcour* (1870: p. lvii) to the effect that 'this novel, which is less immoral than *Justine*, is perhaps more dangerous since the scenes it portrays are less revolting', the implication is that, whatever the books' aesthetic or formal qualities, and whatever their apparent moral position, they provide a channel for a force which is profoundly antisocial, rather than merely immoral. What distinguishes the former quality is that it is taken to be entirely uncontrollable, once unleashed: the immoral individual may always repent, but the truly antisocial individual, it is implied, can only be shut away.

The force in question here is clearly in large part sexual. Jacob's image of two of the women in the Marseilles incident actually dying of the 'fureurs impudiques' brought on by the (purported) aphrodisiac Sade (purportedly) gave them is one sign of this, Jacob's disproportionate attention to the cantharides suggesting he views sexuality as something dangerous and as something which quickly escapes any sort of conscious control. What is most threatening of all is the idea that this force is already present in the women (and in everyone, though the phenomenon is also presented as specifically female in some way), and that the aphrodisiac is merely a catalyst which releases what a later account of the same incident refers to as 'this appallingly excessive uterine frenzy' (*cet horrible excès de leur fureur utérine*) (Anon. 1922: 168).

There are, perhaps surprisingly, certain parallels between, on the one hand, Janin's and Jacob's views and, on the other, those of MacKinnon. All of them apparently share a vision of sexuality as something potentially destructive, especially for women, and especially in so far as it operates unconsciously. All believe that a text's degree of aesthetic sophistication does not necessarily have an inverse bearing on the harm it may cause. For MacKinnon, however, women's self-destruct mechanism is programmed socio-culturally, rather than biologically, and adults are consequently anything but exempt from the problems a text may cause or perpetuate. For her, in other words, being mentally fully-fledged does not mean being fully autonomous. From this perspective, children are not a category apart, texts do not operate on them in a crudely instrumental way, and the supposed purity or 'virginity' of their hearts is a myth. It is a myth, moreover, which engages with discourses on femininity as well as on childhood, since the image of this 'virginité du cœur' which one should try to protect feminizes innocence and seemingly implies that the (controlled) sexual initiation which comes with adulthood (again, especially for women) provides an inoculation, as it were, against the dangerous sort of sexuality to which he is alluding.

How morality fits in with a Janin-type vision of sexuality is complex. On one level, sexual behaviour is clearly a prime area of moral concern and an index of moral character; but, on another, it seems that sexuality quickly moves outside moral boundaries, its excesses occurring in a discrete sphere. Thus Anatole France, in his introduction to an 1881 edition of *Dorci: ou, La Bizarrerie du sort*, comments that Sade used his new-found influence after the Revolution 'with a mildness that one would never have expected of a creature who had been corrupted by raging eroticism [*un être dénaturé par un si furieux érotisme*]' (1881: 18). This implies that France expected a coherence of personality including the sexual within it, and at the same time recognized that the 'denaturing' operated by Sade's sexuality involved a transgression of Natural limits but did not impinge upon his basic good nature. France goes on to reinforce this division, noting that Sade's sexual madness did not affect other aspects of his behaviour (1881: 21).

This approach to Sade's sexuality tended to distance it from the moral sphere, then, and to situate it close to pathology. From this position the necessary positive justifications for publishing his writing were not hard to find, in that sadism could be considered a suitable object of scientific attention. The fact that Sade's work was fictional, or at least used the devices of fiction, was potentially problematic in this respect, but justifications for ignoring or circumventing this fact were also at hand.[9] First, there were Sade's own protestations (along the lines, 'on n'est point criminel pour faire la peinture | Des bizarres penchans qu'inspire la nature') that he was merely producing a copy of natural phenomena, his favoured pictorial metaphors lessening still further the degree of moral responsibility attributable to the 'artist'. (At the same time, though, this argument could also be turned against the books by anyone who did not accept that artistic realism was self-justifying, or who saw the books' fault as lying in their lack of attention to self-conscious aesthetic criteria which might have raised them above their subject-matter. Conversely Anatole France, having pointed out that Baudelaire amongst others also displayed sadistic tendencies in his work, noted (1881: 24 n.) that 'Nevertheless this poem ['Une martyre'] is still normal, since it is beautiful and does not exceed the aesthetic laws which in the end are a matter of public morality').

Secondly, there was again the confusion of the boundaries between life and work in the Sade myth. Thirdly, the scientistic gaze itself served to anchor Sade's books in objectivity, in a way similar to that in which the legal gaze may turn illegally produced photographs into evidence (see Kappeler 1986: 9). Ambiguities about

[9] As I describe different frameworks within which Sade's work has been received—moral, scientific, and so on—and seek to sketch links between these different areas, it is diffcult not to give the impression that one particular framework or another is being posited as originary, or that those who adopted a particular framework invariably found justifications for it only *a posteriori*. Neither assumption can necessarily be made. Furthermore, although my account has a loosely chronological structure, it should be emphasized that different frameworks can be isolated synchronically as well as diachronically.

questions of mediation remain, however. In this instance, the scientistic gaze was generally averted from Sade himself in so far as he could be considered separate from his work (or sickness), in accordance with conventional pathological practice,[10] but this left a problem concerning the type of material Sade's writings provided. On the one hand, his books were treated as an aspect of his disease, of something beyond his control which could manifest itself in— and transfer itself to—another individual. On the other hand, there was a tendency to regard the stories as a *substitute* for the actions his sickness would have had him commit, an account of sadistic behaviour whose efficacy as a substitute depended on its accuracy. In short, the ambiguity lay in whether Sade's writing was best regarded as an account of sadism, or as a sadistic act in its own right.

Though this ambiguity is hard to banish (and as I suggested in the final section of Chapter 1, to attempt to banish it altogether is doubtless already a mistake), it is the former interpretation which has tended to be dominant, and on which claims for Sade's scientific value have generally been based. Given the historical ascendancy of a particular version of the separation of speech or writing from action, this is perhaps unsurprising, especially since Sade's commentators have mostly been obliged to deny any possibility that they themselves have been or could be 'infected', or in any way discountenanced, by reading his works.[11] Anatole France, for example, begins his introduction of 1881 by saying 'I did not seek out this fine, rich example of literary pathology: but finding it before me, I consider it my duty to examine it' (1881: 7). In this remark there is still some ambiguity about the status of textual sadism, but the disinterested, scientific approach of the commentator is in no doubt. Other writers were prepared to make much stronger claims for the scientific utility of Sade's work, seeing it as

[10] One exception is the foreword to *Dorci* written by Anatole France, who, having started out promisingly by dismissing phrenology, goes on to say that a modern physiologist carrying out a postmortem on Sade would have examined his brain, rather than his skull, and that 'the central grey matter of the optic stratum is where he would have looked for the lesion, for that is where genital impulsions, which in this subject were notoriously perverted, are disseminated' (France 1881: 20). France adds, however, that science is probably not yet advanced enough to isolate such a phenomenon.

[11] Again, playing down Sade's own sadism made such an attitude easier to support, and helped discredit simplistic accounts of the dreadful effects of the wrong sort of reading, since Sade was also the texts' first reader.

an active scientific project in its own right rather than as a mere object of scientific curiosity. Iwan Bloch, for instance, who under the pseudonym Eugene Duehren published an influential study on Sade in 1899 entitled *Der Marquis de Sade und seine Zeit* which was translated into French in 1901, and who published the first edition of *Les Cent-vingt Journées de Sodome* in 1904, wrote in his introduction to the latter,

It follows a systematic plan, aiming thereby to group its examples scientifically. These cases of perversion, the Marquis insists, are real and not imaginary [. . .] Often it is as if one were dealing with cases cited by Krafft-Ebing [. . .]

What makes some of the six hundred cases reported by the author all the more interesting, however, is that they are recounted in the form of stories from a brothel; thus the truth of these incidents seems all the more striking and they give us a more accurate idea of the psychological frame of mind [*l'état psychologique de l'âme*] of a sexual pervert, by making all the monstrous, paradoxical, and unnatural aspects of this subject more readily intelligible. (1904: p. iii)

The strength of his claims for its scientific validity are somewhat undermined, however, not only by his recognition that this validity depends on believing Sade—when actually it is far from clear whether even Sade would have expected readers to believe his conventional novelistic assurances that he should be believed—but also by his awareness that the 'cases' are fictionalized and presented 'in the form of stories' (*sous la forme d'aventures*). Again, the account/action ambiguity makes itself felt here, and the attempt to gloss over it by suggesting that the fictional element merely makes the facts more immediate and accessible comes dangerously close to acknowledging that the supposedly neutral observer may be drawn into sympathy with the sadist.

Bloch, however, clearly considered himself immune to this sort of danger. This was partly because he tied his analysis of Sade to a series of racial prejudices against the French, and partly because he justified his interest in Sade in terms not only of a scientific tradition but also of a metaphysical–philosophical one which passed via the flesh on to a higher plane. In his introduction to *Le Marquis de Sade et son temps*, for instance, he writes:

Scientific study of human sexual life can take three forms. First, there is love as a natural phenomenon which as such is subject to the law of causality. Secondly, setting aside unconscious necessity, it is a historical object, the object of a process which, in the eminently original words of Hegel, represents 'progress in the consciousness of moral freedom'. But the goal of love, like that of any human activity, consists in freedom, which is identical with the absolute spiritual principle and perfect knowledge [*science*] [. . .]

Physical love is merely a point of transition—a necessary one—towards the final goal of platonic love. The ultimate metaphysical goal of love is knowledge identical with absolute freedom. The Bible's turn of phrase, 'And Adam knew Eve', is a profound one. (Bloch 1901: 1, 23)

This view of sexual writing such as Sade's as a potential path to perfect knowledge and absolute freedom was undoubtedly to have an influence on the Surrealists, who were appreciative of Bloch's work.

The allusion to Krafft-Ebing which Bloch made in his essay of 1904 was a popular one amongst commentators, used as proof not only of Sade's scientific credentials but also of the fact he was ahead of his times. Similarly, numerous commentators claimed that Sade's writings foreshadowed those of Darwin. Liseux's preface to *Justine* stated in 1884, for instance, that the 'germ' of Darwin's ideas was present in that novel (1884: 7), and Perceau declared in 1923 that 'this extraordinary man [. . .] discovered the laws of natural selection before Darwin' (1948: 40). Even an assessment as negative as that of Paul Bourdin, made in the introduction to his *Correspondance inédite du Marquis de Sade* of 1929, noted that Sade made certain observations which meant one might regard him as a precursor of Lamarck, Darwin, Spencer, Krafft-Ebing, Frazer, and Freud (1929: p. viii).

As I noted earlier, the idea of *science* is a broader one in French than in English, and claims to be *scientifique* were also made from positions closer to the literary tradition. Uzanne, for instance, made the following claim: 'Bibliography [*La Bibliographie*], in and of itself, can quell rather than sharpen compelling desires for [or from] bad books [*les impérieux désirs des mauvaises lectures*] [. . .] scientific in its cold, steady concision, it is useful [*utile*] more than harmful, since its audience consists of mature, cultured minds whose judgement is unassailable' (1878: pp. xi–xii). It is notable, though, that he feels obliged to spell out the moral rectitude of his enterprise in this way, and backs it up with a familiar emphasis both on the 'limited public of refined [*délicat*], educated individuals' for whom it is intended, and on the idea that only fools and scandal-seekers would censure such a project (1878: p. vii).

The first unequivocally positive claims for Sade to appear in an edition of his work came in the shape of the introduction which Apollinaire wrote for a non-clandestine (and fairly tame) selection published in 1909 under the title *L'Œuvre du Marquis de Sade*. Given the influence this essay was to have, and in view of how often one or two of Apollinaire's remarks were to be quoted later, it is a surprisingly insubstantial piece of writing, composed mainly of quotations from Sade, synopses of his novels, and sometimes inaccurate facts about his life and publications. Various familiar arguments in Sade's favour crop up, including the idea that his sadism was less extreme than is generally believed and was brought on by his frustrated love for the younger Montreuil ('The woman he loved having been put in a convent, he felt greatly aggrieved and upset, and abandoned himself to debauchery' (Apollinaire 1909: 3)), and the idea that in *Les Cent-vingt Journées de Sodome*, termed 'rigorously scientific', Sade 'condensed all the new theories and also created, one hundred years before Doctor Krafft-Ebing, sexual psychopathology' (Apollinaire 1909: 24).

Other, less familiar lines of argument were also laid down by Apollinaire, however, albeit rather sketchily. He mentions, for example, that Sade was 'a true republican' (1909: 6), and says that he agrees with Bloch's idea that Sade's doctrines are related to contemporary French politics. In Bloch's case this was part of a theory of French decadence, but to Apollinaire, this relationship seems 'extremely profound and progressive' (1909: 17). Perhaps for the first time in such a context, then, Sade is presented in a positive light in relation to politics, and this light is generated by connecting contemporary political progress to a somewhat mythopoeic vision of the Revolution and of Sade's involvement in it. This is also connected with the more familiar argument that Sade's work was ahead of its time, but Apollinaire, unlike previous proponents of this view, apparently considered the work as in some sense programmatic as well as descriptive. Indeed, by this time Apollinaire himself had already written his own Sadian novelette, *Les Onze Mille Verges, ou Les Amours d'un hospodar* (containing familiar ingredients of violent sex, torture, blasphemy, scatology, and so on), which first appeared in 1907 in a clandestine edition. He was clearly confident that the time had come for Sade's ideas to be more widely accepted, writing in his Introduction of 1909: 'It seems the time has come for these ideas which have matured in the shameful atmosphere of forbidden-books departments [*des enfers de bibliothèques*], and this man, who seemed to count for nothing throughout the nineteenth century, may well dominate the twentieth' (1909: 17). Apollinaire does not go into the details of Sade's politics, except to say that he 'had exceptional ideas on Women, who he thought should be as free as men', illustrating this point by describing Justine and Juliette: 'Justine is the woman of old—subservient, pitiful and less than human; Juliette, on the other hand, represents the new type of woman.' Apollinaire is less concerned with the realities of sexual emancipation, however, than with a particular notion of liberty, and it is unsurprising that the phrase from this essay which has most often been repeated is his reference to Sade as 'the freest spirit who has ever lived' (*cet esprit le plus libre qui ait encore existé*) (1909: 17–18).

'Freudo-sadisme': The Surrealists

It was through Apollinaire's edition that many of the Surrealists discovered Sade's writing, and his enthusiasm was clearly an influence on them. Maurice Heine, who was involved with the Surrealist group and who spent his personal fortune on producing luxurious, painstakingly scholarly editions of Sade's works through the Société du Roman Philosophique which he founded in 1923, dedicated his 1930 edition of *Les Infortunes de la vertu* to Apollinaire and to his Surrealist friends who, he noted, had followed in Apollinaire's footsteps.

By 1924, the year in which the first Surrealist manifesto appeared, and two years before the first of Heine's editions was to appear (the *Historiettes, contes et fabliaux* of 1926), Sade had already emerged as some sort of mascot or role model for the Surrealist group, whose name was itself a tribute to the then recently deceased Apollinaire. In the first issue of *Proverbe* magazine, for instance, published in February 1920 under Apollinaire's aegis, a quotation from Sade ('Come now, I forgive you and I must respect the principles which lead to your aberrations' (*Allons, je vous pardonne et je dois respecter des principes qui conduisent à des égarements*) (*Proverbe* 1920: 2)), isolated in a heavy frame, appeared under the title 'One hundred phrases to repeat', and

Desnos's *De l'érotisme* of 1923 contained an entire chapter on Sade. Aragon, in response to a question about his literary influences for a survey on prominent young authors published in *La Revue hebdomadaire* in 1922, stated: 'my friends and I have all been reading Sade since our childhood' (cited by Bonnet 1975: 243). How true this is must be doubted, however, given the difficulty they would have faced in getting hold of Sade's work, and given that in a manuscript of February 1922 Breton and Aragon referred to *Justice* [*sic*] and to *Les Cent-vingt Jours* [*sic*] *de Sodome* (see Fauskevåg 1982: 205). Certain Surrealists also took up Apollinaire's idea that Sade's example provided a programme of sorts, and this produced a flurry of obscene clandestine literature in 1928, when Aragon published *Le Con d'Irène* ('Irène's Cunt') anonymously, Bataille published *Histoire de l'œil* ('Story of the Eye') under the pseudonym Lord Auch, and Péret wrote *Les Rouilles encagées* (a.k.a. *Les Couilles enragées*, recently translated as 'Mad Balls'), which was eventually published in its entirety in 1954 under the pseudonym Satyremont.

Desnos's chapter on Sade in *De l'érotisme* is full of bold claims concerning Sade's importance. Having said that he will not bother refuting the negative legends surrounding Sade, he goes on to make assertions such as, 'All our current aspirations were essentially formulated by SADE when he, before anyone else, made sexual life in its entirety the basis of the life of the senses and the mind' (Desnos [1923]: 76), 'No prose is more topical than that of SADE' (p. 77), 'From an erotic point of view, Sade's work is of superior intellectual calibre [. . .] creating a completely new universe [. . .] where he would have liked to live' (pp. 77–8), 'The term libertine [*libertin*] as he uses it has its true meaning, referring to liberty of the mind [*liberté d'esprit*]' (p. 80) and 'SADE does not belong with literature but alongside the founders of religions' (p. 82).

Remarks such as these were evidently designed to shock, dealing in extravagant exaggerations and apparent contradictions such as the idea that the notoriously irreligious Sade should be seen as the founder of a religion, or the comment, 'Sade is more of a moralist than anyone' (1923: 78). As Breton suggested in his *Entretiens* of 1952,[12] the early figureheads for the Surrealists were writers who

<hr/>

[12] Though concentrating on the period from 1921 to 1932, I draw in later material where I consider it to be continuous with trends established in that period. I should also note that I assume, with Breton, that he can be considered a mouth-

offered them 'the greatest scope for contestation' (1969*b*: 98); and the Surrealists tended to confuse contestation with confrontation. In Breton's words:

We were a long way from the vast irony [*cette ironie 'énorme'*] in which Flaubert delighted as he dreamed of a *Dictionnaire des idées reçues* which would survey every commonplace and provide, as he said, a 'gloss on every form of human coarseness' [*une 'apologie de la canaillerie humaine sous toutes ses formes'*]. The efficiency of a strategy of that sort seemed questionable to us, or at least too long term. The stance we chose was an aggressive one. (1969*b*: 98)

Though Sade's name is frequently mentioned in Surrealist texts above all for its shock value, then, Desnos's remarks give indications that the Surrealist reception of Sade located his work at the intersection of various discourses which defined Surrealism as something more than the desire to shock. Above all, the notion that Sade 'made sexual life in its entirety the basis of the life of the senses and the mind', and that to do so was one of the main aspirations of Surrealism, conjoined Sade's work with that of Freud in a way which was more dynamic and political than previous claims that Sade was a forerunner of Freud. This conjuncture is made explicit by a writer such as Heine when he refers to the 'obvious freudo-sadism [*freudo-sadisme*]' of Buñuel's *L'Age d'or* (Place 1976: *SASDLR* 3 (Dec. 1931), 12) or when in the fifth issue of the same revue he asserts that 'Sade's views and Freud's doctrine are the same' (Place 1976: *SASDLR* 5 (May 1933), 7).

To understand how an assertion as apparently implausible as this could be made, one needs to examine more closely the Surrealists' understanding of Freud. Breton, according to Bonnet, first became interested in Freud in about 1916 having read about his ideas in Régis's *Précis de la psychiatrie*, which was published in 1884 and which by 1923 had run to a sixth edition. Freud's work was translated extensively into French only from about 1921, and the first edition of *Le Rêve et son interprétation* appeared in 1925—which means, incidentally, that a considerable number of French readers must have come across Freud's ideas for the first time in the work of the Surrealists. Initially Breton was suspicious of Freud's theories and as late as 1921 an article Breton wrote for *Littérature*

piece for the group, and that he is the linchpin of such coherence as the Surrealists achieved as a group.

(1969a: 94–5) after meeting Freud in Vienna, though it dubbed him 'the greatest psychologist of our age', was slightly dismissive of the growing fashion for psychoanalysis. Similarly, reservations about the appropriateness of psychoanalysis to the interpretation of Dada were expressed in his essay 'Pour Dada' of 1920 (1969a: 69–76), and in the course of the Barrès trial of 1921 (to which I return later in this section) Breton remarked 'Nothing today is as overrated as the delights [*les voluptés*] of "analysis"' (Bonnet 1987: 30). Breton later saw his offhand attitude to Freud at that time as 'a regrettable sacrifice to the spirit of Dada' (1969b: 82), but, more than just an example of gratuitous irreverence, his equivocation may have been the sign of an uneasiness about Freud's concern with the control of instinct and the unconscious. In a series of definitions of Dada from this time, Breton wrote in 'Deux manifestes Dada' of 1920: 'DADA, recognizing only instinct, has a prior objection to explanation. According to Dada, we must keep no control of ourselves. No longer can there be any question of the dogmas of morality and taste' (1969a: 61). Clearly this is a long way from Freud, and Breton's distrust of him on this matter may have been enhanced by the idea of sublimation he had gained from Régis, who presented it, in Bonnet's words, as 'an intentional operation [. . .] a curative procedure with a distinctly moral aspect, used by the psychotherapist' (Bonnet 1975: 103). For Freud, it will be remembered, the term described the process by which potentially antisocial sexual energy was transformed into activity of high social worth, most notably artistic and intellectual, and it was not primarily a moral or therapeutic notion. Nevertheless Freud himself was indubitably on the side of high culture, even if his theories could be seen to cut it down to size.

It is perhaps surprising, in view of all this, that by 1924 Freud was, according to Breton in 1952, the Surrealists' 'intellectual guide' (*maître à penser*) (1969b: 108), and that the first manifesto declared that thanks to Freud: 'The imagination may be about to reclaim its rights' (Breton: 1972a: 21; 1969c: 10). Similarly positive and explicit claims for Freud can be found in many Surrealist texts (the second manifesto declared in 1930, for instance, that 'Freudian criticism is the first and the only one with a really solid basis' (Breton: 1972a: 165; 1969c: 160)), and extracts from his work were occasionally reproduced in Surrealist journals. Conversely, unfavourable articles on Freud—such as Crevel's 'Notes en vue d'une psycho-dialectique' (Place 1976: *SASDLR* 5 (May 1933), 48–52), which criticized Freud's political conservatism and his misplaced faith in civilization and high culture—were rare.

What attracted the Surrealists to Freud was the idea that, beneath our conscious thought processes, we have a seething, potentially subversive unconscious, which is censored or kept in check by a set of social norms and its agents. Freud's evaluation of this was, of course, ambiguous, in that he viewed repression as a damaging process in many ways, but at the same time found it difficult to see beyond the cultural and social structures in which he lived and worked, and to which such repression was apparently necessary. The Surrealists, on the other hand, embraced the idea of the subversion which the unconscious seemed to offer, talking in the first manifesto of lifting 'the terrible prohibition' (*le terrible interdit*) which holds down our imaginations and with it our aspirations (Breton 1972*a*: 16; 1969*c*: 5).

Consequently, whereas for Freud, who was concerned to detach his conceptual and therapeutic framework from any political position, the political metaphors which helped constitute psychoanalysis were frequently a source of discomfort, for the Surrealists they provided a welcome passage between personal, artistic, and political concerns.[13] When, for instance, Breton writes in 'Situation surréaliste de l'objet' of 1935 (1972*a*: 267–94; 1969*c*: 255–78) that Surrealist art seeks to draw on the deepest levels of the psychic apparatus and to dissolve the ego into the id, thereby tending, in his words, 'to liberate instinctive impulses more and more, to break down the barrier that civilized man faces, a barrier that primitive people and children do not experience' (1972*a*: 289; 1969*c*: 273), the wider political implications of 'liberate' (*libérer*) and 'break down the barrier' (*abattre la barrière*) are essential to the Surrealist message. On occasion, the Surrealists' analogies and models for the psyche advertised their political roots in a way that would have made Freud shudder, a tendency which must surely have reached its

---

[13] Another concern found particularly in early Surrealism was an interest in the mystical. In his essay 'Une vague de rêves' of 1924, for instance, Aragon discusses automatic writing in terms of 'the beyond, metempsychosis, and the supernatural', and in terms of 'a belief in sleep', of which he writes: 'This belief [. . .] does away with [. . .] the many-faceted censorship [*le faisceau de censures*] which fetters our minds. Freedom, that superb word, takes on meaning for the first time at that point: freedom begins with the birth of the supernatural [*le merveilleux*]' (Aragon 1974–5: ii. 240).

apex (rather belatedly) in an essay by Péret of 1944, in which he wrote: 'Like Hitler or Stalin, who, having been elevated to power by a misled people, took advantage of the opportunity to oppress them, reason today fulfils an analogous role in the mind by crushing intuition with its usurped power' (1944: 13). The Surrealists were also very willing to accept Freud's confusion of phylogeny and ontogeny in his attitude to the working classes, as it suited their conception of revolutionary politics. Likewise Bataille, at the start of the 1930s (a time when he stood in a close, though often antagonistic, relation to the Surrealists) advocated 'renouncing all the moral values associated with class superiority, and renouncing everything which deprives "distinguished" men of proletarian virility' (1970*b*: 99).

While Freud's resistance to the political meant he strove to locate the unconscious deep beyond the influence of politics and history, the Surrealists' gleeful exploitation of the political slippage inherent in Freud's vocabulary meant that, in their use of the concept of the unconscious, the latter sometimes floated up close to the surface of consciousness. In a discussion of found objects in *L'Amour fou* of 1937, Breton, in an account of his attraction to a particular spoon, writes of 'my incapacity, because *censorship* was maintained, to justify fully why I needed that spoon at that moment' (1975: 43; 1987: 35–6). His assumption here is that the necessity is a real one, and that his instinct is making itself felt in a reliable way (i.e. uncensored, in Freud's sense) despite the '*censorship*'—his italics perhaps marking out the concept as one he is borrowing from psychoanalysis, and in any case indicating that the (political) idea of censorship is one which he wishes to stress. Notably, the term Péret chooses in the above-mentioned article to describe what is crushed by reason is not 'the unconscious' but 'intuition'. This fits into a model which constructs all censorship as deliberate, political, and negative, and conversely constructs that which is censored as spontaneous, political, and ultimately positive. Again, this is some way from Freud, and it led the Surrealists to believe that anything that emerged from the unconscious was politically subversive, and therefore good.

So it is that, having apparently embraced the political framework from which Freud's idea of censorship was drawn, the Surrealists end up, like Freud, failing to acknowledge political specificities and their fundamental role in the constitution of the individual. This is one point at which the Surrealists' use of Freudian discourse and a certain discourse on liberty, inherited from the Revolution, most obviously meet, their subject an individual (whom it is considered is best considered *as* an individual) whose freedom is constitutionally (in a dual sense) guaranteed. For the Surrealists, as for the *Déclaration des droits de l'homme*, individuals are, in other words, born free and are or may be entirely free in so far as they can avoid impediments to that freedom. These impediments are only superficially within such individuals, if within them at all, and these individuals are given the capacity, constitutionally, to overthrow them. In Breton's words (from the first manifesto), 'Among all the many misfortunes to which we are heir, it must be admitted that we are allowed the *greatest freedom* of thought. To reduce the imagination to a state of slavery is to betray the ultimate justice deep within us' (*Parmi tant de disgrâces dont nous héritons, il faut bien reconnaître que la* plus grande liberté *d'esprit nous est laissée. Réduire l'imagination à l'esclavage [. . .] c'est se dérober à tout ce qu'on trouve, au fond de soi, de justice suprême*) (1972a: 16; 1969c: 4–5).[14]

The Surrealists' first attempt to overcome the enslavement of the imagination came in the shape of automatic writing, an idea initially inspired, according to Bonnet (1975: 99–106), by Régis's account of free association in *Précis de la psychiatrie*. Automatism was an idea which one found elsewhere in psychiatry at the time, but Freud's use of the idea was original in that he perceived the process as a creative one, and it was this which inspired Breton to begin practising automatism in 1919 and from 1922 to write *récits de rêve*. These techniques became so central to Breton's thought that in the first manifesto of 1924 Surrealism was defined in the following terms:

SURREALISM, n. Psychic automatism in its pure state, by which one proposes to express—verbally, by means of the written word, or in any other manner—the actual functioning of thought. Dictated by thought, in the

---

[14] The same line of argument is all the more striking, and smacks all the more sharply of idealism, when the idea of purity is substituted for that of freedom in an article in *Le Surréalisme au service de la révolution*, where Monnerot writes 'an ethical treatise could be established on the basis of a being's complete self-acceptance, which, using the psychoanalytic technique of dream interpretation, would succeed in rigorously defining the pure human being and explaining the reduction of this purity by the environment' (Monnerot 1933: 37).

absence of any control exercised by reason and exempt from any aesthetic or moral influences. (Breton 1972*a*: 35; 1969*c*: 26)

It is interesting to note that by his own account Freud himself was inspired, at an earlier point on this circle of mutually affirming influence between literature and psychological theory, by an essay entitled 'The Art of Becoming an Original Writer in Three Days', written by Ludwig Börne in 1823. Freud explains in a brief essay entitled 'A Note on the Prehistory of the Technique of Analysis' (1920; *SE* xviii. 263–5), which was published anonymously (and so written in the third person), that Börne's suggestion was that, as an aspiring writer, you should write down 'everything that comes into your head' for three days. Freud first read this at age 14, and notes that it was the only book from his childhood he still possessed some 50 years later in 1920. When he reread it he was astonished, he explains,

to find expressed in the advice to the original writer some opinions which he himself [i.e. Freud] had always cherished and vindicated. For instance: 'A disgraceful cowardliness in regard to thinking holds us all back. The censorship of governments is less oppressive than the censorship exercised by public opinion over our intellectual productions.' (Moreover, there is a reference here to a 'censorship', which reappears in psychoanalysis as the dream-censorship). 'It is not lack of intellect but lack of character that prevents most writers from being better than they are.' (1920; *SE* xviii. 263)

The Surrealist idea was, then, close to Freud's (and Börne's) in its origins, but it differed from Freud's concept in a number of important and largely unacknowledged ways. First, of course, was their fundamental difference of attitude towards their shared assumption that unconscious processes were antisocial, and the difference of their aims. Freud, like Sade, wished to locate his project within rationalism, and Freud perhaps never really relinquished the hope of finding physiological explanations for the psychic phenomena he studied. This rationalist approach is reflected in Sade's and Freud's choice of language, which, though itself buckled by the irrational, aims to present unconscious and taboo material in a readily comprehensible form. In this connection it is notable that the Surrealists tended to choose their heroes on the basis of the subject-matter of their books, and were unperturbed by their formal conservatism.

Secondly, Freud's idea of the unconscious makes it profoundly inaccessible and generally ascribes a high degree of efficiency to psychic censorship. Consequently, although the latter may be relaxed in certain situations, it cannot be completely avoided in any spontaneous, voluntary way, and it continues to distort and disguise the contents of the unconscious even in dreams or in free association. For Freud, the texts which automatism produces are worthless unless interpreted, and he would have seen little value in the raw products of automatism which the Surrealists transcribed. Reading such texts is indeed a problem, to the extent that immediate incomprehensibility is a hallmark of (supposed) outpourings of the unconscious, and the necessary mediations are frequently too personal to be made by anyone other than the text's author.

Freud himself is, of course, inconsistent on this issue, in that he is prepared to supply his own associations to the manifest content of a work of literature or art in order to get beyond the censorship, when one would perhaps expect him to deem it necessary for the writer or artist to provide his or her own associations. Art and literature always had a special place in Freud's theories, though, offering a particularly valued type of articulacy about matters of the unconscious, and another aspect of the Surrealist texts' worthlessness for Freud would have been their declared lack of attention to aesthetics. For Freud, aesthetics are a set of conditions which are met by moulding material from the artist's unconscious into a form which makes it palatable on a conscious level to other people while simultaneously allowing it to speak covertly to their unconscious, and so releasing some of the unconscious's contents in a controlled way. On Freud's economic model, aesthetic pleasure thus derives from the saving the reader or viewer makes on the energy which would otherwise be required to repress the unacceptable unconscious material. For Freud, then, psychic censorship is not only creative in the weak sense that it involves transformations of raw material, but is also the founding instance of artistic creativity, understood as the area of innovation, bounded by aesthetics, within which a manifest level of significance overlies a more fundamental appeal to material which comes from or has been forced into the unconscious.

In an essay of 1933 entitled 'Le Message automatique' (1970*a*: 164–89) Breton discusses at greater length the relation of automatic writing to traditional poetry, claiming that Surrealism has revalorized the idea of inspiration and that its products have a documentary value beyond any aesthetic value. Dreamscripts and automatic poems are thus, in the words of the second manifesto, 'as far removed as possible from the desire to make sense, as free as possible of any ideas of responsibility which tend always to act as a brake' (Breton 1972*a*: 167; 1969*c*: 162). Surrealism is consequently able to proclaim 'the complete equality of all normal human beings before the subliminal message' (Breton 1970*a*: 182), and Breton sees this as the democratization of artistic talent, bemoaning the fact that this artistic democracy is undermined by competition amongst the Surrealists over the poetic qualities of their 'interior language' (1970*a*: 183). Producing documentary evidence of one's unconscious activity is not the same as producing poetry, however, in the sense that it is the 'poetic qualities' of these documents which make them comprehensible and/or pleasurable to other people; and the fact that some documents are more 'poetic' than others is a sign not that their authors have a 'more poetic' inner life, but that they have expressed it in a language with a greater resonance for others.

The relation of all this to democracy is more complex than Breton allows. The idea of a broader social base for artistic activity is an appealing one, but could be understood in two different ways in terms of democracy, either as a more or less metaphorical democratization of a discrete artistic sphere, or as a means to a greater democratization of democracy as a political structure, which would work by allowing more people to intervene in its symbolic systems. Breton, though presumably keen to think of his position as a matter of hard politics, seems closer to the first of these interpretations, given his dismissal of responsibility and of even 'the desire to make sense'. As I tried to show in Chapter 1, this sort of disregard for the impact of one's published writing (or art) may be something democracy is obliged to countenance, but it is hard to see its contributing in any positive sense to a democratic culture: the language and symbols to which we have access are primarily *exterior* and communal, and to regard them as a path starting in a pre-social self and leading only back to the self (if anywhere) is not only theoretically ill founded, but is an instance of an individualist version of self-expression which, I have argued, may be actively damaging to democratic culture in important respects.

Surrealism on Trial

The Surrealists themselves were not unaware of the risks of a directionless individualism. Indeed, it was the attempt to turn away from this impasse which had marked the beginning of Surrealism, as distinct from Dada. One incident signalling this change was the Barrès affair, which took place in May 1921 and which represented one of the earliest attempts by the Surrealists to come to terms with ideas of political commitment and artistic responsibility. That they chose to do this by staging a trial is surely significant. On one level, the gesture was a playful (and provocative) one, by which they appropriated for themselves the censoring authority which would normally, they felt, have been on Barrès's side, directed against the likes of them. On another level, however, the gesture seemed to do little to subvert that authority, and the fact that they made a considerable effort to mimic accurately standard juridical procedure and so to give their judgements a weight they might otherwise have lacked suggests that they shared aspects of the logic by which a juridical censor imputes moral accountability (and a certain instrumental efficacy) to a writer.

Maurice Barrès himself was apparently sufficiently intimidated by their proceedings to arrange to be out of Paris when the trial was being enacted. An inflatable dummy was used in his place in the courtroom. He was an author whom several of the Surrealists had read in their youth, and whose books—such as *Ennemi des lois* of 1893 or the trilogy *Le Culte du moi* of 1888 to 1891—were something of an inspiration to them, with their emphasis on love and on the individual's heroic stand against society, its values, and even its language. From about 1916, however, Barrès was frequently attacked by the Left for his increasingly right-wing sympathies (Sanouillet 1965: 254–66). Quite what Barrès's crime was in terms of the Surrealist ideology of that moment was hard to specify, however. The Surrealists had difficulty settling on an official charge, and eventually opted for 'attentat à la sûreté d'esprit' (conspiracy against mind security) (Breton 1988: 1407), a formula which was again parasitic on legal norms and which gave little clue as to the Surrealist position, beyond the possible implication that, for them, the mind was sovereign in a comparable way to the State. In his role as prosecutor, Breton criticized Barrès's bias (*parti pris*) and 'complete lack of rigour', but he also declared that he was not opposed to contradiction, saying: 'Far be it from me to reproach Maurice Barrès with having contradicted himself' (Bonnet 1987: 31). What was presented as the crucial argument was that, in Breton's words, 'ideas have no value in themselves; they become valuable only in relation to the stakes attached to them' (Bonnet 1987: 32).

The whole trial could indeed be taken to illustrate this point, in that various wider issues accompanied the rather low-level debate. One of these was the development of Surrealism away from Dada. Tristan Tzara, Dada's main representative, participated in the trial but was clearly deeply suspicious of the juridical apparatus of censure which Breton and his friends had put in place, and he did his best to disrupt its conventions, answering 'no' when asked if he swore to tell the whole truth, abusing the other participants, and declaring in his testimony, 'I have no confidence in justice, even if that justice is dispensed by Dada [. . .] we are nothing but a bunch of bastards [. . .] consequently, minor differences—the fact that some people are bigger bastards than others—are completely unimportant' (Breton 1988: 420). At the end of his speech Tzara sang a Dada song then walked out, slamming the door behind him. Those who sympathized with Tzara felt that this helped to reveal the event's inadequacies and to make it a failure; Breton and his allies, on the other hand, considered it a success, Breton later saying that Tzara's flippancy isolated him within the group and that 'Dada, having resolutely declared itself indifferent, had absolutely no part to play' (1969*b*: 74).

The Barrès trial was undoubtedly the site of a power struggle between Breton and Tzara, but it also raised imporant questions concerning the very nature of Dadaist and Surrealist activity. Tzara disagreed with Breton on fundamental issues: he had no time for Freud (who was, according to him, 'a character whose mystery is built on a sort of bourgeois ideal, a prototype of Normal Man' (cited by Sanouillet 1965: 127n.)), and he was disdainful of Breton's growing interest in politics. Tzara wrote of poetry in the following terms in 1931 in *Le Surréalisme au service de la révolution*: 'Poetry which distinguishes itself from novels only by its external form, poetry which expresses either ideas or feelings, no longer interests anyone. To that poetry I oppose the *active poetry of the mind* [*Je lui oppose la poésie* active *de l'esprit*]. It is perfectly evident today that one can be a poet without ever having written a line' (cited by Nadeau 1964: 33; 1978: 74). What, then, was the appeal for Tzara of the notion of the poet? The answer, it would seem, lay in his unspoken, perhaps unconscious assumption—not an unusual one—that poetry was ultimately inconsequential, occupying a cultural area in which one might express oneself in some integral sense beyond ideas or even articulable feelings and which was in other respects severed, causally, legally, and otherwise, from the rest of the world.

Tzara's line of thought in this instance was not far from that of Breton in the Barrès trial when he defined ideas as important only in relation to the stakes which accompany them, for Tzara was simply going one step further, doing away with the ideas altogether, leaving the revolt against everything and nothing which was the hallmark of Dada. The very idea of the trial shows, however, that Breton believed—or wished to believe—that art had consequences, that he was worried by this notion of revolt in a vacuum, and was anxious about the idea of an artistic practice cut off from the rest of the world. He later expressed this anxiety in his essay 'Le Bouquet sans fleurs' of 1925, where he wrote: 'What indirect action could satisfy me? It would seem that as soon as I begin looking, I retreat into art, that is, into some social order where impunity is assured for me but where, to a certain point, I cease to be of any importance' (cited by Nadeau 1964: 65n.; 1978: 110n.). The Barrès trial represented an attempt by Breton to give the group a more positive impetus, and to attribute a significance beyond a few shock waves to their ideas, in other words making those ideas an end as well as a means. The fact that Breton became a far more influential figure than Tzara, and that the group later became involved in politics, are indications that he had some degree of success, but the Dada experience continued to influence profoundly the Surrealists' conception of artistic activity. That one finds Tzara (in the essay quoted above) still promoting a Dadaist idea of poetry in 1931, in a journal entitled *Le Surréalisme au service de la révolution*, is one sign of this.

It is true that, as early as 1919, members of the group were asking themselves, and others, what the point of writing was, via a survey sent out to various writers (mainly non-Surrealists) which asked 'Pourquoi écrivez-vous?'; but no clear sense of direction emerged from the answers, and the question continued to nag at the Surrealist conscience. The responses it elicited in this survey were

published in issues 10, 11, and 12 of *Littérature* (December 1919–
February 1920), arranged within each issue in inverse order of their
interest to the editors (Aragon, Breton, and Soupault). It is difficult
to perceive any consistent criteria behind this order, but certain of
the editors' responses are worth noting. The idea of writing to
change people's opinions did not go down particularly well, for
instance, and the editors were not especially impressed at this stage
by the Freudian answer (which also contained an explicit reference
to Sade) given by Lenormand (no. 11, p. 24). On the other hand,
they seemed keen on answers which implied that the question was
unanswerable, such as Picabia's 'I really don't know and I hope I
never will' (no. 12, p. 26). The favourite responses in the three
successive issues were respectively Valéry's 'Out of weakness' (no.
10, p. 26), André Colomer's 'Why am I alive? Why do I write? Am
I God, to answer Why? I'm aware of being [*Je me constate*] and
that's good enough for me' (no. 11, p. 26), and Hamsun's 'I write
to pass time' (*J'écris pour abréger le temps*) (no. 12, p. 26). All this
suggests that they liked snappy answers whose meaning was in-
determinate, and unsurprisingly that their favoured emphasis was,
if anywhere, on individualism and revolt. When Breton looked
back on this survey in 1923, he said that the only response with
which he agreed, as a partial answer, was the last of these (1969*a*:
12), and he stated categorically that the Surrealists had no literary
ambitions, declaring: 'One *publishes* to seek out men, that's all
there is to it' (*On* publie *pour chercher des hommes, et rien de plus*)
(1969*a*: 9).

The implications of this latter remark would seem to be that
Breton was by this point in a messianic role (at least in his own
mind) in relation to some collective project. The project's purpose
remained unclear, though, defined only as a movement away from
Dada. As Breton put in an essay of 1922, 'People will say that
Dadaism served simply to keep us in the state of perfect availability
[*disponibilité*] which we in are at the moment, and which we will
now leave behind as we respond lucidly to the demands we must
meet' (1969*a*: 108). A couple of years after this was written, it
seemed that these demands had their source in the Communist
Party. They were resisted for a time, and as late as 1925 one could
find Aragon writing, in his polemic with the journal *Clarté*, 'I place
the spirit of revolt way above all politics . . . The Russian revolution? Excuse me if I don't look too impressed. On the level of ideas,

it is at most a vague ministerial crisis. You really ought to be a little less offhand with those who have dedicated [*sacrifié*] their lives to matters of the mind' (1925; cited by Nadeau 1964: 65; 1978: 110). Later in the same year, however, the Surrealists' involvement with the Party began in earnest when they, along with *Clarté* and others, joined their signatures to a declaration entitled *La Révolution d'abord et toujours* which was prompted by the war in Morocco and which stated, amongst other things, 'We are not Utopians: we conceive of this Revolution only in its social form' (cited by Nadeau 1964: 82; 1978: 131).

At this stage, the French authorities' frustration at their own incapacity to quash violent opposition to their occupation of Morocco was leading in France to the arrest of Communist Party members, and to searches of the homes of pacifists, so the Surrealists' gesture was not without risk. A tract such as *La Révolution d'abord et toujours* was necessarily produced in a clandestine atmosphere, and the Surrealists seemingly relished the rituals to which this gave rise, taking an oath of secrecy and inventing (though not using) pseudonyms and a coded vocabulary. The latter included the use of *art/artiste* in the place of *prolétariat/prolétaire*, *poésie/poète* in the place of *communisme/communiste*, *l'horizon* instead of *l'URSS*, and *lyrisme* in the place of *Parti Communiste* (Bonnet 1988: 11, 58). Though all this suggests a playful element in the Surrealists' involvement in politics, an involvement which they initially considered a local, temporary measure, outside the authentic orbit of Surrealism, it was not long before they moved towards a more thorough-going political commitment. In 1926 Soupault and Artaud were excluded from the group for maintaining that literature was worthwhile in itself, and in 1927 a number of the group, including Breton, Aragon, and Éluard, joined the Party.

Despite this important move, there were still considerable tensions between Surrealism and Communism. On the one hand, the Communists generally failed to take Surrealism seriously, and were deeply suspicious of their interest in figures such as Sade and Freud.[15] On the other hand, the Dada inheritance meant it was difficult for the Surrealists to see their work as a serious engagement

[15] Notably, it was on his expulsion from the Communist Party in 1923 that Maurice Heine founded his Société du Roman Philosophique and dedicated himself to Sade.

with the world outside the self, and they were often forced into a
contradictory posture whereby they claimed artistic autonomy but
also claimed to be breaking down the barrier between art and (the
rest of) life, or between art and action. These tensions, and their
implications for the Surrealists' involvement with Communism,
came to a head in the 'Aragon affair' of 1932. This is worth
recounting in some detail for the insight it gives into the group's
attempts to reconcile their art with their politics and the various
issues of censorship the affair raised.

In 1930 Aragon, Sadoul, and Triolet attended an international
conference of socialist writers in Kharkov at which Aragon presented the idea of Surrealism. Initially it seemed his contribution
had been well received, but, shortly before the conference closed,
Aragon and Sadoul were asked to sign a declaration (which was
not intended to be published in France at this stage) to the effect
that they had made errors because of their failure to submit to
the authority of the Party, that the second Surrealist manifesto
was incompatible with dialectical materialism, that they rejected
'all idealist ideology (in particular Freudianism)', and that they
condemned Trotskyism as counter-revolutionary. They duly
signed, Aragon later claiming that he saw this as a matter of
strategic necessity. When he returned to France he was nevertheless 'put on trial' (to use his expression (Aragon 1974–5: v. 143))
by his local cell, who remained suspicious of his Surrealist activities,
and he also had to work hard to persuade the other Surrealists that
his decision to sign had been something other than an act of
cowardice. This balancing act was performed in Aragon's and
Sadoul's tract *Aux intellectuels révolutionnaires!* of December
1930 and continued later in Aragon's essay 'Le Surréalisme et le
devenir révolutionnaire', where he talked openly of Kharkov for
the first time, and also held forth on the subject of censorship,
writing:

In the eighteenth century writers were arrested, books were seized by the
censor, writers had to go to publishers in Holland. We Surrealists are in the
same boat, but new methods are used to deal with us. For example, Crevel
and I simply *cannot* get published any more, and it is obviously the
contents of our writing which alienates publishers. It is censorship without
censors [*La censure agit avant la lettre*], and that is much more elegant.
Moreover, if there is a flaw in the social apparatus and somehow some of
our thought slips through the close-knit net of bastards and big-shots, then

you just have to look at what happened to *L'Age d'or*[16] and later to *L'Immaculée Conception* (which was taken off the shelves). Not to mention suppression in the form of boycotts, silence, and so on. In 1930 and 1931 we have got to the paradoxical point where our thought has been considered a luxury *precisely* because of its revolutionary nature. (Aragon 1931: 3)

As he wrote this, Aragon must have been thinking about the poem 'Front Rouge' which he had written in Russia and which he later (and regretfully) explained as an act of testimony inspired by his anger at anti-Soviet feeling in France, by his 'leftism', and by his 'wish to use poetry to defend and to praise a people whose nature I was discovering to be most moving' (1974–5: v. 148). It was, then, a deliberate attempt to break through the kind of censorship which he believed publishers and editors to impose, and to write a poem whose sheer revolutionary force would prevent it from being aestheticized and recuperated as a 'luxury'.

'Front Rouge' was to appear at the head of a collection entitled *Persécuté persécuteur*, which was printed in October 1931 but whose publication was delayed because Aragon had agreed that 'Front Rouge' should appear first in the French issue of the Soviet journal *Littérature de la Révolution mondiale*. The latter, however, was confiscated in November 1931 by the French police, something Aragon was unaware of until, on 16 January 1932, he was charged with 'incitement of servicemen to insubordination and incitement to murder with the aim of spreading anarchist propaganda' (Aragon 1974–5: v. 145), a crime punishable by up to five years in prison.

The other Surrealists, putting aside their reservations about Aragon's behaviour and indeed about the poem itself, very rapidly rallied in his support and published a document entitled 'L'Affaire Aragon' in which they wrote:

We were unaware until the last few days that poetry [*la phrase poétique*], subject as it is to specific concrete determinations, by definition obeying the laws of intensified language, running its own risks in the field of interpretation *where to consider its literal meaning is by no means to exhaust it*—we were unaware that poetry could be judged on the basis of its immediate contents and, if needs be, brought under judicial attack in the same way as any other, moderate form of expression.

[16] See below, p. 158.

[. . .] We protest against any attempt to interpret a poetic text for judicial purposes and demand an immediate end to the proceedings. (In Losfeld 1980: 204–5)

This collective text was quickly followed by a publication by Breton entitled *Misère de la poésie: 'L'Affaire Aragon' devant l'opinion publique*, which included 'Front Rouge' as an appendix (thereby giving it its first French publication) and which reported the names of the many people who had responded to the Surrealists' call for support. After listing these names, however, Breton acknowledged that some revolutionaries had refused to lend their support. He explained:

people claim that, faced with the first serious threat of repression to one of our number, we are going to evade responsibility for our actions and seek some strange sort of refuge in art. People feign surprise that under these circumstances we could ever have laid claim to the honour of carrying on the revolutionary struggle alongside the proletariat and of running all the risks which that struggle involves. (Breton 1932: 6; in Losfeld 1980: 210)

This accusation seemed, unsurprisingly, to touch a nerve. The Belgian Surrealists argued against such criticisms in their intervention into the debate, an essay called 'La Poésie transfigurée', by writing: 'To put an end to the neutralization of works of art it might be a good idea to see the poetic texts which we consider worthwhile judged *first and foremost* on their immediate content, taken literally' (in Losfeld 1980: 206–8; cited by Breton 1932: 8); but this was a line of argument which Breton, with Aragon's freedom to think about, could scarcely endorse in defence of a poem containing lines such as 'Shoot the cops' and 'I sing of the Proletariat's violent domination of the bourgeoisie' (Aragon 1974–5: v. 160, 165). Breton stressed instead the particularities of poetry and the inappropriateness of taking it literally, when a poem's meaning was 'if not unrelated to, then at least transcendent of, the words it uses' (1932: 12; in Losfeld 1980: 214–15). He also argued that it was arbitrary to take certain phrases (such as 'Shoot the cops') as literal, and others (such as 'The stars descend familiarly on to the earth' (1932: 9; in Losfeld 1980: 213)) as metaphorical. It could well be objected, though, that it is the poem itself which cues such responses, and that a phrase such as '80% of the bread this year | comes from Marxist corn from the collective farms' (Aragon 1974–5: v. 167) does little to release the reader into a flight of metaphorical fancy. Breton, uncomfortably conscious of this and of the fact that 'Front Rouge' was not a Surrealist poem in the sense in which he wished 'Surrealist' to be understood, stated explicitly that it was just an 'occasional poem' (*poème de circonstance*) which others should not imitate (1932: 16; in Losfeld 1980: 218), and that '*returning to exterior subject-matter* and more particularly to *exciting* [passionnant] subject-matter is at odds with all the historical lessons to be learnt today from the most advanced poetic forms' (1932: 15; in Losfeld 1980: 217). He also noted that such considerations were outside the agenda which the Kharkov conference set itself, and warned that there might be an imminent and unfortunate split between 'professional' revolutionaries and revolutionary intellectuals, by which he meant the Party and the Surrealists.

In the case of Aragon, who came under renewed pressure from the Party, this split was not long in coming. The immediate results of this were not especially dramatic, since, on the one hand, the official charges against him were dropped and, on the other, the Surrealists continued to be involved with the Party. Both *Paillasse!* and *Certificat*, two tracts which put the Surrealists' seal on the split with Aragon, were basically personal attacks on him, and did little to clarify the ideological stakes of the affair. Breton apparently objected to these texts for that very reason, but if the issue had not been obscured in this way, it is doubtful if his association with the Party could have carried on as long as it did. Indeed, he even became a member of the Association des Écrivains et Artistes Révolutionnaires later in 1932, and remained a member of the Party until the end of 1933.

On another level, however, the Surrealists' claims that their work was inseparable from their politics had been irreparably undermined. Ever since the Barrès affair, a crucial aspect of the Surrealist project had been the idea that a radical artistic practice went hand in hand with a certain attitude of revolt in the face of society, and the censorship of 'Front Rouge' created a chance for the kind of well-publicized confrontation which one might have expected the Surrealists to seize. After all, Breton had already said in the first manifesto: 'I would like to know how the first punishable offences, the Surrealist character of which will be clearly apparent, will be *judged*' (1972a: 52; 1969c: 44n.). He had also suggested in this passage that the techniques of automatism meant the Surrealists could not really be held responsible for what they wrote, and that 'surrealism, as I conceive of it, asserts our complete *nonconformism* clearly enough that there can be no question of summoning it [or translating it], at the trial of the real world, as a witness for the defence' (*le surréalisme, tel que je l'envisage, déclare assez notre non-conformisme absolu pour qu'il ne puisse être question de le traduire, au procès du monde réel, comme témoin à décharge*) (1972*a*: 55; 1969*c*: 47). The idea of diminished responsibility for Surrealists was always a questionable one, however, and, though Aragon's poem was not a work of automatism, by 1930 the Communist Surrealists had indeed decided to put their ideas on trial in the real world.

In fact, the 'Front Rouge' affair was not the first time a Surrealist had run into trouble with the law. *L'Age d'or*, which had its début in Paris on 28 November 1930, was banned five days later, after a showing had been violently disrupted by the Ligue des Patriotes. Moreover, one reason why Sadoul went to Kharkov in the first place was to avoid the three-month prison sentence with which he was threatened for sending a provocative letter to a schoolboy prizewinner whose name he had found in the paper. The Sadoul incident was trivial and did not involve Surrealism as such, however, and the *Age d'Or* incident, in which the personal freedom of the Surrealists was not at stake, provided an uncomplicated opportunity for opposition to the bigots behind the censorship and to their anti-Semitism, fascism, and disregard for freedom of expression. In the case of 'Front Rouge', by contrast, a Surrealist's personal freedom was at risk, but a show of solidarity in the face of this risk proved impossible to maintain under the pressure of a series of conflicting demands. First amongst these were the demands made by the censoring authorities, which the Surrealists attempted to counter with conventional references to the 'moral and intellectual worth' of the poem (Breton 1932: 5), to the weight of public opinion behind them, and to the 'freedom of thought', compromised by censorship in a way that was—as only a 'philistine' could fail to see—'infinitely more arbitrary and more profound' in the case of poetry than in the case of other genres (Breton 1932: 11). Next were the demands of the Communist Party, which was deeply suspicious of the Surrealists and of their perceived aversion to materialist hard-headedness and true political commitment; and, thirdly, there were the demands created by Surrealism itself, which Aragon's poem evidently failed to meet.

The Aragon affair was an unmistakable sign that reconciling such diverse demands in any practical sense was a dream. It was a dream without which Surrealism had little meaning, however, since to collapse together artistic, cognitive, aesthetic, and political categories (foreclosing any careful examination of the categories' interrelation) was one of the defining gestures of Surrealism, and it was a dream which the Surrealists were consequently unwilling to relinquish. One explanation for the appeal which the Sade myth held for them was that it provided a locus in and from which the dream of an exemplary dynamic relation between art and life could be kept alive, and that as myth it was able to cover the junction of art and life in such a way as to suspend the resolution of the tensions this relation enclosed. Thus Sade symbolized at once the liberated existence which the mind can lead irrespective of exterior circumstances, and the inscription of artistic activity within a project of revolt with a real impact in the world. The very fact of being associated with the Sade myth gave the Surrealists the impression of moving into the area of action, in other words, bringing them into apparent confrontation with the law, politics, and sexual politics; but the myth *as* myth mediated this confrontation and allowed them to avoid the compromises inflicted on them by the real world.

The Surrealists' mythopoeic vision of Sade reveals itself most clearly in the way they, like others before them, adapted Sade's biography to their own ends, at a time when a reasonably reliable version of the facts (first provided by Heine's *Le Marquis de Sade* of 1950 and then Lély's *Vie du Marquis de Sade* of 1952–7) was still unavailable. Éluard, for instance, claimed that Sade may well have been innocent of all the sexual crimes imputed to him, and that he was persecuted purely for his 'revolutionary intelligence'; in Éluard's words:

Because he never allowed any barrier to impede his frenzied passion for freedom, because his genius unblushingly uncovered human instincts and denounced man's hypocritical relationship with his peers, because he developed the system capable of giving back to humans of both sexes their natural freedom and of allowing them a truly communal existence, Sade was persecuted throughout his life. (1926a: *Clarté*, 6: 20)

This version of the Sade myth emphasized the liberty of his thought, then, and de-emphasized the relevance of his actions (other than his writing). On the other hand, Sade fitted in with a broader myth of Revolution, and to this end his contribution to the revolution of 1789 was greatly exaggerated: another article by Éluard, for instance, claims that 'he dedicated himself body and soul to the Revolution' (1926*b*: 9), and Desnos, in *La Liberté ou l'amour!*, writes: 'We should recognize—for justice's sake, we must recognize—that he was the instigator of the 14 July, the day on which freedom was born!' (1962: 113).

The notion that freedom was born on 14 July 1789 is an indication of the extent to which the Surrealists adopted an idealized image of the Revolution and to which they inherited the idealist concept of freedom which formed the backbone of revolutionary rhetoric. From its earliest stages the Surrealists' own rhetoric of revolution bore the imprint of this inheritance, such that in an essay of 1922 Breton, after declaring that 'a revolution of some sort, as bloody as you like' was what was needed to move away from the *impasse* in which Dada found itself (and everyone else), went on to remark that 'It wouldn't be a bad idea to re-establish for the mind the laws of the terror' (1969*a*: 161)—which suggests at once that the 'revolution of some sort' was modelled on the Revolution of 1789, and that the historical realities of that Revolution, including the blood and the physical Terror which he absorbs into his rhetoric, were not being given due weight. Conversely, freedom was at times discussed by Breton as if it were some unearthly essence. In an indirect reference to Sade, for instance, he remarked: 'Freedom will allow itself to brush the earth only with respect to men who have had little or no idea of how to behave in life, having loved freedom to distraction' (1971: 20).

Other examples of rhetorical borrowings from the Revolution are not hard to find, such as Éluard's phrase, 'The mind has its *bastilles* to which it banishes anything which raises too violent a protest at the accepted order' (1926: *Clarté*, 4: 27), or Breton's remark, 'We have resolved unanimously once and for all to have done with the *ancien régime* of the mind' (1925: 2). Even in their claims for the life of the unconscious and the imagination, then, they fell back on revolutionary models. These included the language of rights: the first edition of *La Révolution surréaliste* was launched under the slogan 'Our goal must be a new declaration of human rights' (1 December 1924, cover page), an injunction first found in Aragon's 'Une vague de rêves' of autumn 1924 (1974–5:

ii. 225–51). Furthermore, there was a tendency to refer to the rediscovery of these 'Surrealist' rights (for example, in Breton's statement from the first manifesto, 'the imagination may be about to reclaim its rights' (1972a: 21; 1969c: 10)), as if they had always existed—perhaps at the time of the Revolution, or perhaps always, immanent in the world, underneath the social and cultural conventions which disguised them. Again, this notion of rights and the related concept of an individual (or a certain class of individual) who was essentially free and whole and whose freedom could be realized and secured through a set of measures preventing vagaries of government or society from impeding it owed a considerable debt to the Revolution. The 'spirit of the French Revolution' which Aragon, in *Le Libertinage* of 1924, asserted explicitly was the object of the Surrealists' quest ('Today it's the spirit of the French Revolution that we are chasing and hunting for everywhere' (1977: 271; 1987: 16)) was in fact surprisingly pervasive in their work.

Surrealist Sex

I have argued that, for the Surrealists, Sade provided a means of tapping the dynamism of the Revolution in a way which allowed them to show themselves in the reflected light of his (still shocking) revolt, without grappling with the political specificities of Sade's era or their own. Surrealist activity was driven, in other words, not so much by the revolutionary will to which it was attributed as by quasi-metaphysical revolt. Sade was combined with a purportedly 'politicized' version of Freud in an attempt to anchor the Surrealists' revolt in instinct and the unconscious, but ultimately, I have suggested, this 'politicization' was largely oblivious to politics. The shortcomings of this make themselves felt not only as theoretical inadequacies, but also in the Surrealists' practice: one is promised an expression of the deepest, pre-social unconscious, but one is frequently delivered nothing more than conventions and stereotypes which the Surrealists adopted unthinkingly from the society in which they lived.

The area in which this is most obvious is the Surrealists' attitude to women and to sex, and to the depiction of women and sex in Sade's work.[17] Various conventional strains of limited thought are

[17] I am assuming here that the dominant perspective of Surrealism is masculine, for reasons which should become apparent, if they are not apparent already. The

apparent here. First, women are viewed as creation's highest achievement, and the answer to all men's problems. Breton, for instance, wrote in 1933: 'It is the earth which, somehow, gives orders through woman [*ordonne à travers la femme*]. "One only loves the earth and through woman the earth loves us in return." That is why love and women are the clearest solution to all the world's mysteries' (1970a: 143); and in 1944 he was still talking of 'earthly salvation through woman' (1971: 53). Secondly, and relatedly, women are considered close to nature and so to provide access to the 'real' world ('C'est la terre qui [. . .] ordonne à travers la femme'), an idea linked to that of the 'woman-child' which Breton promotes in *Arcane 17* (1971: 71). Thirdly, this ties in with an idea of women as irreducibly other and mysterious: in the second manifesto, for instance, Breton notes that 'The problem of woman is the most marvellous and disturbing thing in the world' (1972a: 182; 1969c: 180n.). Similarly, sex retains something dark and enigmatic about it: in Breton's words, 'even these days the sexual world, despite the supremely memorable investigations carried out in modern times by Sade and Freud, has not, to the best of my knowledge, stopped setting against our desire to penetrate the universe its indestructible nucleus of *darkness* [nuit]' (1970a: 142). Finally, women are thought of as loci of resistance or as objects, and it is here that the Surrealists are closest to Sade. In the first manifesto, for instance, Breton covertly adopts the model of Silling castle from *Les Cent-vingt Journées de Sodome*, fantasizing about an isolated château filled with his friends and with beautiful women, and asking: 'the main thing is surely that we are our own masters, and the masters of women and of love, too, is it not?' (1970a: 28). This attitude also surfaced occasionally when they were being actively 'surreal', rather than programmatic, for example in the Surrealist proverb 'You must beat your mother while she

fact that women Surrealists existed at all was something that was largely ignored until recently (see Suleiman 1990: 18–19, 210, for a summary of recent work on women Surrealists). In the later period of Surrealism a certain sensitivity to masculine bias did establish itself, but it was very limited. Breton writes in 1944, for instance, 'the time may have come to valorize women's ideas over men's ideas [. . .] It falls to the artist in particular [. . .] to bring everything pertaining to the female world system to the fore as far as possible [. . .] to glorify or, better yet, to appropriate and guard jealously everything which distinguishes woman from man' (Breton 1971: 66). It seems not to occur to him that some artists may be women.

is young' (proposed by Éluard and Péret; cited by Nadeau 1964: 107), or in Breton's poem 'L'Union libre' of 1931, which consists of a verbal dissection of his wife into a series of body parts, each prefaced with a proprietorial 'Ma femme' (my woman/wife) ('My woman with a tongue like a stabbed communion host | With the tongue of a doll that opens and closes its eyes', etc. (1948: 65; 1982: 49)) or in the exchange between Breton and Valentin in the eleventh session of the *Recherches sur la sexualité*[18] (discussed at greater length below), which went:

> —Valentin, what do you think of the idea of masturbating and coming in a woman's ear?
> —It's out of the question.
> —It's a purely surrealist question.

(In Pierre 1990: 183; 1992: 146)

It was this many-layered oblivion to the realities of sexual politics which allowed the Surrealists to regard Sade unconditionally as one of the 'great emancipators of desire' (Breton 1969b: 270), and simultaneously to add their voices to the claim that his work was a forerunner of psychopathology (see, for example, Breton 1939: 39–40). They thereby obscured the very obvious sexism of much of Sade's writing and its role in reinforcing far from emancipatory sexual stereotypes. When Aragon, presumably inspired by Sade, declares in *Le Libertinage* that 'all means are valid in the immediate satisfaction of the body's desires' (1977: 208; 1987: 150), the potential violence which is implied is intended to set the phrase against a background of unfettered revolt, but when it is considered more closely the background reveals itself to be a profoundly conventional one in which supposedly neutral formulations disguise gender bias, in which masculine desire is constructed in terms

---

[18] The *Researches on Sexuality* were a series of twelve discussions about sexuality which took place from January 1928 to August 1932, under the guidance of a rather pompous and egocentric Breton. The proceedings of the first two sessions were published in issue 11 of *La Révolution surréaliste*, but the transcript of the other ten sessions saw the light of day only in 1990, when the full set was published in book form. (For the first two sessions, to which I refer most extensively, I will give page numbers from *La Révolution surréaliste*. Page numbers for subsequent sessions are necessarily taken from the book, which was presented and annotated by José Pierre.) Despite this lack of publicity, the fact that the sessions continued over several crucial years in the Surrealists' development suggests that they were of some importance to them.

of victory over the resistances offered by its feminine object, in which the social mediations of bodies and of their sexual satisfaction are mistaken for unchanging components of human nature; and in which it is believed that true works of literature are objects whose creative autonomy makes them invulnerable to pitfalls of this kind.

Though all this shows that the Surrealists' own creative autonomy was a myth, and that they drew unconsciously on conventions which in fact created or supported conditions of social inequality, there is nevertheless a gap on another level between their rhetoric of a (supposedly) radical practice and their own behaviour, which was not apparently sadistic or murderous.[19] In fact, as the *Recherches sur la sexualité* show, their attitudes to sex were in general unexceptional. In these discussions, though the group's candour in discussing their sexual experience was unusual and was presumably inspired by Freud, their approach was generally expository rather than analytical,[20] and, though Sade's influence can also be detected (for example, when Breton says he would like to have sex, 'with every possible refinement', in a church, and Péret agrees enthusiastically, 'While I was there I would like to profane the hosts and, if possible, leave excrement in the chalice' (*La Révolution surréaliste*, 11: 35; Pierre 1992: 14)), their comments show little self-consciousness about the orthodoxy of most of their opinions. In the eleventh session Breton makes an isolated attempt to give the proceedings a surreal element by asking 'Since men have a cock between two balls, how is it that women have nothing between their breasts?' (in Pierre 1990: 181; 1992: 145), but it is tempting to see this in context as nothing more than one of his many ploys for taking the lead in the debate, and he, in particular, is mostly quite content to give voice to some vehemently conservative opinions. On several occasions, for instance, he inveighs against

[19] This gap was something of which Bataille was critical. He accused the Surrealists of treating Sade as ultimately a literary phenomenon, 'exempt from all practical applications' (Bataille 1970b: 70), and thereby robbing his work of its revolutionary potential. In Bataille's account, needless to say, Sade's revolutionary potential turns out to lie in his value as an illustration of Bataille's own quirky metaphysics of revolt, and even he is forced to admit that 'when one [sic] meets a young woman it is pretty much [sic] out of the question to cut her throat or to dismember her alive' (Bataille 1970b: 425 n.).

[20] Pierre notes that explicitly Freudian terminology and references had even been retrospectively eliminated (presumably by Breton) from the manuscript. The reasons for this are open to debate.

male homosexuality, which in the first session he comments on as follows:

> I accuse pederasts of confronting human tolerance with a mental and moral deficiency which tends to set itself up as a system and to paralyse every enterprise I respect. I make exceptions, among them one for the unparalleled case of Sade [. . .] By definition everything is permitted to a man like the Marquis de Sade, for whom moral freedom [*la liberté des mœurs*] was a matter of life and death. (*La Révolution surréaliste*, 11: 32; Pierre 1992: 5–6)

Other conservative opinions of Breton's are not hard to find. He has a remarkably genital-centred idea of sex, something one sees in his description of men who engage in oral sex together as 'an embryonic form of pederasty' (*La Révolution surréaliste*, 11: 33; Pierre 1992: 8), or in his opinion that, although it is highly desirable and highly unusual for men and women to reach orgasm simultaneously, he cannot countenance the use of 'artificial methods' to help it occur. (In his words, 'I refuse to have recourse to artificial methods when it's love, and I consider it a moral issue. The alternative would be libertinism' (*La Révolution surréaliste*, 11: 37; Pierre 1992: 22)). Quite what 'artificial methods' are is not actually defined, but the notion seems to cover everything other than the penis. Aragon, to his credit, raised the objection in this session that much of what was being said was made invalid by its masculine bias, but Breton was unable to recognize this, and even when women were present at a couple of the later sessions the male participants were uninhibitedly sexist. Breton's opinions and attitudes are also frequently contradictory (though not in any particularly unconventional way): in the third session he insists, for instance, that love and sex are inseparable, and apparently sees no problem in asserting this only moments after saying, 'I would like Péret to describe an imaginary woman whom he would find particularly tempting. Her eyes, hair, breasts, waist, bottom, and legs' (in Pierre 1990: 91; 1992: 48). He is intolerant of male masturbation (which he insists should be accompanied by 'images of women' (*représentations féminines*) (*La Révolution surréaliste*, 11: 33)), says he is repelled by the idea of having sex with a black woman (in Pierre 1990: 99; 1992: 57), and rejects as 'unbearable' the idea of having sex with a woman who did not speak French (*La Révolution surréaliste*, 11: 36; Pierre 1992: 16). In view of all this,

Breton's affirmation, in response to a question from Queneau, that he is interested in 'everything connected with sexual perversion' (Queneau's phrase: *La Révolution surréaliste*, 11: 39; Pierre 1992: 28) rings a little hollow, and it almost seems necessary to suppose he wishes to be taken literally when, in support of his contention that he is becoming increasingly depraved, he says: 'At 20 I liked blondes; at 30 I prefer brunettes: therefore I have become depraved' (a remark he says he is quoting from Théodore Jouffroy: *La Révolution surréaliste*, 11: 34; Pierre 1992: 10).

Though such remarks seriously undermine Breton's claims to be a sexual nonconformist, the more unorthodox attitudes of participants such as Queneau and Prévert are not necessarily any more 'radical', in the sense that they are not necessarily any freer of convention-bound discourses on sexuality, or any more sensitive to issues of sexual freedom. Like Sade, they often build their pleasures on the *idea* of transgression and so reinforce negatively the very conventions which they apparently breach. While Breton and others condemn the idea of rape, for instance, and Breton even declares that he has no predetermined physical demands of women (*La Révolution surréaliste*, 11: 36; Pierre 1992: 15), Queneau proclaims rape to be 'the only thing that appeals to me' (in Pierre 1990: 138; 1992: 94). On another level, Queneau's attitude is like Sade's in that he clearly seeks to unleash his sexuality with a complete disregard for the conventions of social propriety, and ends up doing away not only with those which are indeed oppressive, such as the (conventional) homophobic attitudes which Breton displays, but also with those which keep misogyny and sexism (which are also conventional, of course) in check. It is unsurprising, consequently, to find that Queneau declares himself to be something of a sadist (*La Révolution surréaliste*, 11: 39; Pierre 1992: 31), that he joins in with the chorus of aversion to menstruation and to pregnant women (in Prévert's words, 'It's comical if she's ugly, but it's sad if she's beautiful' (in Pierre 1990: 103; 1992: 62)), that he sees nothing wrong with brothels (unlike Breton), and makes statements such as 'I do not trust anyone, especially not a woman' (*La Révolution surréaliste*, 11: 38; Pierre 1992: 25). In terms of sexual politics, there is perhaps little to choose, on balance, between the prejudices circulated by someone like Breton, and those released by the urge to transgression of someone like Queneau, or Bataille, or Sade.

TEL QUEL, SADE, AND THE SCENE OF CENSORSHIP

Sade from Surrealism to Tel Quel

After the Second World War, increasing numbers of writers and publishers in France began to build on the foundations of Sadian enthusiasm which the Surrealists had laid. Heine found a successor in Lély, who took over Heine's task of carefully editing Sade's work and of paying homage to Sade's promoters, and who in his preface to Heine's *Le Marquis de Sade* wrote, 'the birth of Maurice Heine was, on the level of destiny, the promise of a resurrection, the announcement of the rebirth of the Marquis de Sade under incomparable auspices' (Lély 1950: 9). Later, his work on Sade brought him into contact with *Tel Quel* he occasionally published new fragments of the Sadian *œuvre* and his own comments upon them in the journal (see *TQ* 78, 79, 86).

The other major figure in Sade publishing after the war was Pauvert, who began his extended campaign to publish reliable editions of all Sade's writing in 1947. He too paid hommage to Heine's work (in his introductions to *Les Cent-vingt Journées de Sodome* in 1953, and to *Les Infortunes de la vertu* in 1954), and was fond of quoting Apollinaire to vouch for Sade's importance (see Pauvert's introductions to *La Philosophie dans le boudoir* (1953), *Œuvres* (1953), *Juliette* (1954)). As recently as 1991 he was still speaking up for the Surrealists, joining Le Brun in her distaste for those whose interest in the Surrealists is purely historical, and describing supporters of the 1991 Beaubourg exhibition on Breton[21] as 'necrophagists who live on what they believe to be a corpse' (in Le Brun 1991: back cover).

Though there were intellectual continuities between the Surrealists and figures such as Lély and Pauvert who dominated the publication of Sade after the war, the increasing availability of Sade's work in the post-war period was part of a qualitative as well as a quantitative change in its reception. As Pauvert points out (1981: iii. 83), Sade's major works had been consistently seized, pros-

---

[21] This was an exhibition which collected together in a fairly haphazard way a wide range of Bretonalia—letters, his copy of *The Interpretation of Dreams*, some African dolls which decorated his flat, pictures he liked, and so on. The exhibition's sheer size and its lack of structure (such as supporting historical information) were signs, I would argue, that its organizers erred on the side of generosity in their appraisal of the vitality of Breton and his ideas, contrary to what Pauvert suggests.

ecuted, condemned, and destroyed until 1947 (when the first Pauvert edition of *Juliette* appeared), and, at the time that the Pauvert trial started (in 1956), little of Sade's work was available outside this first Pauvert *Œuvres complètes*, which comprised ten titles in twenty-four volumes. Initially only 2,000 copies of each were printed, and for only two titles (*La Philosophie dans le boudoir* and *Juliette*) had demand been sufficient for there to be reprints. In other words, though the demand for Sade had increased since Heine published *Les Cent-vingt Journées de Sodome* from 1931 to 1935—an edition which, though limited to 400 copies, had to be remaindered—it was scarcely overwhelming. Pauvert notes that Lély's *Vie de Sade* was also selling slowly, and concludes that, although Sade's name was frequently mentioned in literary articles and conversations, Sade's work was still little read. As I noted in the Introduction, this situation changed dramatically after the Pauvert trial, and in part because of it.

After the trial, Pauvert continued to publish Sade's work (as he had said all along that he would) and was never again prosecuted for doing so, and the seized books took up their place as part of France's cultural heritage in the Bibliothèque Nationale. Following this, the Cercle du Livre Précieux complete edition (billed as definitive) was published, first from 1962 to 1964 and then reissued from 1966 to 1967, heavily equipped with introductions by well-known critics, psychoanalysts, psychiatrists, and so on. These editions, which are those most commonly found in libraries at present, considerably increased the availability of Sade's work, though they were still purchasable only by subscription and in limited numbers. In the 1970s the first paperback editions started to appear (Hachette's paperback *Justine* came out in 1973, for instance); and it is from that time, according to Pauvert, that Sade's work truly entered the public domain. A collection of Sade's work is now available in the prestigious *Pléïade* series, and the most recent *Œuvres complètes*, more comprehensive and more systematically ordered than its predecessors, started to appear in 1986, edited by Pauvert and Le Brun.

The introductions of the various post-war editions of Sade are in many cases similar to those of earlier editions. Preface writers continued to draw on themes such as Sade's political and psychological insight and prescience, or his literary originality and influence. In other instances, though, it is clear that there had been changes in the cultural horizons against which Sade was perceived.

First, the war itself was occasionally a more or less explicit reference point. In an essay entitled 'Lectures pour un front', for instance, which was published in 1950, Queneau—partly arguing against Breton's use of Sade in his *Anthologie de l'humour noir* of 1939—suggested that the goal of Sade's heroes was the same as that of the concentration camps—namely, to dehumanize humans —and that in various ways Sade's world prefigured that of the Gestapo. Nevertheless, in spite of this and despite his mixed feelings about Sade's impact on the reader, Queneau continued to accept that Sade's work had 'profound human value' (Queneau 1965: 216).

For other writers, the war made Sade's value all the more incontrovertible: Paulhan, for instance, who insisted in 1945, in an article entitled 'Sade, ou Le Pire est l'ennemi du mal',[22] that there was no longer any reason to deny that people could take pleasure in making others suffer, and even in cutting people up (or at least imagining it), clearly believed that intellectual honesty compels us to face up to the unspeakable, and also seemed to believe, or at least to hope, that voicing the unspeakable is a means of averting it. The hopes invested in Sade from this point of view were given perhaps their most unreserved articulation by Lély in an essay of 1948, where he wrote,

If the Marquis's unrelenting thinking had been understood, if ignorance and repression had not, for five generations, made people recoil in horror from his works, if they had not been thought of as the product of an insane criminal's imagination [. . .] perhaps the unspeakable period from 1933 to 1945 would never have happened and left its permanent blot on the character of the human race. (Lély 1948a: pp. xxxiv–xxxv)

Secondly, in the longer term the post-war reception of Sade was marked by various 'strong' and at times idiosyncratic readings carried out by writers such as Klossowski, Blanchot, and Bataille, which I will refer to and draw on in due course. I should note preliminarily that, although their approaches to Sade were fairly diverse (not only from author to author but also across time, especially in the case of Bataille), I think it would be accurate to suggest that all three had concerns which, though psycho-

[22] This title is difficult to translate, being a play on the saying 'le mieux est l'ennemi du bien' literally meaning something like 'Better chases out Good', more idiomatically rendered as 'let well alone'. Paulhan's version means 'Worse chases out Bad/Evil', the sense of which is understandable from my summary of his argument, I hope.

analytically informed and though involved in certain ways with the social, were primarily metaphysical, turning around notions of religious feeling, evil, the absolute, the essence, and so on. Although they were fairly close to the Surrealists in important respects, then, they also differed from them in the significant respect that they were not obviously concerned to make Sade an exemplary figure within an explicitly political project, and so were not central to the tradition of counter-censorship which is my main concern here.

A third salient characteristic of Sade's reception in this period was that it was becoming possible to approach Sade's work relatively unselfconsciously, not only in the sense that it was simply becoming materially more readily available, but more importantly in the sense that the critical vocabularies applied to it were increasingly the same as those applied to the work of other authors. One of the most eminent examples of this is Beauvoir's essay 'Faut-il brûler Sade?' (Should we burn Sade?) (published in *Les Temps modernes* in 1951–2, and in book form in 1955), in which her critical tools were drawn from existentialism, psychoanalysis, and Marxism. Something of a turning-point was marked by the conference on Sade held in Aix-en-Provence in February 1966, which, according to a report in the *Revue des Sciences humaines*, showed the way forward for the study of Sade, now constituting itself as a legitimate (though still controversial) area of academic concern 'for those who refuse to treat the Marquis's works as revealed texts whose critical exegesis is forbidden on pain of excommunication' (Goulemot 1966: 413). Indeed, the tone of the conference was set by the opening speech by the conference president, who declared: 'We are here neither to idolize nor to censor, and our approach is above all scientific' (Aix-en-Provence 1968: 7).

This conference was an important sign that the stakes were being lowered with respect to Sade's work, in a process of which the Pauvert trial and appeal had constituted an earlier, ambiguous moment. Even excepting those who objected fundamentally to Sade's work, however, not all of Sade's commentators were happy to see him accepted into the literary fold in this way. Blanchot, for instance, declined an invitation to participate in the Aix conference, and sent a letter in which he enjoined the participants, 'At least show some respect for what is scandalous in Sade' (*En Sade respectez au moins le scandale*) (cited in Aix-en-Provence 1968: 172). For writers influenced by the Surrealist approach to Sade, it was hard to see Sade as anything other than thoroughly exceptional, and for most it was also hard to accept the view that the potential for psychic and political subversion perceived by the Surrealists in Sade's work could be contained within the tame categories of literature, or explained away historically, or simply ignored.

In the period between the end of the war and the mid-1960s, in summary, the impulse towards a complex psychic/political counter-censorship which had inspired much of the Surrealists' activity, particularly their approach to and understanding of Sade, became dispersed across the literary landscape along the lines of tension which I have attempted to sketch out. To resume broadly, these tensions were created between (i) a certain pessimism about humankind in the period immediately after the war, (ii) various influential, 'strong' (but not enthusiastically political) readings of Sade, (iii) the normalization of Sade criticism within intellectual circles, (iv) 'specialized' readings such as the psychoanalytic essays used (amongst others) in the Cercle du Livre Précieux edition, or such as various relatively orthodox Marxist readings, and (v) the continued awareness of the possibility of censorship, an awareness brought into focus by the Pauvert trial.

Littérature interdite

My purpose in the rest of this section is to examine the way in which a notion of counter-censorship was revitalized by the *Tel Quel* group, who, like the Surrealists, sought to explore the subversive potential of creative writing and situated their notion of subversion at the intersection of psychoanalytic and political discourses on censorship. To this end I will be looking primarily at the special Sade number of the *Tel Quel* journal which came out in winter 1967, and at Barthes's book *Sade, Fourier, Loyola* of 1971, the first chapter of which is a slightly altered reprint of his essay 'L'Arbre du crime' from the Sade number of *Tel Quel*. I will also be referring to various essays and interviews published (many of them in 1972 in a volume called *Littérature interdite* ('Banned Literature')), in connection with Pierre Guyotat's *Éden, Éden, Éden*, which was censored in October 1970.[23]

---

[23] There is no single, unified *Tel Quel* perspective on censorship, and no programmatic statement on the subject was ever made by the group. Furthermore, some of the writers to whom I will be referring, such as Klossowski or Foucault, were not

A sense of how strongly the *Tel Quel* group sought to define itself against other writers with a claim to a different understanding of the Surrealist heritage (including, broadly, the political uses to which psychoanalysis should be put), or of the way forward for literature and literary criticism, or of Marxism, or of Sade, is gained from two short texts in the 'Selected Criticism' section at the back of their Sade number. The first of these, headed simply 'André Breton', deplores the mediocrity of the homilies prompted by Breton's then recent death, and presents the *Tel Quel* group as the true inheritors of 'what Breton, beyond any individual limits, actually *is*' (*ce que Breton, en dehors de toute limite individuelle*, est *une fois pour toutes*) (*TQ* 1967: 84). In a later edition of *Tel Quel*, where he set out the group's 'General Theses', Sollers was more explicit about what this inheritance meant, noting that the Surrealists had 'located/mislocated every nerve centre in our culture' (in Sollers's words, they had carried out 'une reconnaissance-méconnaissance de tous les points névralgiques de notre culture' (Sollers 1971: 96)). By this latter point, in other words, the *Tel Quel* group disagreed with much of what the Surrealists wrote and did, but nevertheless felt indebted to them to the extent that it was the Surrealists who had opened up the politicized cultural space, the space of the *avant-garde*, which *Tel Quel* was continuing to explore. It is typical that Kristeva in *La Révolution du langage poétique* should make substantial criticisms of the Surrealists at points in her argument—notably, she is critical of their 'censuring/censoring fetishization' (*fétichisation censurante*) of women (1974: 513)—but nevertheless states in her concluding section that 'Jarry's and Queneau's texts or Breton's and Aragon's positions, tell us more about subjective and social revolution than does any philosophical or political metalanguage' (1974: 618).

The second text at the back of the Sade number, written by Sollers (which the first may have been, too: the context makes it unclear if it was by him, or was collectively authored), is an attack on some remarks which Sartre made in an interview published by *La Quinzaine* on 15 October 1966. Sollers explains briefly that in this article Sartre, claiming to speak for Marxism, collapsed together linguistics, structuralism, and the work of Foucault, Robbe-Grillet, Lacan, Althusser, and *Tel Quel* in an attempt to

members of the central core of the group, but they expressly associated themselves with it in the texts I cite here by having them published in the *Tel Quel* journal.

'demonstrate the impossibility of historical reflection' (*TQ* 1967: 84). Sollers gives no more details of Sartre's overall argument, but quotes a passage from Sartre in which the latter has referred to Sade and has stressed that Sade was an aristocrat, a man whose rights were theoretically limitless, but who was prevented from exercising them by the decline of his class. Sartre argues, somewhat elliptically, that Sade overcame this situation subjectively in sadism, which he had to discuss in terms of 'nature' simply because that was the language available to him in eighteenth-century French society. Sartre concludes: 'Sade is forced to work with [*passer par*] the idea of nature. So he builds a theory of nature similar to the bourgeois version, with one difference: instead of being good, nature is bad, it wants man to die. Thus *Juliette* ends on the image of a man jerking off into a volcano' (cited in *TQ* 1967: 85). Sollers underlines these last two sentences (from 'So he builds'), and says that Sartre's use of the expression 'with one difference' (*avec cette seule différence*) and of the word 'thus' (*ainsi*) is 'comical'. He also objects that Sartre is incapable of discussing a 'text' (a word Sollers underlines), constructing instead 'a biographical scenario where the writer's name functions like a character in a bourgeois novel' (*TQ* 1967: 85). Having made these points briefly, he then writes:

What is serious, and indeed inexcusable, is that in discussing a *banned* book Sartre should put forward an untruth such as the one which provides his peremptory conclusion. One would search in vain for the *image* on which Sartre claims that *Juliette* 'ends' ['*s'achève*']. If in a discussion of Proust he were carried away by a burst of the same phantasmic enthusiasm and concluded that in his flight from reality 'Marcel', as a perfect bourgeois gentleman, had imprisoned himself in language and that *Le Temps retrouvé* ended on a detailed description of an aesthetic orgasm in front of the Eiffel tower, I imagine there would be something of an outcry. The thing is, the bourgeoisie do not need to ban *Le Temps perdu* explicitly, whereas it is hard to imagine how they could allow people to read *Juliette*, which ends on something quite other than an 'image' and quite specifically on some remarks concerning the role that philosophy must fulfil.[24] It seems to me that such irresponsible talk from Sartre about literature of the past and of the present says little for his understanding of Marxism, of which one is entitled to have different expectations. Once again it must be recognized that this is an example of profound obscurantism, revealed by

[24] This is an allusion to *tout dire*, which I discuss in my Conclusion.

a slip which really ought to go down to posterity. In the name of *history*, in fact [*Cela, au nom de l'histoire, justement*]. (*TQ* 1967: 85)

There are various signs here of the ways in which the tensions and influences to which I have referred were negotiated by *Tel Quel*. First, Sollers clearly objects to the way in which Sade is treated by Sartre as just one possible example amongst others which he could use to illustrate his point, and to the way in which Sartre treats Sade like 'a character in a bourgeois novel' (*TQ* 1967: 85)—the objection being not only to the specific inadequacies of Sartre's model in Sade's case, but also to Sartre's use of a simplistic psychology of a type called into question by Freud. Secondly, Sollers, like the Surrealists before him, is staking a claim for the radical potential of certain types of writing, to the exclusion of other types. From here, thirdly, Sollers is engaged in a struggle to decide who is authorized to speak in the name of Marxism, and who has greater authority to mobilize the rhetoric of freedom (in a footnote, Sollers writes, '*in the name of Marxism* [. . .] our task is to erode from the inside, through a questioning of forms [*par une contestation formelle*], the language of the bourgeoisie's naturalist ideology' (*TQ* 1967: 86)). And finally, Sollers emphasizes that Sade's work, though treated as banal by a writer such as Sartre, is still exceptional because subject to a prohibition, and that the critic is therefore obliged both to set the record straight and, more radically, to disrupt the criteria by which the record (including Sade's criminal record) is established.

Quite how much weight there was in the interdiction which hung over Sade was by this point far from clear, but the *Tel Quel* group's anxieties about censorship and its sense of marginalization were vindicated, at least in certain respects, by what happened to *Éden, Éden, Éden*. The work's author, Pierre Guyotat, had made a name for himself in 1967 with the publication of a novel entitled *Tombeau pour cinq cent mille soldats* ('Tomb for Five Hundred Thousand Soldiers'). He was compared to Sade, amongst others, and in an interview of 1967 declared that Lély's *Vie de Sade* had changed his life, though he had not read much of Sade's own writing (*LI* 21). In the period between the publication of *Tombeau pour cinq cent mille soldats* and that of *Éden, Éden, Éden* in 1970, Guyotat became a Communist and became involved with *Tel Quel*. His style of writing altered considerably, and was created according to a technique, he explained, whereby he first made a series of notes for himself, 'with precise political intentions' (*LI*, 68), then secondly abandoned these ideas as he tried to give himself over to his unconscious by writing a 'wild text' (*texte sauvage*) (*LI* 71) while masturbating, then thirdly revised this text so as to produce a more rigorous text, a *texte savant*, (*LI* 71), supposedly purged of those phrases, words, rhythms, and structures (such as notions of psychology) which did the work of bourgeois ideology. The end result was, he hoped, 'a sort of psychoanalysis of language' (*LI* 72), a text inspired by psychoanalysis on two levels: first in that, in his words, 'its words, its rhythms, its bodily patterns [*ses trajets de corps*] and its tone [pass] into the unconscious' (*LI* 89), and secondly in its decentring of the human subject and in its attention to 'the sexual' (*le fait sexuel*). The text involves a series of bodies (some named, some not) in a series of sexual encounters and an unstoppable stream of bodily fluids and excretions including sperm, faeces, pus, tears, wind, sweat, eye-gunge, blood, mucus, saliva, milk, and bile. There are indications that it is set in Algeria, and a great number of the bodies involved belong to soldiers, though it deploys so few of the novelistic elements which would normally constitute a setting that it is difficult to say that it takes place anywhere in particular. Indeed, it is impossible to make much sense (as one would make sense of a plot, for instance) of the text overall, which flows on in a semi-continuous sentence (there are no paragraphs or full stops), and whose scatological and sexual insistence seemingly provides the only connection, other than the recurrence of a couple of names, between the various 'scenes'. There is little reason to pick out any one part of this text as representative and it is impossible to give a sense of the flat relentlessness of the text as a whole, but to give an idea of Guyotat's style, here are two brief extracts:

at the changing of the guard the sentry has come down again, and runs, his organ caught in the elastic of his underpants, drags the woman, by her feet, behind the tree trunk, into a salt marsh, lies on top of her and she's no longer breathing, pulls the withered lips of her vagina apart with his fingers, thrusts in his penis which draws back from the now cold flesh, kisses the woman's dried lips, the eyes where the saliva which the soldiers spat on to the iris is evaporating. (*ÉÉÉ* 22)

the strongest pushes Wazzag, held by his penis, into the first bogs on the corridor where the metal worker, squatting, excrement bursting beneath his buttocks, his hands all sticky, is eating a pomegranate picked up off the cement, his spare hand pulling a filament of come from his penis grown hard again at the panting, the grating of muscles of the apprentices pressing against Wazzag. (*ÉÉÉ* 22)

In an interview published in *Tel Quel* in summer 1970, Guyotat explained the evolution of his style by reference to the political events of May 1968, remarking: 'It is obvious that the events of May 1968 have hardened the political situation and so have hardened texts and the battles being fought about them' (*LI* 26). Here and elsewhere he talked specifically about censorship, and there are signs that his suspicion that *Éden, Éden, Éden* would be censored was shared by the writers who provided prefaces for it, namely Leiris, Barthes, and Sollers. Sollers, for instance, instructed his readers, 'Challenge both censorship and counter-censorship,[25] one moral, the other psychological' (in *ÉÉÉ* 10), while Barthes, reflecting on the 'reciprocal, indissoluble metonymy' of desire and language in Guyotat's text, stated still more explicitly:

Considering the weight of this metonymy, which is supreme [*souveraine*] in Guyotat's text, weighty censorship can be foreseen which will find that its two habitual stamping grounds, language and sex, are combined; but consequently this censorship, which could take many forms, will immediately be unmasked by its very weight: condemned to be excessive if it censors sex and language *at the same time*; condemned to hypocrisy if it claims to be censoring just the subject and not the form, or vice versa: in both cases condemned to reveal its essence as censorship [*son essence de censure*]. (In *ÉÉÉ* 10)

In the event, the censorship took the mitigated form of an order banning any type of publicity for the book or its sale to minors (an 'interdiction de vente aux mineurs de moins de dix-huit ans; interdiction à l'affichage et à l'exposition; interdiction de publicité' (see *LI* 163). This order also meant that the book became classed as a 'luxury object' subject to value added tax, unlike 'proper' literature (*LI* 87), and that the book's publishers, Gallimard, could be placed under an obligation to submit all books 'of the same nature' (*de même nature*) to prior inspection, if any other two books they published were subjected to a similar ban. Such a measure was

---

[25] Sollers is evidently using 'contre-censure' in a different, almost opposite sense to that of Barthes and to that in which I have used it in the title of this section. I return to this quotation later.

designed, then, to make publishers more cautious about the sort of material they would publish; and it must also have had a financial impact on Guyotat, who made his living from his writing ('they are censoring a job of work', *Humanité* explained (*LI* 166))—though it seems likely that Guyotat's sales in fact increased as a result of the ban. It was eventually lifted in December 1981 under the new presidency of Mitterrand, who had himself raised the issue in the Assemblée Nationale at the time the ban was imposed.

A petition was launched in protest at the ban by Jérôme Lindon, who was the head of Minuit publishers and a member of the commission which should have been consulted on such an issue, the Commission de Surveillance et de Contrôle des Publications Destinées à l'Enfance et à l'Adolescence (which I discussed in Chapter 1). Lindon wrote an article in which he argued that, if obscene, *Éden, Éden, Éden* should have been prosecuted in court—pointing out that Apollinaire's considerably more accessible and undoubtedly obscene *Les Onze Mille Verges* had been published unchallenged in 1968. He also underlined the literary credentials bestowed on *Éden, Éden, Éden* by its prefacers and others; and argued that, even if certain youths got their kicks from *Éden, Éden, Éden* or from *Les Cent-vingt Journées de Sodome*, this was not necessarily a good reason to ban them—especially since, in the words he borrowed from a 'scientific commission', 'statistics prove that as a general rule sex offenders have no erotic experience' (*LI* 189). Finally, Lindon invoked the precedent of *Madame Bovary* and *Les Fleurs du mal* as evidence of the kind of errors censors tended to commit, and concluded, 'it cannot be ignored that imposing "moral order" by way of books is today the prerogative of totalitarian states and that freedom, on the other hand, is the sign of the most democratic nations—which means, in fact, the healthiest ones' (*LI* 190).

The petition itself followed this article, stating briefly that its signatories objected to the censorship of a work of recognized literary importance, and to the manifest abuse of a law designed to protect children.[26] It was signed by a great many people, including

[26] As an article in *Les Lettres françaises* (a revue directed by Aragon) pointed out, the action against *Éden, Éden, Éden* took place at a time when pornography was increasingly widely available and when sexual material was easy to find on television as well as in the press, in forms considerably more intellectually accessible to minors (or anyone else) than Guyotat's book. For instance, photos of naked women had

not only individual members of the *Tel Quel* group and the journal collectively but also writers such as Aragon and Sartre who may have had limited sympathy for Guyotat and his books *per se*. Similarly the article from *Les Lettres françaises*,[27] though it showed little interest in *Éden, Éden, Éden* in itself, defended the writer's right to experiment, and concluded, in an echo of Guyotat's remark on the events of May 1968, 'Isn't their aim to destroy anything which—in the area of freedom of expression as elsewhere—might pass for an achievement of May 68?' (*LI* 165).[28]

The censorship of *Éden, Éden, Éden* took place in a political atmosphere which was highly charged, not only because of the events of May 1968, but also because of lingering political sensitivity created by the Algerian war, notably in the area of freedom of expression. *Éden, Éden, Éden*'s 'Algerian' elements must have been a factor in its selection as an object of censorship, though this was an issue on which most commentators on Guyotat—including Barthes, Leiris, and Sollers—were strangely silent. Having said this, exactly why *Éden, Éden, Éden* was picked on remains a matter for speculation. Partly, there was again undoubtedly a circular process independent of the text itself whereby Guyotat and *Tel Quel* de-

started to appear in French magazines (amongst which *Lui* was a trendsetter) in the second half of the 1960s, and the first sex shop (not intended for minors, admittedly), selling mainly books and magazines, opened in 1965. At this point almost everything it sold would have been from abroad, but by 1970 20% of pornography sold in France was home-produced, and by 1975 as much as 90%—though subsequently this figure declined (Faligot and Kaufer 1987: 196). Slogans from May 1968 had included 'Jouissez sans entraves' (a call for limitless (sexual) pleasure) and 'Inventez de nouvelles perversions sexuelles'; and in that year, at the same time that the idea of women's liberation began to gather momentum, the circulation of *Lui* doubled from 350,000 to 700,000 (Faligot and Kaufer 1987: 69). In the early 1970s written pornography, too, had great success: a new venture of 1971 was the magazine *S*, which aimed, according to its editors, to avoid both aesthetic and scientific glosses on sexuality and to provide a more direct approach by publishing readers' letters in which they described their fantasies and sexual encounters. After various problems with the vice squad this particular magazine closed down in July 1974, but other magazines of its type took its place and were so successful that by 1974–5 about forty titles were sharing a market of some five million readers a month.

[27] See n. 26.

[28] Though it is doubtless true that there was a backlash against freedom of expression after May 1968, it is worth noting that the *soixante-huitards* themselves were not necessarily in favour of greater liberalism in this area. Several committees of *lycéens* called for *Histoire de l'œil* to be banned, for instance, on the grounds that it was a product of bourgeois decadence (see Pauvert 1981: 405).

clared the text's subversive potential and identified his project as a Marxist one, and by which these declarations were believed by people who were hostile to Marxist subversion and perhaps also to the defilement of the sacred space of literature. Such a circle of censorship clearly offered benefits to both parties, with the censoring authorities reassured, in the face of baffling formal changes in writing and still more baffling new ways of reading, that they were on the right track; the writers and critics likewise.

For Guyotat, though, this circle meant that the political particularities of every level of his text were open to theorization. In his explanations of his work he constantly stretched political (especially Marxist) vocabulary into new applications, displacing the scene of political struggle on to various interconnected areas—on to language (talking of 'the daily struggle against the syntax, vocabulary, and grammar of a determinate, outmoded ideology' (*LI* 51)); on to psychoanalysis (ideally, Guyotat noted, his readers were 'influenced by the facts of psychoanalysis' (*travaillés par le fait psychanalytique*));[29] on to the unconscious (his initial 'precise political intentions' were, as I noted earlier, 'abandoned as soon as they had been written down *in favour of the irrepressible movement of the unconscious*' (*LI* 68); on to sex ('I observe, and all of this is very coherent, that the bourgeoisie are still good at selling their literary merchandise, everywhere. So it is very important that we, as Communists, permanently and in practice reject this bourgeois literary merchandise, and that we pay heed ever more rigorously and audaciously to the sexual (*au fait sexuel*)' (*LI* 49); and even on to 'the act of excretion' (his aim being 'not to rehabilitate nor glorify so-called "base" functions but to *emancipate* them by reintegrating them into sexual activity [*ré-insertion dans le mouvement sexuel*]' (*LI* 31).

In the work of the *Tel Quel* group more generally, too, the notion of censorship was a mobile one, which shifted away from its

[29] Guyotat's version of psychoanalysis was an idiosyncratic one. In parentheses after the phrase quoted above, he writes, 'breaking up the familial economy and dominant ideology, political instability, the problems posed by sexual prohibitions, sexual repression, the need for physical contact with other civilizations' (*LI* 89)—a series of condensed propositions which, though individually doubtless approachable (with varying degrees of ease) in psychoanalytic terms, scarcely constitute a recognizable summary of 'le fait psychanalytique'. Guyotat also recasts Freud's link of the proletariat with the instinctual, writing, 'sexual drives have always, for me, masked [*recouvert*] a drive towards the proletariat' (*LI* 110).

political groundings as the group sought to find the true locus of
literary subversion in a writer such as Guyotat or Sade. Roland
Barthes, on possibly the only occasion in *Sade, Fourier, Loyola*
when he alludes to censorship in its most obvious form (namely in
the brief 'Vie de Sade' at the end of the book, where he mentions
that Sade was refused a copy of Rousseau's *Confessions*), writes,
'censorship is abhorrent on two levels: because it is repressive,
because it is stupid; so that we always have the contradictory urge
to combat it and to teach it a lesson' (*SFL* 185; 1977c: Barthes
181). This gives a fair indication of the *Tel Quel* approach to Sade,
which involves at once a refusal of overt censorship and a desire to
bring Sade out into the open, vaunting his merits and condemning
the censor's failure to understand him, and at the same time a
fascination with what *really* makes Sade censorable, and a desire to
teach people to read Sade so as to understand how and why he is
indeed subversive. Censorship, in other words, is taken as a clumsy,
back-handed compliment concerning the power of writing, and its
sphere of operation is shown to be other than it would at first
appear, as the notion is metaphorically transplaced then literalized
in a new position.

Methodologically this approach to censorship is clearly close to
that of Freud, and, even if Freud's own notion of censorship is used
explicitly only infrequently, its influence is often felt. Klossowski,
for instance, in a text published in the *Tel Quel* journal, discusses
psychic censorship, transgression, and Sade in relation to 'impulsive
forces', and censorship as he describes it is of a type familiar from
Freud, situated between the unconscious and the conscious, acting
against forces which threaten the integrity of the ego, and constantly overwhelmed and then rebuilt in a cycle of gratification and
guilt. Though he goes beyond Freud in suggesting how censorship
is actively complicitous in the cycle of transgression, Klossowski is
also close to Freud in that he, unlike Sade, does not necessarily take
a (supposedly) radical stance against the censorship. The passage
where Klossowski explains his understanding of censorship is
worth quoting at length:

in one of the structures that these [impulsive] forces, individuated in the
subject, have developed under the pressure of the institutional environment, that is, of norms, [Sade] seems also to have recognized a *self-
consciousness*. This structure suffers variations and instability, though
these become clear only after the event [*ne se vérifient qu'après-coup*].

Sometimes these forces put the subject *beside himself* [hors de soi] and make him act *against himself*; they transgress the structure of consciousness and decompose it. Sometimes, in particular when they have made him act against himself, they recompose the (remembering) consciousness of the subject during his inaction; in this case these same forces are inverted. The inversion of the same forces constitutes the consciousness that *censors* the subject. What exercises censorship is the feeling the subject has that *being put beside oneself* is a menace to the subject, who is dependent on the norms of the species. This censorship is exercised already in the very act of transgression and is the necessary motive for it. For Sade, moral conscience simply corresponds to an exhaustion of the impulsive forces (the 'calm of the senses'); this state of exhaustion opens up an interval in which the repellent image of the act committed represents itself in the form of 'remorse'.

  In fact, from the first time the act was committed, it presented itself as a a promise of pleasure because its image was repellent. And if now the reiteration of the same act is to 'annihilate' conscience, it is because each time it is the same forces that, through their inversion, re-establish conscience. Inverted into censorship, they will then provoke the act *again*. (*TQ* 1967: 14–15; Klossowski 1992: 30–1)

In other cases, too, Freud's ideas were drawn on, and sometimes adapted, in an unobtrusive way which shows how fully they were integrated into the *Tel Quel* critical perspective. Damisch, for instance, uses Freud's notion of sadism as 'a displacement of the sexual goal' (*TQ* 1967: 53), and goes on to postulate that Sade's fiction provides 'natural reserves' (an expression he has taken from Freud) which are not subject to the jurisdiction of reality and in which desire can turn away from the objects and goals which society prescribes and towards those it labels as perversions (*TQ* 1967: 62). Tort uses Freud's idea that sexuality in general is perverted, in that it is not dictated by need (*TQ* 1967: 71); and Barthes, having contended that the only type of torture in all of Sade which is terrifying is that which involves sewing up the vagina or the anus, explains this in relation to castration (*SFL* 172–3; Barthes 1977c: 168–9). Barthes especially is willing to adapt Freudian vocabulary to his own ends, making broad use of the term *après-coup* (in an untranslatable way that indicates Lacan's influence[30]), or, in an appreciation of the horizontal 'furnishings of

[30] The central members of the *Tel Quel* group, though interested in Lacan's work, were not uncritical of it. Sollers was specifically critical of Lacan's essay 'Kant avec Sade' of 1963, implying that it was inaccurate and reductive (*TQ* 61 (spring 1975)

debauchery', of 'the censorship imposed by our vertical, legal, moral, separative stance' (*SFL* 144; Barthes 1977*c*: 140). Similarly, he concludes his 'Vie de Sade' by discussing as a form of censorship the way in which Sade was sometimes denied writing materials:

The repression of writing doubtless, as anyone can see, serves as censorship of the book; but what is poignant here is that writing is forbidden in its material form [*dans sa matérialité*]; Sade is denied 'any use of pencil, ink, pen or paper'. What is censored is his hand, his muscle, his blood, the finger on the pen pointing to the word. Castration is circumscribed, the scriptural sperm can no longer flow; detention becomes retention; lacking exercise and lacking a pen, Sade becomes *blocked up* [s'engorge], becomes a eunuch. (*SFL* 186; Barthes 1977*c*: 182)

This idea of the symbolic equivalence of pen and penis is one that Barthes had already used, writing that, for Sade, 'speech and posture [*la parole et la posture*, metonyms here for language and sex] are of exactly the same value, they are equivalent: giving one, one can get the other back as change [. . .] So it is not at all surprising that, anticipating Freud, but also inverting him, Sade makes sperm the substitute of speech (and not the opposite)' (*TQ* 1967: 34; *SFL* 37; Barthes 1977*c*: 32). This idea is in fact some way from that of Freud, who, in an essay entitled 'Inhibitions, Symptoms, and Anxiety', had written:

Analysis shows that when activities like playing the piano, writing, or even walking are subjected to neurotic inhibitions it is because the physical organs brought into play—the fingers or the legs—have become too strongly eroticized. [. . .] As soon as writing, which entails making a liquid flow out of a tube on to a piece of white paper, assumes the significance of copulation, or as soon as walking becomes a symbolic substitute for treading upon the body of mother earth, both writing and walking are stopped because they represent the performance of a forbidden sexual act. The ego renounces these functions, which are within its sphere, in order not to have to undertake fresh measures of repression—*in order to avoid a conflict with the id*. (1926; *SE* xx. 89–90)

16). Similarly, in an article of 1971, *Tel Quel* rejected Lacan's claim to be at the cutting edge of studies of the relation of psychoanalysis and literature (*TQ* 47 (autumn 1971), 144), a position which they wished to claim for themselves. Although Lacan doubtless shared many influences and certain ambitions with the *Tel Quel* group, his project in general was distinguished from theirs, crucially for my purposes, by its relative inattention to politics, and his reading of Sade sheds little light on the discourse of counter-censorship with which I am concerned.

Freud is arguing that, once someone sees writing as sexual, that person's ego will inhibit writing activity, rather than risk releasing the dangerous sexual contents of the id. His comments are, of course, ambiguous, in that he himself makes the link of sex and writing and gives it a rationale, and one might suppose that the neurotic's problem thus lay in his or her attitude to sex rather than to writing (or walking): but, contrary to what Thérèse Réveillé, another *Tel Quel* collaborator, implies in an interview with Guyotat (*LI* 91), Freud is not arguing prima facie that a writing practice grounded in an awareness of its own link to sex will encounter censorship, but rather that it will provoke self-censorship in the form of neurotic inhibitions. Barthes's point is a different one again, for he inverts the Freudian symbolic hierarchy of sperm and ink, suggesting that Sade's urge to write was as sexual as any sexual urges which his imprisonment frustrated.[31]

Barthes on Sade

Though perhaps surprising if presented in this way, Barthes's argument regarding Sade's sexual/scriptural urges is nothing more than the last example of the overriding thrust of his interpretive strategy with respect to Sade, which is to examine all questions pertaining to his work in relation to a particular notion of writing and of pleasure. What links Sade, Fourier, and Loyola for Barthes is that they are 'founders of languages [. . .] men who invented and formulated ways of writing [*des formulateurs, des inventeurs d'écriture*], textual operators' (*SFL*: back cover). In his introduction Barthes states that he intends to look, not for the secret, the contents, or the philosophy of Sade's texts, but for their 'felicity of writing' (*bonheur d'écriture*) (*SFL*: 15; Barthes 1977c: 9), in order to detach them from sadism and from the moral framework in which they are usually discussed. His aim, he explains, is to 'displace (but not to suppress; perhaps even to accentuate) the text's social responsibility' (*SFL* 15; Barthes 1977c: 9), moving this responsibility away from the historical class position of the author and towards the site

---

[31] As we have seen, the link of sex and writing was an important one for Guyotat, too. In an explanation of how he created his 'texte sauvage' while masturbating, he wrote: 'the desire to write is directly linked to sexual desire, the desire to ejaculate is the desire to write (the title of my *texte sauvage* is "The Other Hand is Jerking Off")' (*LI* 69–70).

of reading. The rationale for this is that one cannot set oneself outside 'bourgeois ideology' (*SFL* 15; Barthes 1977c: 10), and cannot confront or destroy its language, but can only fragment it and rework it into unfamiliar forms. He argues that what is important is 'the animation of the message, not the message' (*l'emportement du message, non le message*) (*SFL* 16; Barthes 1977c: 10), and that Sade's work constitutes a triumph for the 'signifying text' (*texte signifiant*) (*SFL* 16; Barthes 1977c: 10) from which the received wisdoms and meanings of repressive, liberal discourse peel away like unwanted skin. He then states that the impact a text has on a society (when it is written, or later) cannot be assessed in terms of its popularity nor of its sensitivity to socio-economic conditions, but depends on the violence which permits it, in Barthes's words, 'to go beyond the laws that a society, an ideology, a philosophy set themselves in order to agree with themselves in a fine movement of historical intelligibility' (*d'excéder les lois qu'une société, une idéologie, une philosophie se donnent pour s'accorder à elles-mêmes dans un beau mouvement d'intelligible historique*). And Barthes concludes: 'This excess has a name: writing [*écriture*]' (*SFL* 16; Barthes 1977c: 10).

This is to be compared with the very end of 'L'Arbre du crime', where he writes that the function of discourse is not (i.e. ought not to be) to create impressions or emotions, but to conceive the inconceivable, 'i.e. to leave nothing outside the words and to concede nothing ineffable to the world'. This, he concludes, is Sade's guiding principle, a principle of *écriture*: in Barthes's words, 'such, it seems, is the watchword repeated throughout the Sadian city, from the Bastille, where Sade existed only through writing, to the Château of Silling, a sanctuary not of debauchery but of the story/history [*l' "histoire"*]' (*TQ* 1967: 37; *SFL* 42; Barthes 1977c: 37).

Both at the end of the introduction to *Sade, Fourier, Loyola* and in the concluding part of 'L'Arbre du crime', then, writing is conceived of as a surpassing of limits, and is grounded politically through the use of elements of Marxist (or *marxisant*) vocabulary—the idea of intervention against bourgeois ideology in the first case, and the notion of *histoire* in the second. What this play on *histoire* aims to suggest, it seems, is that, through their very excesses, through their very 'unrealism', stories of the type told in and about Silling reveal the 'materiality of the signifier' (to use Sollers's term: *TQ* 1967: 86) and, from there, the constructedness of ideology, jolting us out of the false consciousness engendered by 'transparent' writing which 'reflects'—and accepts—the (social) world as it is. To Sadian *histoire*, in other words, Barthes is attributing, however elliptically, a heuristic political role, whereby it helps the reading subject to understand his or her position within a mutable history.

Barthes's critical approach is not entirely consistent, however, and it is not always clear in what sense his analyses are political, despite these nods towards Marxism. In spite of his declared attention to reading over writing, and his statement that he is not interested in the author (any author) as a 'biographical hero' (*SFL* 13; Barthes 1977*c*: 8), his allusion to Sade's time in the Bastille in the above quotation suggests that he is not completely detached from the critical tradition which has built Sade up into just such a hero, and also suggests that he accepts overriding political continuity between Sade's biography and his writing practice. There is an implication, in other words, that Sade himself is politically an exemplary figure. A more serious objection is that Barthes's punning use of *histoire*, and the implied opposition of *histoire* to debauchery, empties the term of its meaning (at least in so far as it would normally mean 'history'). To raise this objection may seem to be to miss Barthes's point, his antipathy to the idea of 'content': but I wish to argue that his rejection of content is theoretically weak, hinging on a simple reversal of the view which he condemns, that of language as potentially 'the neutral instrument of a triumphant content' (*SFL* 15; Barthes 1977*c*: 10).

Barthes is not unaware of specific historical determinations in Sade's work, and sets out briefly, in a section of 'Sade II' entitled 'Social', how the social structures found in his novels are drawn from the society of Louis XV (*SFL* 134–5; Barthes 1977*c*: 130–1). He argues that, rather than reproducing these relations as Balzac might have done, Sade re-produces them in a new context, and that therefore, in his words, 'It follows that the Sadian novel is more real than the social novel (which is realistic)' (*SFL* 135; Barthes 1977*c*: 131). There seems little justification, however, for establishing a hierarchy of reality amongst different types of literary representation in so far as these are viewed from outside, as it were—in which case Barthes's distinction ceases to indicate any real difference; and Barthes insists that, if one views the representation from the inside, the fictional world is not answerable to exterior reality.

In his words, 'Sade makes a fundamental contrast between language and the real, or more precisely he places himself under the sole authority of the "real of language" [*sous la seule instance du "réel du langage"*] [. . .] The "real" and the book are *cut off* from each other [*sont* coupés]: they are not linked by any obligation' (*SFL* 141; Barthes 1977c: 137).

In certain obvious respects, Barthes is right about this division of language from reality. He is obviously right, in the passage from which this last quotation is taken, to accept, for theoretical as well as for practical and historical reasons, Sade's statement that he had not done and would never do many of the things he described. He is right to point out that language can evoke things which in reality do not and could not exist, and can deny or forget things or aspects of things which in reality do exist. Barthes insists that Sade is an *écrivain* rather than a realist author, that Sade chooses 'discourse' (*le discours*) over the referent, semiosis over mimesis, and that he should be read 'on the level of meaning, not of the referent' (*au niveau du sens, non du référent*). Barthes argues that the society which bans Sade, however, heeds only 'the call of the referent' (*l'appel du référent*), that for that society, 'the word is nothing but a window on to the real; the creative process it envisions and on which it bases its laws has only two terms: the "real" and its expression', and that legal action against Sade's work is based on a narrowly realist conception of literature (all *SFL* 41–2; Barthes 1977c: 37). In Barthes's words:

The legal condemnation brought against Sade is therefore founded on a certain system of literature, and this system is that of realism: it postulates that literature 'represents', 'figures', 'imitates'; that the faithfulness [*conformité*] of this imitation is what is being offered for judgement, aesthetic if the object is touching and instructive, or penal if it is outrageous; that in the end to imitate is to persuade, to captivate [*entraîner*]. This is the perspective of one school alone, but a whole society and its institutions are committed to it [*vue d'école, dans laquelle pourtant s'engage toute une société, avec ses institutions*]. (*TQ* 1967: 37; *SFL* 41–2; Barthes 1977c: 37)

A similar point was made by Guyotat in an interview with *Tel Quel*, when he said that *Éden, Éden, Éden* should be read 'outside any notion of representation' and that censorship was a 'a fate [*fatalité*] tied to the fate of representation' (*LI* 27). Both Barthes and Guyotat are right that any given instance of censorship is linked implicitly to a certain notion of representation: but, in countering censorship or in revealing its shortcomings, one cannot abandon the notion of representation altogether. It is misleading to establish an opposition between discourse and referent, or between semiosis and mimesis, because the reader cannot in practice—or in more rigorous theory—read for the *sens* of the discourse without some notion of reference.[32] Indeed, it is implicit in Barthes's position that he has measured and does measure Sade's discourse against reality, in order to decide that Sade cannot realistically be read realistically.

On the model Barthes is using here, language and reality are not only separate, but separated by a void into which any sense of history disappears. Though it is indeed absurd for the censor to read Sade's texts as straightforward imitations of reality, and to assume that such an imitation is inherently persuasive, encouraging a retranslation of the text back into reality, it is equally absurd for Barthes to suggest that the erotic charge of the Sadian text is purely textual,[33] or that *libertinage* is nothing other than 'a fact of language' (*SFL* 140–1; Barthes 1977c: 137) with no determinate relation to the material practices which the word *libertinage* is used to describe. Furthermore, it is a mistake to assume, as Barthes seems to, that censors, having established a model of the relation of reality to its expression as an unmediated one, are able to pass directly via this model into reality, as it were, in order to censor features of reality which are considered offensive or dangerous, rather than themselves approaching reality via the mediations of language, including the discursive category of the censorable or of that-which-should-be-censored. This is a point to which I will return later.

Barthes's determination to view Sade's works as 'pure' text leads to a series of distortions in the specific interpretations he makes of them. In 'L'Arbre du crime', for instance, having postulated that Sade's descriptions of his characters become progressively more

[32] This is an issue to which Barthes is generally sensitive, of course, and elsewhere he often 'figures (without solving the problems of) the process of reference', as Andrew Brown puts it (1992: 163; see e.g. pp. 206–15 of 'Le Mythe, aujourd'hui' in Barthes 1957). I am suggesting that in *SFL*, however, he too often simplifies or ignores these problems.

[33] This idea is repeated, in a more general form, in *Le Plaisir du texte*, where Barthes writes: 'The pleasure of representation is not attached to its object: pornography is not *sure*' (1973: 88; 1990: 55).

rhetorical and less visually suggestive and 'real' (in the conventional sense as applied to literature) as one descends the hierarchy of libertines, their aides, and their victims, Barthes states that, 'It is therefore neither ugliness nor beauty but the discourse in and of itself, split into illustrating portraits and signifying portraits, which determines the way Sadian humanity is divided up' (*Ce n'est donc ni la laideur ni la beauté, c'est l'instance même du discours, divisé en portraits-figures et en portraits-signes, qui détermine le partage de l'humanité sadienne*) (*TQ* 1967: 28; *SFL* 28; Barthes 1977c: 22–3). To this, it night be objected that counter-examples could be cited (Justine as a 'real' victim, for example); and, furthermore, since the visually suggestive in writing is never just visual, in that it always engages the rhetoric of beauty, ugliness, and so on, that the division of *portraits-figures* from *portraits-signes* is a crude one. Most importantly, though, it must be recognized that the divisions and hierarchy to which Barthes is referring are overdetermined by factors such as class and gender, and that these may have priority over the *figure/signe* dualism even within the Sadian universe.

For similar reasons, it is difficult to accept the disembodied notion of the victim which Barthes uses when he writes, 'the victim is not: he or she *to whom things are done* [qui subit], but he or she *who uses a certain language*' (*SFL* 148; Barthes 1977c: 144), or 'the scream is the mark of the victim: it is because she(/he) chooses to scream that she becomes a victim; if, in the same unpalatable circumstances [*sous la même vexation*] she were to come [*jouir*], she would cease to be a victim, and would be transformed into a libertine: *to scream/to ejaculate*, this paradigm is the point of departure of (Sadian) choice, i.e. of Sadian meaning [crier/décharger, *ce paradigme est le départ du choix, c'est-à–dire du sens sadien*]' (*SFL* 147; Barthes 1977c: 143). Again, there is a problem with the factual exactness of Barthes's terms, in that *crier* and *décharger* (in reality as in fiction) are not necessarily mutually exclusive; and, on another level, even for Sade, *crier/décharger* is not necessarily a choice (the ambiguities around *départ* may be intended to hint at this), since numerous factors *make* certain people victims, in Sade's texts as in reality (and these factors are largely the same in Sade's fiction as in reality (the historical reality Sade knew), even if other aspects of Sadian victimhood are sometimes unrealistic). On the subject of transgressive sexual behaviour, too, Barthes tends to empty Sade's vocabulary of content, writing: 'incest [. . .] is only a surprise of vocabulary' (*SFL* 142; Barthes 1977*c*: 138) and stating that for Sade,

The addition of pleasures provides a supplementary pleasure, that of addition itself [. . .] This superior pleasure, completely formal, since it is in sum only a mathematical idea, is a pleasure of language: that of unfolding a criminal act into different nouns: 'I am thus simultaneously committing incest, adultery, sodomy': it is the homonymy that is voluptuous. (*SFL* 161; Barthes 1977*c*: 158–9)

Perhaps led astray by an urge to couch his criticism in the neutral, scientific-sounding vocabulary of linguistics (and perhaps punning, more or less consciously, on the prefix 'homo-': describing his own writing, Barthes writes: 'you practise a pseudo-linguistics, a metaphorical linguistics [. . .] and like a poetic language, it enables you to express the desire that is distinctively yours [*le propre de votre désir*]' (1975: 127; 1977*b*: 124)), Barthes not so much metaphorizes as misuses the term homonymy here (homonyms being words pronounced or spelt in the same way but having different meanings). He presumably means to say that *synonymy* is voluptuous (in that the same act can be described by different words, in his example), but this statement is already less plausible for using a more commonplace word which allows counter-examples to spring more readily to mind (how voluptuous, for instance, is the synonymy of 'spectacles' and 'glasses'? And how voluptuous is the 'synonymy' of incest, adultery, and sodomy for the victim?). Furthermore, incest, adultery and sodomy are evidently not synonymous: the libertine's pleasure derives from the sense of intensified transgression and power provided by the combination of these *different* transgressions, which are defined as such and given a material specificity within a linguistic community of which the victim, too, is a part.

I want to give one final example of the way Barthes hollows out Sade's texts. In 'L'Arbre du crime' he suggests that the various functions in the Sadian 'grammar' can be fulfilled by anyone and that pleasure is therefore available to everyone. He writes:

above all in Sadian grammar, no function is reserved for anyone in particular (with the exception of torture). In any scene all the functions can be interchanged [. . .] This is a cardinal rule, first because it means Sade's erotics is close to a truly formal language in which there are only classes of action and not groups of individuals, which greatly simplifies its grammar: the subject of an act (in the grammatical sense of the term) may just as easily be a libertine, an assistant, a victim, a wife; secondly, because it discourages us from dividing up Sadian society on the basis of erotic traits [. . .] everyone can be sodomist and sodomized, agent and patient, subject and object [. . .] pleasure is possible anywhere, for victims as well as for masters. (*TQ* 32)

Again, Barthes's model of a Sadian grammar is imperfectly matched with its fictional object, first because the uneven distribution of torture seriously undermines his analysis, rather than incorporating itself comfortably into it as an insignificant exception, and secondly because, again, numerous factors come into play to determine who is the subject of the act. It is, of course, true that the grammatical subject is mobile, but this observation is in itself an uninteresting one, and is misleading if it obscures the fact that the struggle for full, unassailable subjectivity (i.e. that of the philosophical, not the grammatical, subject) is a fundamental theme—and a structuring principle—of Sade's work. Gender, for instance, is evidently once again a factor in this, yet Barthes makes the claim—which is at the very least problematic—that all Sadian characters can engage in 'active' sodomy.

What, then, is at stake for Barthes in such a statement? A clue to a possible answer lies in an addition which Barthes made to this passage for *Sade, Fourier, Loyola*. Where in the original he states that the rule of the exchangeability of sexual roles 'discourages us from dividing up Sadian society on the basis of erotic traits' (*dissuade de fonder le partage de la société sadienne sur des traits érotiques*), in the second version the elliptical 'traits érotiques' is expanded upon, and one gets: 'This rule [. . .] discourages us from dividing up Sadian society on the basis of particular sexual practices (just the opposite of what happens in our own society; we always ask ourselves whether a homosexual is "active" or "passive"; with Sade, sexual practices never serve to identify a subject)' (*SFL* 35–6; Barthes 1977c: 30). This makes the ideological thrust of Barthes's argument, here and in certain other cases, somewhat clearer. His reading of Sade creates a Utopia in which there is an unending plurality of sexual possibilities and a refusal of sexual identity, and he suggests that to read Sade in any other way is to slip into the sterile, self-perpetuating dualisms of conventional politics (in his essay on Fourier he writes 'can a Utopia ever be political?

Isn't politics *every language bar one*, that of Desire?' (*SFL* 90; Barthes 1977c: 85)). It is perhaps in the light of this refusal of sexual identity and this impatience with the type of politics which is oblivious to 'Desire' that one should read Barthes's remarks on censorship and counter-censorship in 'Sade II', where, having cited two obvious forms of censorship (that of overt intervention and that of aesthetic marginalization), Barthes argues that more important than these, more *real*, is the censorship which takes the form of stereotypes, that which is built into the chatterings of 'common opinion' (*l'opinion courante*). What is most subversive in relation to this, he argues, is inventive writing. In full, Barthes's comments, under the heading 'La Censure, l'invention', read as follows:

Sade is apparently censored twice: when, in one way or another, the sale of his books is banned; when he is declared to be boring, unreadable. Yet true censorship, the most profound censorship, does not consist in banning (in cuts, abridgements, deprivations), but in providing undue nourishment, in keeping up, keeping in, smothering, entangling in stereotypes (be they intellectual, romantic [*romanesques*], erotic), to feed only with the accepted word of others, the repetitious matter of current opinion. The real instrument of censorship is not the police, it is the *endoxa*. Just as a language is better defined by what it makes it obligatory to say (its obligatory rubrics) than by what it forbids to be said (its rhetorical rules), so social censorship exists not where speech is prevented but where it is compulsory [*là où l'on contraint de parler*].

The most profound type of subversion (counter-censorship) does not, then, necessarily consist in saying what shocks public opinion, morality, the law, or the police, but in inventing a discourse that is paradoxical (pure of any *doxa*): *invention* (and not provocation) is a revolutionary act: the latter cannot be accomplished except by founding a new language. Sade's greatness lies not in having celebrated crime, perversion, nor in having used a radical language to do so; it lies in having invented a vast discourse founded on its own repetitions (and not those of others), a currency of details, surprises, journeys, menus, portraits, configurations, proper nouns, etc.: in short, counter-censorship meant starting with prohibitions and making something novel [*la contre-censure, ce fut, à partir de l'interdit, de faire du romanesque*]. (*SFL* 130; Barthes 1977c: 126)

The first sentence of this passage (up to 'unreadable') is unambiguously about Sade, but for the rest of this paragraph Barthes drifts away from Sade's writing and towards the concerns I set out above—namely, his refusal of sexual identity and his impatience with conventional politics. The 'social censorship' which makes speech 'compulsory' could, of course, be a description of the social forces which encourage people to declare Sade 'boring' and 'unreadable' (those people may do so even if they have read him and have found his books exciting, after all), but it is other constraints which Barthes seems to have in mind. What is truer and deeper than politics or aesthetics, in this passage, what constitutes the site of 'true censorship [. . .] the most profound censorship', seems to be—stereotypically—sex, and it is being suggested, in the less than categorical terms that may be the sign of Barthes's own self-censorship, that it is in the compulsory categories of sexual identity that deep censorship acts. Again, the circle of censorship closes around the topic of sex, Barthes trying to distance himself (a gay man unwilling (at least at this point in his life) to *identify* himself as one), from the conventional fixities of sexual definition by which he suffers, trying to do so by fragmenting those fixities into eroticized details spread across the body of a text (Sade's, or his own);[34] but at the same time eliding the specificities of that eroticism as it is found in Sade (and as it transfers itself to Barthes), an eroticism full of inequalities. Underneath this eroticism sex works as a value against which society is measured and found lacking (less true, more superficial), and as such is actually an anchor-point for the sexual identities Barthes wishes to disperse.

Barthes's choice of vocabulary here ('subversion', 'revolutionary', 'radical') indicates that he considers his approach a political one in a way which is close to that of the Surrealists. Indeed, when one reads in the earlier essay, 'we are beginning to recognize that transgressions of language possess an offensive power at least as strong as that of moral transgressions, and that poetry, which is the very language of transgressions of language, is therefore always revolutionary' (*TQ* 1967: 35), the sense of political–historical progress in art ('we are beginning to recognize . . .') and the faith in poetry could easily be Breton's rather than Barthes's. Kristeva too was developing arguments similar to these at this point, presenting literature as an exemplary form of 'productive violence' which, she

---

[34] Seemingly describing a personal Utopia, Barthes writes in *Roland Barthes par Roland Barthes*: 'there will be, for example, only *homosexualities*, whose plural will baffle any constituted, centred discourse, to the point where it seems [. . .] virtually pointless to talk about it/them' (1975: 73; 1977*b*: 69). One might compare this with his remark on his own writing, 'in what he writes, everyone defends his own sexuality' [*chacun défend sa sexualité*] (1975: 159; 1977*b*: 156).

explained, was 'a practice comparable to political revolution: one brings about in the subject what the other introduces into society' (1974: 14; 1984: 16–17). It is notable that 'poetry' (*poésie*) has entered inverted commas and 'revolutionary' (*révolutionnaire*) has been replaced by 'contestatory' (*contestataire*) in the *Sade, Fourier, Loyola* version of Barthes's essay (cf. *SFL* 39; Barthes 1977*c*: 34), and it is tempting to see his change of vocabulary, and also his scepticism concerning 'what shocks public opinion, morality, the law, or the police', as signs of a change of attitude produced at least in part by the events of May 1968 ('L'Arbre du crime', it will be remembered, first appeared in 1967, and *Sade, Fourier, Loyola* was published in 1971); but this apparent lowering of stakes is not systematic and does not prevent Barthes from talking about revolutionary writing in the above passage on censorship and invention, for instance. Nevertheless, as Barthes displaces political vocabulary in this passage away from what is apparent—external censorship, the police, the law—and towards stereotypes, writing, and inventiveness (not to mention 'surprises, journeys, menus, portraits, configurations, proper nouns, etc.'), a certain amount of political force is inevitably lost.

Sade's writing is far from 'pure of any *doxa*', and to conceive of writing that would be 'pure' in this way is impossible. To the limited extent that any text could be 'pure' in this sense, it would presumably not be shocking; but Sade's writing *is* shocking to 'public opinion', and the refined pleasures a reader can gain from Sade's descriptions of meals, for instance, depend to a large extent on those descriptions' position within a text which is marked and defined as Sadian largely by its shockingness. Barthes is tempted to ignore this shockingness because he measures Sade and other writing that is to be considered 'contestatory' by criteria which are presented as being above all formal. Barthes insists that what makes Sade irrecuperable is that he creates 'a world that exists only in proportion to its writing' (*TQ* 1967: 35; *SFL*: 39; Barthes 1977*c*: 34), and goes on to state:

Thus the singularity of Sade's *œuvre* is established—and at the same time, the prohibition upon it is adumbrated [*du même coup se profile l'interdit qui la frappe*] [. . .] Inside the Sadian novel there is another book, a textual book of pure writing [*livre textuel, tissé de pure écriture*] [*TQ*: a primal text of pure words [*livre originel, tissé de pure parole*]] which determines what happens 'imaginarily' in the former: it is not a question of telling a story, but of telling that one is telling.[35] (*TQ* 1967: 36; *SFL* 39; Barthes 1977c: 34–5)

The book as Barthes describes it is about nothing outside itself—it is, he argues, 'arbitrary' to move one's attention to 'the reality which it is supposed to represent or imagine', as opposed to 'the performance of the discourse' (*TQ* 1967: 36–7; *SFL* 41; Barthes 1977c: 36)—and has little to do with politics, despite the unexpected uses Barthes makes of political vocabulary. In a similar vein, in his introduction to *Éden, Éden, Éden*—which he reads much as he reads Sade—Barthes writes that criticism, 'since it cannot say anything about the author, nor his subject, nor his style, can do nothing with this text: we have to "enter" Guyotat's language: not believe in it, or play along with an illusion, or participate in a fantasy, but write that language with him' (in *ÉÉÉ* 9). *Éden, Éden, Éden*, he argues, is 'a free text: free of any subject, any object, any symbols' (in *ÉÉÉ* 9). The type of 'freedom' this represents is arguably an extreme version of the freedom of expression conceived of as a guarantee of the individual's autonomy, such that the writer is not only unassailable in his or her opinions but also invents new forms of expression and a new language severed from the world, which the reader has no choice but to accept. For Barthes here it is as if 'expression' has taken on a life of its own and has its own liberty autonomously of any writer or speaker and the society in which he or she lives. This is, then, recognizable as an instance of the idealist conception of freedom of expression which divorces it from the conditions under which it is exercised; and this, as I argued in Chapter 1, is a notion which tends to be oblivious to the directions in which greater freedom of expression may actually lie.

Ultimately, of course, Barthes cannot but be aware that the crude meaning of Sade's text is difficult to ignore, for all his intimations that the truest reading is one which is radically non-referential. 'Sade II', for instance, ends with the following thoughts:

Of course, Sade can be read in terms of a plan of violence [*selon un projet de violence*], but he can also (and this is what he recommends us to do) be read *delicately* [selon un principe de délicatesse]. Sadian *délicatesse* is not a class product, an attribute of civilization, a style of culture. It is a potency

[35] Barthes's argument is weakened, here and elsewhere, by the fact that what are at first sight generalizations about Sade's writing seem on closer inspection to be statements specifically about *Les Cent-vingt Journées de Sodome*, Sade's most 'singular' work.

of analysis and a power to achieve pleasure [*un pouvoir de jouissance*]: analysis and *jouissance* join together to achieve an exaltation which is unknown in our societies and which for that very reason constitutes the most formidable of Utopias. Violence follows a code worn out over millennia of human history; and to return violence [*retourner la violence*] is still to speak in the same code. The *principe de délicatesse* postulated by Sade can alone constitute, once the basis of History/the Story (*l'Histoire*) has changed, an absolutely new language, the unheard-of transformation destined to subvert (and not to invert, but to fragment, pluralize, pulverize) the very meaning of pleasure [*le sens même de la jouissance*]. (*SFL* 174; Barthes 1977c: 170–1)

Again, one sees Barthes's evasion of conventional politics (specificities of class, civilization, or culture), and his hope that Sade may represent a subversive third dimension in relation to the pendulum swings of history. What is slightly different here is the suggestion that the 'absolutely new language' for which Barthes yearns is not to be found in Sade's text other than as a potentiality bearing the promise of a *jouissance* whose meaning would be dispersed, perhaps to the point where it had no meaning at all— where it was, in other words, pure *jouissance*.

In the end, then, Sade's texts represent for Barthes less a Utopia of writing than a locus favourable to a Utopia of reading, reading as *jouissance*. In his introduction to *Sade, Fourier, Loyola*, Barthes writes: 'Nothing is more depressing than to imagine the Text as an intellectual object (for analysis, speculation, comparison, reflection, etc.). The Text is an object of pleasure [*plaisir*]' (*SFL* 12; Barthes 1977c: 7). What this pleasure consists in, according to this introduction, is the ability to *live* with Sade, which means 'introducing into our daily lives fragments of intelligibility ("set phrases" ["*des formules*"]) from a text we admire' (*SFL* 12; Barthes 1977c: 7). What this in turn means is elusive, however: it does *not* mean treating the text as a programme to be acted out, it does not mean becoming sadistic, it does not mean internalizing its contents, convictions or even images: it means only 'receiving text, a kind of fantasmatic order' (*recevoir du texte, une sorte d'ordre fantasmatique*) (*SFL* 13; Barthes 1977c: 8).

The type of pleasure which forms Barthes's Utopia is, then, a strangely disembodied one, and he is keen to demonstrate that it does not derive in any obvious way from the sexual content of Sade's texts. He argues that Sade is not erotic, stating that, in our

society, 'eroticism cannot be defined except by a perpetually allusive word [*une parole perpétuellement allusive*]. On that basis, Sade
is not erotic' (*TQ* 1967: 30; *SFL* 32; Barthes 1977c: 26). 'Our'
society, contemporary society in Britain, or France, is not necessarily the same as that of Barthes, of course, and the language of
eroticism may well have changed, becoming more direct; and, in
any case, it would seem hard to justify a general statement that Sade
is not erotic (i.e. never erotic for anyone), even if some of his
writing is too shocking to be erotic (for some people), and even if
one wishes to delimit a category of allusive 'erotica' from which
Sade would be excluded. As far as this latter category is concerned,
however, Barthes suggests that Sade's writing should not be classed
as pornography, either, claiming that 'pornography [*SFL*: current
pornography] could never recuperate [*récupérer*] a world which
exists only in proportion to its writing' (*TQ* 1967: 35; *SFL* 39;
Barthes 1977c: 34).

Despite this statement, Barthes does conceive of Sade as a pornographer elsewhere—for example, in explaining Sade's 'politeness' as a gesture by which, in his words, 'the libertine or the writer:
in fact, let's say the *pornographer*, he who literally writes debauchery, imposes his own solitude, and refuses cordiality, complicity,
solidarity, equality, the entire morality of human relationships, i.e.
hysteria' (*SFL* 136; Barthes 1977c: 132). Again, however, his emphasis is on the autonomy of the written word (rather than on the
erotic link established between the pornographer and the reader,
say). Similarly, he goes on to write that 'in Sade, libidinous practice
is truly a text—so that we must speak about it as *pornography*,
which means: not the discourse usually used for amorous conduct,
but this tissue of erotic figures, cut up and combined like the
rhetorical figures of written discourse' (*SFL* 137; Barthes 1977c:
133). Despite his suggestion a few pages later (a surprising one, in
the case of Sade) that one might consider fiction as 'programmatic
rather than as a portrait' (*SFL* 140; Barthes 1977c: 136), he rejects
the idea that the eroticism of the text might translate into (and out
of) actual sexual practices, and might become entangled in the mesh
of morality, power, sexual identity, and so forth in which they are
played out. His objection to 'conventional' erotica, in other words,
is an objection to the conventions whereby its function is, as he puts
it, one of 'conduction' rather than of 'substitution' (*SFL* 119;
Barthes 1977c: 114).

A similar aversion to erotica is expressed by Sollers in his introduction to *Éden, Éden, Éden*, where, in a passage from which I have already quoted, he writes:

Reject both censorship and counter-censorship, one moral, the other psychological. That is to say the exploitation of sexual representation (sexuality instead of sex). Persist, *repeating yourself as often as necessary*, in preventing any sublimation and in particular sublimation which believes it can appear in the form of pseudo-nudity. Censorship is repression of the first degree: counter-censorship is repression of the second degree (preciosity, eroticism). (*ÉÉÉ* 13)

What Sollers seems to want, rather like the Surrealists, is a *true* nudity, a complete absence of sublimation, an absolute refusal of the conventions of sexuality. Like Barthes, Sollers is doubtless more radical than the Surrealists in his perception of where conventions start, as one sees in his sideswipe at 'sexuality' (and implicitly at the false identities it offers), but in other respects his vision still points towards an asocial Utopia. Barthes, whose positions are more elusive, is arguably more sensitive to this kind of problem, and he seems close to Freud in viewing both censorship and sublimation as processes at once limiting and creative.

Barthes wishes to believe that pleasure is political precisely because it is normally excluded from politics. He writes, for instance, that: 'the crudest of censorships (that of morality [*celle des mœurs*]) always masks some ideological profit: if the Sadian novel is excluded from our literature, it is because its novelistic peregrinations are never a quest for the Unique (the essence of time, of truth, of happiness) but a repetition of pleasure' (*SFL* 153; Barthes 1977c: 149–50). From this perspective, the very act of reading or writing for its own sake, for the pleasure it brings, with no thought of getting anything *out* of it, is a subversive act;[36] what comes to be

---

[36] The idea that reading and writing might be subversive in themselves is naturally an appealing one for certain readers and writers, and it is an idea which found an interesting embodiment in a French film of this period, Truffaut's 1966 adaptation of Raymond Bradbury's story *Fahrenheit 451*. It is the story of a 'fireman' in a future totalitarian society, whose job is not to put out fires but to burn books—including those of Sade, which can be seen in a protracted shot of various famous works going up in flames. In 1966 more than today, this situation may have been broadly reminiscent of the Nazi regime; but it is crucially different in that, in the film, *all* books are burnt. The fireman stumbles across the pleasures of reading, which broaden both his political and his emotional horizons. The culmination of this process is his decision to join the outlawed *hommes-livres* (a pun on *hommes libres*,

198 Metaphors of Censorship

at stake in the struggle for freedom of expression is the freedom to express nothing. As I have tried to show, however, expressing nothing is not really a possibility. It is, of course, possible to write nonsense—though the urge to interpret is hard to arrest—but the gesture is a unidimensional one that does not bear repetition; and it is certainly not the gesture made by Sade. Indeed, it is in part a semi-acknowledged awareness of this that prompts Barthes to shift his Utopia from the scene of writing to that of reading, where he attempts to open up a space in which his pleasure (which is in a broad sense sexual) can be innocent, non-responsible, and disengaged from the 'outside' world. Barthes wishes to celebrate the sexual power of writing, but gives writing (and reading) an ultimate autonomy which denies the relation of this power to sex as it is practised, shot through with sexual representations and with power relations which are themselves fantasized, eroticized, and real.

The Scene of Censorship

To conclude this section, I now want to summarize briefly and uncritically the many different levels on which censorship is perceived by *Tel Quel* to act, before summing up in broad terms what I take to be the weaknesses of the group's approach to this issue.

For *Tel Quel*:

- Censorship acts against the body, as Barthes suggests when he describes how Sade was denied the physical release of writing ('What is censored is his hand . . .' (*SFL* 186; Barthes 1977c: 182)), but also *through* the body, according to Barthes's reference to 'the censorship imposed by our vertical, legal, moral, separative stance [*stature*]' (*SFL* 144; Barthes 1977c: 140).

- Censorship acts against pleasure, Barthes suggesting that it is the undirected 'repetition of pleasure' of Sade's writing (*SFL* 153; Barthes 1977c: 150) which makes it unacceptable.

- Censorship acts against the link of sex and politics: (Sollers, explaining the reasons why Bataille's 'Le Toit' was censored,

'book men/free men'), a community on the margins of society whose members have all memorized an entire book to recount to each other and to pass on to future generations. Thus the historical links of the novel with urbanization, capitalism, and individual consumption are severed, and it becomes the oral art form by which the members of an egalitarian bucolic commune display their political radicalism—irrespective of the contents of the books they have learnt.

writes: 'The reasons are sexual, and they are also political: a relationship is played out between them which we must consider unconscious and fundamental' (*TQ* 42 (summer 1970), 103).

- Censorship acts in the very structures of language. It censors nonsense: Klossowski writes: 'Traditional language, which Sade himself uses with amazing effect, can put up with everything that conforms with its logical structure. It corrects, censors, excludes, or silences everything that would destroy this structure—all non-sense' (*TQ* 1967: 21; Klossowski 1992: 40). It also obliges the speaker to speak a particular version of (common) sense, the *endoxa* of Barthes's statement, 'The real instrument of censorship is not the police, it is the *endoxa*' (*SFL* 130; Barthes 1977c: 126). Kristeva treats the split between the signifier and the signified as 'the first censorship of a social order [la première censure d'ordre social]' (1974: 46, 47, 62, 150; 1984: 48, 49, 63, 164), since this split materializes as the subject enters ('thetic') language and becomes separated from the mother.

- Censorship acts in the teleology of conventional fiction (the 'quest for the Unique (the essence of time, of truth, of happiness)' to which Barthes refers (*SFL* 153; Barthes 1977c: 150)); it acts against writing and reading which split apart the illusionist amalgam of nature and culture in which such fiction is embedded, and against reading and writing which resist the idealist oblivion to the 'materiality of the signifier'. Thus Sollers asks:

> How is it that Sade is at once banned and accepted, banned as fiction (as writing) and accepted as reality; banned as reading matter taken in its entirety but accepted as a point of psychological or physiological reference?
> [. . . The thing is] that Sade, if the truth is told, provides a radical denunciation of the type of reading which we continue to practise and to teach on a wide scale. He does this to the extent that in his work there is a relationship, masked by discourse but wholly active, to thought, not as the cause of language, but to language without a cause, to the very writing of the signifier as effect. (*TQ* 1967: 38–9)

- Censorship acts against the reality which it believes to be reflected unproblematically in the text, and which it believes could always become reality once again (Barthes writes that the society which bans Sade's work sees in it only 'the call of the referent' (*TQ* 1967: 37; *SFL* 41; Barthes 1977*c*: 37)). Specifically, it acts against sex, or against a true understanding of sex: Guyotat explains that what makes *Éden, Éden, Éden* threatening, in a way pornography is not, is the fact that the former displays, in Sollers's words, '*knowledge* of sex' where pornography, in his words, 'distorts [*dénature*] knowledge of sex' (*LI* 61).[37]

- Censorship acts through a certain conception of the self-identical individual, a viewpoint sketched out by Barthes in his explanation of how, in the wake of the Revolution, 'a confusion arises (under which we are still labouring) between morality and politics'; whereas Sade's imprisonment under the *ancien régime* was, according to Barthes, neither penal nor moral but quite simply an abuse of feudal power, his imprisonment of 1801 was demanded by 'the apparatus of an entire State (justice, education, the press, criticism) which, stepping in for a faltering Church, censors people's morals [*les mœurs*] and regulates literary production' (both *SFL* 182; Barthes 1977*c*: 178). The ideological stakes in these two instances were thus quite different; as Barthes puts it:

> Sade's first detention was segregative (cynical); the second was (and still is) penal and moral; the first stemmed from a practice, the second from an ideology; this is proved by the fact that in order to lock Sade away the second time it was necessary to mobilize a philosophy of the subject, founded entirely on the norm and deviation: for having

[37] What this 'knowledge' might tell us is spelt out by Foucault in an article addressed to Guyotat and first published in September 1970, where he writes:

My impression is that you have touched on something which has been known about sexuality for a very long time but which is carefully kept in the background to protect the primacy of the subject, the unity [*unité*] of the individual and an abstract concept of 'sex': namely that sexuality [. . .] is not a means of communication, nor even the fundamental or primitive desire of the individual, but the very framework [*trame*] of its processes is considerably anterior to it; and the individual is merely a precarious extension of it and is provisional and quickly effaced. The individual is ultimately nothing more than a pale form which springs up for a few brief moments from a repetitive, obstinate base [*souche*]; individuals are short-lived pseudopods of sexuality. If we wanted to know what we know, we would have to renounce the things we imagine of our individuality, of our self [*moi*], and of our position as subject. Your text may be the first place where the relationship between the individual and sexuality has been frankly and decisively stood on its head. (In *LI* 161)

These remarks are strangely similar to those of Sollers on the law of normality (see p. 201).

written his books, Sade was locked away as a madman. (*SFL* 182; Barthes 1977c: 178)

- Lastly, even beyond sex, censorship acts against the amorphous force of desire. Sollers contends that if we followed the models offered to us in society by religion, mythology and any philosophical system founded on the idea of normality, we would say to ourselves: 'the law is written outside me, I am merely its provisional metaphor, a particular instance of what, in general, "people say" [*un cas particulier du "on dit" général*], so I have simply to repress and deny what I find written within me, "in my heart of hearts" [*"dans mon âme"*]' (*TQ* 1967: 40). He counters this with what Sade can teach us:

  what does this writing teach me if I do not misrepresent it as the voice of conscience? Desire. Desire, i.e. a complete absence of limits, the interminable and irresponsible energy without an opposite whose force every society has to divert and channel. Sade highlights the moment at which sexuality is transformed into God, the Law, and Conscience; the moment when man makes himself into the servile animal whose cruelty will be justified in the name of the cause he has given himself [. . .] The alliance of the throne and the altar—of power and belief—is at the base of human organization which must, to avoid disappearing, censor desire and cover it with causal language. Sexual repression is primarily a repression of language. (*TQ* 1967: 40)

Inevitably, there are tensions between these different levels on which censorship is seen to act, many of them arising from ambiguities in the *Tel Quel* group's understanding of language, and the relation of language to consciousness and to extra-linguistic reality. There is a tendency, as I argued earlier, to point out the errors built into the censor's model of representation, but then to proceed to accept the transparency of language postulated by this model, in so far as it is believed that it is the *reality* of sex or of desire which is censored. This is a mistake which, as I argued at the end of Chapter 1, MacKinnon and other opponents of pornography often make, too. If the objection to this model is an epistemological one rather than (or as well as) a contingent political one, however, then one must question the accessibility of this reality. This is not to say that an epistemologically ill-founded model cannot have real effects, of course, because it may have a socio-psychological reality (a psychological reality which produces, and is produced by, a social reality) in which real censorship takes place: but these real effects provide no evidence that what was censored was singled out on the basis of some inherent quality it possessed, or that it was more 'real' than what was left untouched.

Much is made by *Tel Quel* of the 'materiality of the signifier', a phrase intended to indicate the arbitrariness of the relation between the signifier and the signified, and the freedom of the text in relation to the reality it supposedly represents; and a writer such as Sade is appreciated partly because it is felt that his writing displays an awareness of these issues, and works to pass this awareness on to its readers. However, the materiality of the signifier is a feature of any other text, too, and what brings it to the fore in Sade, if anything, is precisely the reader's sense of reality which the signification (as opposed to the mere signifiers) of Sade's text in some way contravenes. This sense of reality is not necessarily to be relied upon, of course, and it is constantly modified, not least by what we read: but it is not a sense which we have the option of abandoning.

This over-emphasis on the signifier is part of a wider tendency in *Tel Quel* to consider phenomena only in their linguistic aspects. When Barthes writes, for instance, 'a language is better defined by what it makes obligatory to say (its obligatory rubrics) than by what it forbids to be said (its rhetorical rules)' (*SFL* 130; Barthes 1977c: 126), he raises the important issue of the relation of our consciousness to our language in such a way as to imply a deterministic interpretation of that relation, one which leaves little room for consideration of its changeable, political aspects. The view of language as a rigid structure capable on its own of compelling us irresistibly to say certain things and forbidding us from saying others breaks down if conceived of in such a way that it allows no possibility of differences of consciousness within a linguistic group, either historically or from one person to another. Similarly it is misleading for Klossowski to talk about the way in which traditional language 'censors' nonsense: for, though it may be true that a certain traditional language is used in fictional and other structures to establish the predominance of a particular version of sense, and to brand other interpretations of the world as nonsense, this is not a fact of language. It could be argued that Kristeva's understanding of the subject's entry into language, on the other hand, does make this type of censorship a fact of language, inherent in its very structures; but one must ask what one gains from terming the signifier/signified split 'censorship' in this way. To do so implies that the subject actually wants to say things which are *structurally* unsayable, a proposition which seems to be self-contradictory.

Kristeva's understanding of language and of the censorship which inheres in it is in many respects close to that of Lacan, who doubtless both influenced and was influenced by her on these issues. Censorship, for Lacan, 'is part of the interrupted character of discourse' (1978: 155; 1988*b*: 127) within a scheme where the unconscious is a product of the subject's entry into language and is defined as 'that part of the concrete discourse, in so far as it is transindividual, that is not at the disposal of the subject in re-establishing the continuity of his conscious discourse' (1966: 258; 1977: 49). Again, the negative and political connotations of the term 'censorship' must be treated with caution if the process it describes is considered both constrictive and constitutive of the (semi-abstract philosophical) subject, and, though Lacan's intro-duction of otherness at source may seem to offer the possibility of making sense of this duality in relation to a socially situated, politicized conception of the unconscious, the shifting, epigram-matic style and drive towards abstraction of Lacan's theory finally render that possibility elusive. Lacan's minute attention to language, like that of Barthes in *Sade, Fourier, Loyola*, is frequently of a type which tends to efface any reality which is not linguistic: in Lacan's theory, the 'Real', as Bowie argues (1987: 116), 'is radically extrinsic to the procession of signifiers', and comes close to representing 'the ineffable'.

Conversely, it may be unhelpful to think of Sade as truly having 'invented' *a* new language, as Barthes does. As I tried to establish at the beginning of Chapter 2, there are sound epistemological grounds for taking a literal-minded approach to metaphorical for-mulations of this sort: Sade's French itself is not new, and the degree to which it is conceived of as such, I have argued, becomes the degree to which one undermines the basis from which any critical engagement with his writing can take place. Barthes's dis-course of counter-censorship, as it emerges in his work on Sade, his dream of finding a new language, tends to become a dream of stepping outside society, a dream of giving expression to a funda-mentally asocial body whose pursuit of pleasure perpetuates itself in a state of pure self-reliance. This impossible body is Barthes's

Utopian counterpart of the desire which Sollers presents as a universal and absolute force which different societies (and the bodies which constitute them) struggle to divert and contain.[38] Something that is clear from reading Sade, after all—despite the lip-service which he pays, in contradictory ways, to the 'natural'—is that desire of the type circulated in his texts and communicated to his readers thrives on the limit, which is to say that it thrives on specific ideas and metaphors of the limit; and such ideas and metaphors are evidently not a transsocial, transhistorical constant. Moreover, any pleasure the text offers cannot be detached from our affective relationship to factors such as class and gender which help structure the sexual encounters and their narration within Sade's texts. These factors are, in reality, inseparable from the representations we make of them, within texts and without.

---

[38] Indeed, the word 'desire', a highly charged one in modern French writing, is not really a Sadian term, as Henri Coulet points out in an essay entitled 'La Vie intérieure dans *Justine*' (Aix-en-Provence 1968: 85–95). Sade, Coulet argues, talks in terms of *besoin or excitation*, which have very different connotations.

Conclusion: Tout dire

❦

You will be tempted to say to yourself that this or that is irrelevant here, or is quite unimportant, or nonsensical, so that there is no need to say it. You must never give in to these criticisms, but must say it in spite of them—indeed, you must say it precisely *because* you feel an aversion to doing so. Later on you will find out and learn to understand the reason for this injunction, which is really the only one you have to follow. So say whatever goes through your mind. Act as though, for instance, you were a traveller sitting next to the window of a railway carriage and describing to someone inside the carriage the changing views which you see outside. Finally, never forget that you have promised to be absolutely honest, and never leave anything out because, for some reason or other, it is unpleasant to tell it.

(Freud, 'On Beginning the Treatment' (1913: *SE* xii. 135))

Allons, mes amis, réjouissons-nous, je ne vois dans tout cela que la vertu de malheureuse: nous n'oserions peut-être pas le dire, si c'était un roman que nous écrivissions.
— Pourquoi donc craindre de le publier, dit Juliette, quand la vérité même arrache les secrets de la nature, à quelque point qu'en frémissent les hommes? La philosophie doit tout dire.[1]

(Sade, *Histoire de Juliette*: OC ix. 586)

When the *Déclaration des droits de l'homme et du citoyen* of 1789 noted that the right to communicate thoughts and opinions was 'one of man's most precious rights', what was supposed to make it precious was above all precisely that it helped to make the man (though not the woman) into a citizen, an active participant in a political community in which he had his say. As I noted in the first section of Chapter 1, the *Déclaration* initially defined itself against

---

[1] 'Come, good friends, let us all rejoice together, it seems to me that virtue is the only loser in all this—though we would perhaps not dare say so if it were a novel we were writing.'
'Why fear publishing it', said Juliette, 'when truth itself lays bare the secrets of nature, however terrifying men may find them? Philosophy must say everything [tell all]' (Sade 1991: 1193).

a long history of censorship, carried out first by the Church, which as the embodiment of absolute authority had to be *seen* to carry out that censorship; and later by the Crown, which also had to be seen to carry out a clearly defined policy of censorship, but whose policy in practice became relatively flexible and helped to hollow out from the inside the notion of absolute authority on which it too was built. This loss of authority in the centre was in dialectic, however, with a gain of authority away from the centre. Heterodox opinions under a system claiming absolute authority were political, in some important sense, through their very heterodoxy, and increasingly found political sources of legitimacy; and, conversely, orthodoxy in itself was only decreasingly a guarantee of authority.

Sources of legitimacy since the Revolution have been multiple, and have changed. They have included the Church, secular leaders, public opinion, science, and the market, to name some of those I have examined. Heterodoxy is a complex matter in a situation where different authoritative discourses are heterodox to one another, and discourses which offend against censors or would-be censors can no longer be assumed, as I have tried to show in relation to pornography, to be opening up a new space from which oppressive, univocal authority is challenged. To put this another way, the fact that a work is censored cannot be taken as a guarantee by the counter-censor that the work is doing something right. This is partly because the censor cannot be relied upon to know in whose interests he or she is working, partly because those interests may, in fact, be legitimate, or contradictory, to a greater or lesser extent, and partly because, once one allows for ambiguities and contradictions in the theory and practice of the censor, one must allow also for ambiguities and contradictions in the object of censorship.

The case of Sade's work is exemplary in this respect, rather than unique. The politics of his writing is complex—and indeed, often contradictory—and in it one finds amongst other things attacks on the Church, lectures on Republicanism, an antipathy to Enlightenment optimism, an attention (however tendentious) to female desire, and, as I have stressed, profound misogyny and sexism. The fact that Sade himself was caught up in the Revolution makes it easier, of course, to think that his purposes were indeed subversive (rather than both subversive and reactionary, say), but this is already to settle for too simple an understanding both of the Revolution and of Sade's involvement in it. Even in the somewhat different case of Flaubert and *Madame Bovary*, the politics are far from clear-cut; on the one hand, the mobility of narrative perspective, for instance, could be seen as the very embodiment of a post-revolutionary dispersal of oppressive authority, and could be evaluated positively on that basis; but, on the other hand, it could be seen negatively as an acquiescent avoidance of the political and moral ground on which censorship is played out. Flaubert's notion of realism is, after all, similar to the idea of art for art's sake (as Ludwig Marcuse has pointed out (1965: 93)) to the extent that it seems indifferent to its own effects except in so far as those effects are aesthetic.

In this respect, of course, Sade's work is importantly different. Pornography, as Angela Carter puts it, 'is always art with work to do' (1979: 12), and this is doubtless part of what made a writer such as Sade appealing to avant-garde groupings such as the Surrealists and *Tel Quel*. It must be repeated, though, that the work which Sade's writing does is politically ambiguous. The counter-censorship of the *Tel Quel* group, and the Surrealists, including their enthusiasm for Sade, tended to be elaborated as if the pre-revolutionary model of authority (the theoretical model of absolute authority, to which reality was always resistant) were still predominant in twentieth-century France, and as if any confrontation with the censor were at bottom a simple clash between forces of oppression and forces of freedom. The claim that any challenge to the censor's authority is potentially liberating is a claim that still has a certain force, particularly in a tradition of freedom of expression where the abstract formulation of the right carries considerable weight and where the right's main benefit is considered to be the way it protects the autonomy of the individual with regard to the State; but in practice, as I have argued in connection with pornography, this challenge may not be an unambiguously liberating one.

The stance of counter-censorship which the Surrealists and *Tel Quel* practised was in any case not an indiscriminate stance against censorship, and involved viewing Sade's work in itself as an exemplary practice of counter-censorship. The claim made by the Surrealists and *Tel Quel* was that Sade's work is profoundly subversive: is, in other words, eminently censorable. Sollers, for instance, in a passage quoted earlier, wrote that 'the bourgeoisie do not need to ban *Le Temps perdu* explicitly, whereas it is hard to imagine how they could allow people to read *Juliette*, which ends on something quite other than an "image" and quite specifically on some remarks concerning the role that philosophy must fulfil' (*TQ* 1967: 85). The 'remarks' in question are those I have quoted from Sade at the head of this Conclusion, including his famous remark, 'La philosophie doit tout dire', which has frequently been taken to be the essence of the Sadian project and the guarantee of its importance.[2] As Marcel Hénaff points out (1978: ch. 2), Sade's notion of saying everything or telling all contains at once an impulse towards totality, and an impulse towards excess. The impulse towards totality is seen most clearly in the encyclopaedic ambitions of *Les Cent-vingt Journées de Sodome*, but this idea of totality betrays itself as a fiction in the arbitrariness with which that work marks out a certain ground which it can then claim to have covered in its entirety. This arbitrariness is disguised, however, by the impulse towards excess, which links *tout dire* to truth: when one threatens to 'say everything', after all, one is threatening to overstep limits and to reveal the hidden truth which will undermine or overturn the superficial truth which others, not realizing it is superficial, accept as their yardstick. The notion of *tout dire* depends, then, on a notion of limits, and the effect of 'saying everything' depends on its being a matter of power as well as a matter of knowledge, the basis of a threat as well as of a statement.

This notion was clearly an appealing one to the Surrealists or to *Tel Quel*, for various reasons. First, if the censoring authority is taken, as it tended to be taken by them, to be monolithically oppressive, and to be self-identical in its choice of object—which is to say perfectly self-perpetuating—then the task of the counter-censor is, quite simply, to say the unsayable (i.e. what the censor declares unsayable), to proclaim the truth which is guaranteed as truthful and made powerful because it surges up from an area outside the circle drawn by the censor, and which for that reason is threatening to it.

---

[2] Pauvert, for instance, in his introduction to an edition of selected works by Sade, wrote appreciatively that Sade's domain was that of truth ('le terrain de la vérité') and that he was part of an intellectual current which gave the writer the right to say everything ('le droit de tout dire') (1953: 52); Blanchot, in his essay 'L'Inconvenance majeure' (Major Impropriety), wrote: 'The first amongst freedoms is the freedom to say everything' (*La première des libertés est la liberté de tout dire*) (1965: 19; and cf. p. 51); and, in the Sade number of *Tel Quel*, the idea of *tout dire* featured in the essays of Sollers, Damisch (in an essay entitled 'L'Écriture sans mesures'), and Tort, for whom 'La philosophie doit tout dire' was also an epigraph.

Secondly, the notion is appealing because as articulated by Sade it concerns artistic conventions, which both the Surrealists and *Tel Quel* were keen to challenge. 'We perhaps would not dare say so if it were a novel we were writing', wrote Sade in his novel, mocking (and disrupting) the conventions which delimited and limited that genre and which made its fictions normative and less strange than fact. This is to be compared with Barthes's remark to the effect that the force of a text's socio-political impact comes from the violence behind (or of) its writing (he writes: 'a text's social impact [. . .] can be measured [. . .] from the violence which allows it to go beyond [*d'excéder*] the laws that a society, an ideology, a philosophy set themselves in order to agree with themselves in a fine movement of historical intelligibility. This excess has a name: writing [*écriture*]' (*SFL* 16; Barthes 1977c: 10)), or his remark a little earlier in the introduction to *Sade, Fourier, Loyola* that, in Sade's writing, everything can be articulated: in Barthes's words, 'there is nothing inexpressible, no irreducible quality of *jouissance*, of happiness, of communication: nothing exists that is not spoken' (*SFL* 9; Barthes 1977c: 4). These remarks represent the two facets of *tout dire*, excess and totality, though the Barthesian version of them is a slippery one: the totality is recognized and understood as a fiction (the Sadian world, in other words, is an apparently hermetically sealed one of writing, and *therefore* one in which everything is articulated), the excess is (one of) *écriture*. Nevertheless, Barthes is trying to keep hold of a notion of the text's social impact ('intervention sociale'), and the Sadian totality can only be understood against (and compromised by) the outside world from which any notion of totality must be derived. The excess of *écriture*, similarly, is dependent on a violence which is not merely linguistic, though Barthes's slippage from violence to excess to *écriture* obscures this fact. It should be noted in passing that the conventions which govern sense-making in the novel (Barthes's 'beau mouvement d'intelligible historique' (fine movement of historical intelligibility)) were at stake in the *Madame Bovary* trial, too, alluded to by Pinard (who viewed them from the other side of the political fence, as it were) in his remark 'Art without rules is no longer art' (*L'art sans règle n'est plus l'art*). On one level, Flaubert's project too was *tout dire*, and what he sometimes pretended were total descriptions governed only by the demands of accuracy (though, of course, they were not) were deemed by his critics to be excessive, and in some way subversive. Conversely, the Surrealists would probably have agreed with the statement that 'L'art sans règle n'est plus l'art' if it had been applied to their own work, but would have understood it as praise for the way in which their unchained art broke out of the cage of aesthetics and bounded dangerously into the real world.

Thirdly, and crucially, there was the congruence of the Sadian *tout dire* with the discourse of psychoanalysis. 'Say everything' is, as the quotation from Freud at the head of this Conclusion indicates, the watchword of psychoanalysis, too. Freud's idea of *tout dire*, like Sade's, masquerades on one level as a command to relate everything, even the 'irrelevant', or 'unimportant', or 'nonsensical' (and, as Hénaff points out, Freud, like Sade, is ever attentive to the apparently trivial detail); but it is underpinned by a sense that such indiscriminacy leads inevitably, and fortunately, to indiscretion—to stories which one has an 'aversion' to telling, in other words, and to narrative material which is 'unpleasant'. The same slippage occurs, consequently, each time Freud discusses the 'fundamental rule' of psychoanalysis: in his essay 'Freud's Psycho-Analytic Procedure', for instance, in which he describes his own procedures in the third person, he writes:

Before he asks them for a detailed account of their case history he insists that they must include in it whatever comes into their heads, even if they think it unimportant or irrelevant or nonsensical; he lays special stress on their not omitting any thought or idea from their account because to relate it would be embarrassing or distressing for them. (1904; *SE* vii. 251)

Indeed, when Freud writes, in the passage quoted earlier from 'On Beginning the Treatment', that you, the analysand, must say the things that are disagreeable to you 'precisely *because* you feel an aversion to doing so', he is making it clear that the excessive impulse behind the *tout dire* imperative is the path to, and the guarantee of, psychoanalytic truth. Psychoanalysis, to put it another way, aims to uncover that which has been censored, and the idea that that which is censored is more important, more *fundamental*, than the social conventions which marginalize, distort, and hide it, is both a starting hypothesis and a conclusion of this process.[3]

[3] Various writers, most prominently Foucault, have pointed out similarities between the practice of psychoanalysis and that of confession. For Foucault, psychoanalysis, like Catholicism, produces self-policing subjects; as McNay puts it (1992: 87), 'for Foucault, the liberating power of psychoanalysis as therapeutic practice is illusory since, in effect, it serves to implicate individuals even deeper in the network of disciplinary power by instilling in them the urge to confess'. The analyst, like the

It is also worth noting that at moments Freud tends to assume that, once he has uncovered censored material, then his work is done and beneficial results will follow automatically. The same assumption is prominent in the work of the Surrealists, but amongst other fans of Sade's, too, it is assumed that to present 'censored' material, material which was previously (supposedly) unspeakable or unimaginable, in as raw a form as possible, is to expand the reader's imaginative horizons in some important way. In certain cases this may be true, but it should also be realized that in a society such as modern France, people are regularly exposed to horrific images—more often of a violent than of a sexual-violent type—which nevertheless remain unimaginable in the crucial sense that they take on very little imaginative weight. Simple exposure to the unimaginable is not necessarily enough, in other words, to expand or redefine the viewer's or reader's psychic framework, and in order to expand, that framework needs to be given some means of encompassing the unimaginable—which psycho-analysis can sometimes provide—rather than allowed merely to brace itself and to have such material impact inconsequentially upon it.

An attention to the metaphoricity of Freud's discourse can indi-cate to us, as I suggested in Chapter 2, some of the other short-comings of his approach, by revealing some of the hidden assumptions which are at work in it. One might look, for instance, at the metaphor he chooses to illustrate the fundamental rule, the rule of *tout dire*, in the passage quoted from 'On Beginning the Treatment', where he advises the analysand, 'Act as though, for instance, you were a traveller sitting next to the window of a railway carriage and describing to someone inside the carriage the changing views which you see outside'. It is not possible, however, simply to turn one's 'gaze' inwards and to watch the landscape of the mind rolling past, as the metaphor implies one might. The observing part of the mind and the observed part are, in such a situation, intimately bound up together; the observing part does not have the detachment of the railway traveller, and the changing views of the observed part change partly *because* they are being

confessor, is recognized by the analysand/confessant as having a privileged relation to the truth of the confessing subject and grants him- or herself the right both to reveal as illicit and to pardon illicit fantasies and behaviour, before returning the unruly subject to the unstable social medium where that subject is supposedly free to behave as he or she wishes. As Legendre points out in his book *L'Amour du censeur* (1974), this role bears similarities to that of the censor, too.

observed, and in response to the observer's expectations (including the expectation of finding the landscape dotted with unimportant, nonsensical, or embarrassing features). Such criticisms may not, in fact, be particularly damaging to psychoanalysis as a practice, for reasons I will come to: but these criticisms are damaging to psychoanalysis as a theory, and as a theoretical inspiration to the literature of counter-censorship. To an important extent psychoanalysis finds what it is looking for, in the sense that its conclusion is also its starting-point, and the path from one to the other is a circular one: and it is damaged as a theory if it fails to recognize this circularity.

Psychoanalysis sets out on its journey under the banner of *tout dire*, and sees itself pushing past barriers and over frontiers into the realm of the censored: sees itself, as I suggested in the first section of Chapter 2, as both a witness to and a participant in forceful territorial conflict. The Surrealists and the *Tel Quel* group used similar spatial metaphors to describe their own projects. Sollers, for instance, defined literature as 'a constant struggle against repression and prohibitions [*les interdits*]', and explained that literature, in his words, 'battles on the borders where the individual makes himself other than is allowed' (*TQ* 24 (winter 1966), 95). The *Tel Quel* 'Mouvement de Juin 71' numbered amongst its aims 'true avant-garde and scientific experimentation' which would challenge the 'intolerable impediment [*frein*] to cultural development' represented by bourgeois ideology (*TQ* 47 (autumn 1971), 140). These metaphors of lateral space and movement, in psychoanalysis as in the theory of *Tel Quel* or the Surrealists, gain much of their force by interacting with a system of vertical spatial metaphors, in which the discourse's starting-point is not the centre but the surface, and the censored is not marginal (or supra-marginal) but subterranean, a scheme which both assumes and comes to show that the surface is indeed superficial, and that the subterranean is profound.

Such schemes were obviously not invented by Freud, and if I call them metaphorical it is above all to draw attention to the way in which they work rather than to render them transparent with regard to some hypothetical underlying literality. The same schemes, after all, have been used by censors, who have seen their task as drawing and policing limits, thereby marginalizing and excluding material which (and at this point, the scheme switches) threatens to sap the very fundamentals of society; and though these

'limits' and these 'fundaments' are, in important respects, metaphorical, they are taken 'literally' enough by censors to inform their
behaviour and to have real effects. This is a point I made in Chapter
2 in slightly different terms in connection with Pinard's remark, 'the
judge is a sentry who must protect the border', and it should be
noted, as I noted then, that in such a case the boundary between the
metaphorical and the literal (and, relatedly, between mental and
physical censorship) is blurred.

Metaphorical schemes of lateral and vertical space also come into
play in those comments of Pinard's (which I first quoted in the
second section of Chapter 1) in which he criticized Flaubert for
writing 'unbridled and with no sense of moderation' (*sans frein,
sans mesure*) and then remarked 'Art without rules is no longer art:
it is like a woman ready to take all her clothes off' (*L'art sans règle
n'est plus l'art; c'est comme une femme qui quitterait tout
vêtement*). The first scheme underpins Pinard's use of terms such as
frein, *mesure*, and *règle*, and the second scheme guides the movement from the superficial, social, and transient (clothes) to the
fundamental and pre-social (the naked body). This latter movement
was considered by Pinard to be a dangerous one because he conceived of the values which art, in his view, should help reinforce, as
those of the Christian morality which a society needed in order to
contain and control the pre-social, unchristian body's carnality.
Pinard was more explicit about this in the *Fleurs du Mal* trial,
where he spoke out against 'this unhealthy fever which brings
people to portray everything, describe everything, say everything'
(*cette fièvre malsaine qui porte à tout peindre, à tout décrire, à tout
dire*) (in Baudelaire 1930: 336), and where he argued that dangerous material brought to light within this *tout* could not simply be
balanced out by other, virtuous material, since humans lacked the
necessary equilibrium to weigh one against the other with impunity, being themselves fundamentally unbalanced by original sin. In
Pinard's words:

Even amongst your educated readers, mature men, do you think there are
many who coolly weigh up arguments for and against, who set pros against
cons, men whose minds, imaginations and senses are perfectly balanced?
Man does not want to admit it, for he is too proud, but the truth is this:
man is always somewhat infirm, always somewhat sick, and the burden of
his original fall weighs the heavier on him when he has doubts about it or
wishes to deny it. (In Baudelaire 1930: 334)

This point of view was evidently at odds with that of the *Déclaration* (which is to say the point of view necessarily inscribed in the rhetoric of the *Déclaration*, rather than the actual point of view of its authors, or of the Revolutionaries, or of the *philosophes*), since the *Déclaration* presumed, as I suggested in Chapter 1, that adults indeed possessed the equilibrium and the capacity for detachment necessary for arriving at balanced views, and that censorship should act only against 'that which is harmful to truth' (*ce qui blesse la vérité*), as the *Encyclopédie* had it (ii. 819). From Pinard's perspective, the metaphorical scheme of the naked truth, which seems at first to be operating a subversive pull on his disapproving image of 'a woman ready to take all her clothes off', may in fact fit rather well: precisely what Pinard wished to avoid was what he saw as the naked truth of naked animality, from which social conventions—including those of art—help protect us. Having said this, it is also doubtless true, as I noted in Chapter 1, that Pinard, whose discourse was clearly shaped by other factors in addition to Christianity, would have liked to find evidence for his values inherent in the world, and would have liked to have truth of all sorts, empirical as well as moral, on his side. Indeed, his criticism of *Madame Bovary* as *invraisemblable* was, as I argued in Chapter 1, an attempt to make empirical truth and his moral vision coincide.

What this should remind us of is that censorship has no inherent relationship to truth. That which is censored is usually considered by the censor to represent a threat in some way to the values which he or she (or it) seeks, or is employed, to protect, but, as I have argued, one can assume neither that the censor is fully aware of what those values are, nor that those values are internally consistent, nor that the censor knows the best way of protecting them; and though in some cases (particularly those of political censorship) that threat may come from, or be perceived to come from, the fact that the censored material offers truth or an alternative version of truth, the threat may also come from elsewhere.[4] The countercensor may consequently be mistaken not only in assuming that that which is censored is subversive, but also in assuming, on the

---

[4] Lacan is often misleading on this point, writing, for instance, that repression is 'censorship of the truth' (1966: 358), that censorship acts against 'facts of history' (1966: 261; 1977: 52), and that 'the task of censorship is to deceive through lying' (1975: 220; 1988a: 195).

basis of its being censored, that it is true. Both the censor and the counter-censor are invariably obliged to speak as if they know the true reasons for censorship which lie behind the tautological (but mobile) category of that-which-should-be-censored, though in many cases there is no outside perspective on censorship, or on the 'limits' it enforces. Much of Sade's writing actually turns around this issue, in its own way, driven by the contradictory impulse to show, on the one hand, that there are no natural limits on transgression, and, on the other hand, that consequently nothing one does can truly be called 'transgressive'. As Bennington puts it:

Sade's fiction grows from the frustration born of the philosophical demonstration that transgression is strictly speaking impossible, there being no transcendent order to transgress [. . .] The effect of this is that any attempted legitimation of Sade's writing in terms of truth, is *itself* only a fiction allowing for the production of *jouissance*, through the creation of simulacra of limits to be transgressed. (1985: 192)

It should be repeated, though, that these 'simulacra' have a reality which is social as well as fictional and individual-psychological. Transcendent transgression is indeed 'strictly speaking impossible', but what matters with regard to censorship and counter-censorship (Bennington's concerns are elsewhere) is the status of non-transcendent transgression, which, since non-transcendent, is itself convention-bound, and not only in the sense that it is the obverse of the non-transgressive or 'conventional'. What one sees in Sade's writing, or in that of the Surrealists or even of *Tel Quel*, is that, when writers try to break away from conventions and out of the circle of censorship, they are liable to come up with that which, according to convention, is the unconventional and that which is connoted as the censorable or the censored but which is not necessarily censored in the fullest sense. This is true above all of sexual representations, which, as I argued at the end of Chapter 1, are caught up in a circular process whereby it is both assumed and confirmed that the fundaments of human existence, beyond (or below, or behind) its social avatars, are sexual, and whereby the (simulacrum of) movement towards these fundaments and away from their social restraints is itself (really) sexualized. This clearly applies to Sade's writing and, as MacKinnon and others argue, to a great deal of pornography, and it also applies to Pinard's comparison of 'art without rules' with 'a woman ready to take all her clothes off', where his simile brings into play not only the metaphor of the naked truth, but also a metaphor of seduction, a porno-graphic metaphor of the way in which sexual desire, embodied in woman (*le sexe*) behind the fragile veil of decency (*la pudeur*), lies close behind the barrier of censorship, ready to overwhelm morality's and rationality's attempts to keep it in check. That which Pinard wishes to censor is to be censored, in other words, not because it is true, or false, but because it is considered seductive, and is liable to unbalance the precarious moral subject. Or, to take another example, this model, in which sex (and women) operate a subversive pull on the controlled exchanges of rationality, is folded in on itself in metaphors of seduction such as Freud's idea of 'the seduction of an analogy',[5] which makes sexual seduction at once the model and the basis of any force which is in some way illegit-imate with regard to rationality, or morality, or literality, but which is at the same time difficult to resist, and difficult to resist also *because* it is illegitimate.

I should clarify that to place such emphasis on the inclusiveness of the circle of censorship in the case of sexual representations is not to deny that sexual desire can indeed buckle rational discourse, or that desire will ebb and flow within discourse which purports to be 'purely' rational, or that powers of seduction can indeed be hard to resist. Nor is it to deny that to read Sade, say, can be a disturbing experience and this experience even a liberating one in certain respects; nor that in modern France, certain forms of sexual censorship or sexual repression exist, in forms which are distinc-tively modern or which persist from an older France, and in generalizable ways but also to different degrees for different people. What I am insisting on is that conventions not only channel but also constitute desires, and that the desire 'liberated' by a Sade novel may turn out to travel well-worn tracks of misogyny and sexism, class prejudice, and so on; and furthermore, that even to the extent that it *does* depart from these tracks, one is taken into territory where conventions are still in play (though at moments perhaps only in a metaconvention of unconventionality), a territory which is no more real nor more fundamentally bound to truth than the

---

[5] The word in Freud's text which the *Standard Edition* renders as 'seduction' is *Verlockung*, which is less explicitly sexual. *Verlockung*, too (which is close to the English 'temptation'), has sexual connotations, however; and similar metaphors of seduction are very common in French.

realm of conventions from which one departed. As Annie Le Brun has pointed out, commentators on *Les Cent-vingt Journées de Sodome*, for instance, particularly those informed by psychoanalysis, have tended to suggest that the effect of reading that book is to find one's identity disrupted by the discovery of a hidden, true erotic identity; but, Le Brun argues (1986: 39), the experience is better described as one which disrupts erotic identity. This is, I think, correct in certain respects, but I wish to underline that, in other respects, erotic identity (and identity, more or less eroticized, more generally) may be reinforced by such an experience. Moreover, on another level, erotic identity may allow for, and even thrive on, such 'disruptions'.

This observation could bring us back to psychoanalysis, where the idea of identity allows for such complexities and contradictions, and where it presupposes a fundamental type of 'censorship' without which there would be, in Samuel Weber's words (1982: 47), 'the interminable and indeterminable play of the primary process under the rule of the pleasure principle'. Much of the novelty and potential importance, for all its problems, of the psychoanalytic concept of censorship is this notion that it is constitutive of (a specific, historical) consciousness and that there is consequently no unmediated access to the unconscious. The 'primary process' should be seen as a fiction and at times a misleading one, in other words, since, as Lichtman points out, if individuals were governed by pure primary processes at any stage there could be no development, as there would be no means of conceiving of reality and none of subordinating those processes to an other principle of organization. Freud, however, frequently treats censorship as if it were a secondary phenomenon. This is what leads him to write, for example, in *Jokes and their Relation to the Unconscious* that certain jokes may evade censorship through their use of the 'technique' of displacement (1905: viii. 171–2), when it would be less misleading to say that such jokes *consist* in the movement of displacement, a movement which is at once an evasion of censorship and the constitutive moment of censorship in his terms.

Freud's models, in practice if not in theory, depend on much that is culturally specific: as Lacan once noted, to interpret the unconscious as does Freud, one must be an encyclopaedia of the arts. There may be a circularity about this, Freud illustrating and supporting certain conceptions by reference to literature which is likely to share the same conceptions irrespective of whether or not they are true, but at least this can form a real, practical link with the patient or reader within a certain historical context. It is in this sense that my criticisms of Freud's theory of censorship earlier in this Conclusion may not be too damaging to psychoanalysis as a practice. It is important theoretically that one cannot simply bypass psychic censorship through free association, and that the trajectory of *tout dire* does not necessarily carry one towards the domain of truth. Fictions of broader truths, such as a fiction of material which is inherently censorable, may, however, serve a useful purpose in the context of psychoanalytic practice, in that they may help that subject to make sense of his or her own experience: and a metaphor such as Freud's instruction to the analysand to act as if he or she were 'a traveller sitting next to the window of a railway carriage', though objectively misleading, may aid the patient (through temporarily lowering his or her sense of responsibility, say) in a context where objectivity counts for little. I have stressed that, contrary to what Freud sometimes suggests and to what the Surrealists and the *Tel Quel* group wished to believe, *tout dire* does not necessarily carry one outside the circle of censorship: but people can get better, as well as fall ill, within that circle.

It is evidently a mistake, however, to think that all the problems which an individual faces can be solved by the individual. The political version of the Freudian idea of censorship is, for that reason, preferable to the depoliticized models which Freud came to favour, and which, as I have tried to show, served as an inspiration to the Surrealists and to *Tel Quel*. The politicized psychoanalytic model can encompass facets of censorship which are not political in any direct sense, and it can encompass the idea that censorship (in a psychoanalytic sense) is a condition of consciousness: but also, crucially, it is a model which insists that consciousness—and the unconscious—are always produced in a particular society, and that the psychoanalytic sense of censorship cannot be understood except in relation to its political sense. Politics and the psyche are bound together within the circle of censorship, but this circle is not so much a complete or static shape as a motion, and one which takes place through history. This model should also allow politics a certain autonomy, consequently, and should allow the possibility that the individual intervene meaningfully in his or her society and against forms of censorship which are illegitimate.

Writing is one form of intervention, of course, and in a way, as I have implied, it can be gratifying for a writer that the censor, perhaps above all others, takes this intervention seriously. It can be experienced as gratifying, however, only to the extent that the threat of censorship is actually not very threatening (in that it is limited, or actively counter-productive in terms of sales, say), and to the extent that the writing in question tends otherwise to be treated as inconsequential: and in this context, as I have stressed, the censor's opprobrium is no guarantee that the writer's intervention is actually of any consequence. Similarly it is, at best, unhelpful to suggest that censorship promotes creativity in a writer, when it is clear from the case of the Surrealists, for instance, that it can also be plausibly asserted that a *lack* of censorship promotes creativity. Comparing degrees of creativity is in any case surely a hopeless task, and appears worthwhile only if creativity is tacitly assumed to be linked to some other quality, such as the capacity to give pleasure, or to tell profound truths. Against the author-centred, individualistic, aestheticist aspects of this approach, I would propose that if anyone is made more 'creative' by (an awareness or suspicion of) censorship it is the reader, who is likely to work harder at finding significance in a text if he or she assumes that its 'message' is occulted or oblique, and assumes that texts which are at first sight obscure conceal hidden depths. This is certainly true of Freud's reading of dreamtexts, for instance, and was reportedly true of readers and theatre-goers in certain former Eastern bloc countries. These examples indicate, however, that the 'creativity' of this type of reading is constrained and directed by the reader's assumptions about the *sort* of censorship to which the text is subject. The trajectory of such readings, in other words, is perhaps best considered not as passing beyond the text into the truths which the empirical author was secretly offering, but as following a circle of censorship via a projected author (with whom the empirical author may coincide only imperfectly, or in contradictory ways) and back to the reader, within a medium of shared assumptions.

This trajectory evidently also passes via, and is deflected by, actual texts, and takes place in time, and its starting-point will never be quite the same as its end point. Consequently, to stress the role of the reader is not to absolve writers of their responsibilities. It is true that the way a given text will be read and the effect it will have can never be fully foreseen or described, depending partly on factors outside the realm of consciousness and beyond the writer's control; but nor is a text's impact entirely unforeseeable, enigmatic, or unconscious, and it is something for which the writer should surely strive to *take* responsibility as far as possible. Relaxing back into the supposed indiscriminacy of *tout dire* and its pleasures is a poor moral and political grounding for writing, in other words, as well as a poor theoretical one. This fact can be obscured by a version of artistic freedom of expression (or freedom of artistic expression) which stresses the uniqueness of the individual (so that Sade's singularity, for instance, once a reason to fear and despise him, has come to be a reason to admire him; whereas in itself it should probably be neither), and stresses the artist's responsibility to *express* (in the sense *to squeeze out* almost as much as to communicate) himself or herself. Freud, too, can be misleading on this point, writing, for instance, 'Surely we write first of all to satisfy something within ourselves, not for other people. Of course, when others recognize one's efforts, it increases inner gratification, but nevertheless we write in the first place for ourselves, following an inner impulse' (cited by Weber 1982: 32, from E. Jones 1955: 397). Freud's own writing serves to refute this argument, in fact, not only in that it is so obviously written for others, marshalling every power of persuasion which Freud can muster and bearing the marks, as I argued in the last section of Chapter 2, of his mental negotiations with the society which was his first audience, and in that it has had such a profound effect on twentieth-century culture, in France and elsewhere, but also in that as a theory it is capable of refuting the idea that our 'inner gratification' is truly inner and purely impulsive. As Samuel Weber argues:

Freud's entire theoretical effort to articulate the importance of the uncon-scious belies the clear-cut distinction between 'inner impulse' or gratifi-cation, and 'other people'. If the unconscious means anything whatsoever, it is that the relation of self and others, inner and outer, cannot be grasped as an *interval between polar opposites* but rather as an irreducible disloca-tion of the subject in which the other inhabits the self as its condition of possibility. (1982: 32–3)

It is important, then, that any idea of a constitutive censorship fits into a politicized scheme in which we recognize that our concep-tion of self depends on a conception of the other, within a particu-lar society. It is important, too, that this idea of constitutive censorship is not used in such a way that the poles of the metaphor are reversed to leave political censorship as a kind of metaphorical effect of psychic censorship. When Derrida writes, for instance, in his essay 'Freud et la scène de l'écriture', that 'the apparent exteriority of political censorship refers to an essential censorship which ties the writer to his/her own writing' (*l'apparente extériorité de la censure politique renvoie à une censure essentielle qui lie l'écrivain à sa propre écriture*) (1967: 335; 1978: 226), there is a danger that the individual and the psyche are given priority over the political context in which they exist—though the ambiguity of 'apparent' may mean that political censorship is *obviously* exterior, as well as exterior in appearance. This ambiguity is worth retaining in so far as it suggests at once that censorship (in its primary sense) *must* be seen as exterior, and at the same time that political censorship is itself shaped partly by psychic censorship and its exclusion of that which is perceived, more or less rationally, to threaten one's identity and integrity within the body politic. The idea that on this model some level of psychic censorship is 'essential' should not, in other words, obscure the fact that any *act* of censorship is contingent, exterior in a crucial sense, and always open to question.

References

Adorno, Theodor, and Horkheimer, Max (1989), *Dialectic of Enlightenment* (first published, as *Dialektik der Aufklärung*, in 1944; London: Verso).

Aix-en-Provence (Colloque de) (1968), *Le Marquis de Sade* (Paris: Armand Colin).

Alméras, Henri d' (1906), *Le Marquis de Sade* (Paris: Albin Michel).

Anon. (1883), Introduction to *Aline et Valcour* (Brussels: J. J. Gay), pp. v–viii.

Anon. (1922), Introduction and Afterword to *Zoloé et ses deux acolytes* (Paris: Bibliothèque des Curieux), 1–5, 155–81.

Apollinaire, Guillaume (1909), Introduction to *L'Œuvre du Marquis de Sade* (Paris: Bibliothèque des Curieux), 1–56.

—— (1973), *Les Onze Mille Verges, ou Les Amours d'un hospodar* (first published 1907; Paris: Pauvert).

Aragon, Louis (1931), 'Le Surréalisme et le devenir surréaliste', *Le Surréalisme au service de la révolution*, 3 (Dec.), 2–8.

—— (1974–5), *L'Œuvre poétique* (Paris: Club Diderot), ii (1921–5); v (1930–3).

—— (1977), *Le Libertinage* (first published 1924; Paris: Gallimard).

—— (1987), *The Libertine* (London: John Calder).

Article 19 (1988), *Information, Freedom and Censorship: The Article 19 World Report 1988* (London: Article 19); includes Preface by W. Shawcross, and 'Censorship and its History: A Personal View' by M. Scammell.

—— (1989), *Freedom of Information and Expression in France* (London: Article 19).

Assister, Alison (1989), *Pornography, Feminism and the Individual* (London: Pluto).

Aymard, Camille (1929), *La République est en danger* (Paris: Éditions de la liberté).

Balkis, (1928), Introduction to *Pages curieuses du Marquis de Sade* (Paris: Éditions de la Grille), pp. i–iv.

Barthes, Roland (1957), *Mythologies* (Paris: Seuil).

—— (1960a), 'Le Problème de la signification au cinéma', *Revue internationale de filmologie*, 32–3 (Jan.–June), 83–9.

—— (1960b), 'Les "Unités traumatiques" au cinéma', *Revue international de filmologie*, 34 (July–Sept.), 13–21.

—— (1963), 'La Métaphore de l'Œil', *Critique*, 770–7.

—— (1966), *Critique et vérité* (Paris: Seuil).

—— (1970), *S/Z* (Paris: Seuil).

—— (1971), *Sade, Fourier, Loyola* (Paris: Seuil).

—— (1972), *Le Degré zéro de l'écriture* (first published 1953; Paris: Seuil).

—— (1973), *Le Plaisir du texte* (Paris: Seuil).

—— (1975), *Roland Barthes par Roland Barthes* (Paris: Seuil).

—— (1977*a*), *Fragments d'un discours amoureux* (Paris: Seuil).

—— (1977*b*), *Roland Barthes by Roland Barthes* (Basingstoke: Macmillan).

—— (1977*c*), *Sade, Fourier, Loyola* (English; London: Cape).

—— (1980), *La Chambre claire: Note sur la photographie* (Paris: Éditions de l'Étoile, Gallimard, Le Seuil).

—— (1982), *Camera Lucida* (London: Cape).

—— (1984), 'L'Effet de réel' (1962), *Le Bruissement de la langue* (Paris: Seuil), 167–74.

—— (1990), *The Pleasure of the Text* (Oxford: Blackwell).

Bataille, Georges (1955), Preface to *Justine* (Paris: Pauvert), pp. vii–xxxvii.

—— (1966), *Ma mère* (Paris: Pauvert).

—— (1970*a*), *Histoire de l'œil* (first published 1928; in *Œuvres complètes*, i (Paris: Gallimard).

—— (1970*b*), *Dossier de la polémique avec André Breton*, in *Œuvres complètes*, ii (Paris: Gallimard), 49–109 and nn.

—— (1979). *La Littérature et le mal* (first published 1957), in *Œuvres complètes*, ix (Paris: Gallimard).

—— (1986), *Erotism* (San Francisco: City Lights).

—— (1987), *L'Érotisme* (first published 1957), in *Œuvres complètes*, x (Paris: Gallimard).

Baubérot, Jean (1990), *Vers un nouveau pacte laïque?* (Paris: Seuil).

Baudelaire, Charles (1930), *Les Fleurs du mal* (1857), in *Œuvres complètes*, v (Paris: Louis Conard).

Beauvoir, Simone de (1946), 'Œil pour œil', *Les Temps modernes*, 5 (Feb.), 813–30.

—— (1955), *Faut-il brûler Sade?* (Paris: Gallimard).

Bécourt, Daniel (1961), *Livres condamnés, livres interdits: Régime juridique du livre. Outrage aux bonnes mœurs. Arrêtés d'interdiction* (Paris: Cercle de la librairie).

Beller, Steven (1989), *Vienna and the Jews 1867–1938: A Cultural History* (Cambridge: Cambridge University Press).

Benayoun, Robert (1965), *Érotique du surréalisme* (Paris: Pauvert).

Bennington, Geoffrey (1985), *Sententiousness and the Novel: Laying Down the Law in Eighteenth-Century French Fiction* (Cambridge: Cambridge University Press).

Bersani, Leo (1978), *A Future for Astyanax: Character and Desire in Literature* (London: Boyars).

—— (1990), *The Culture of Redemption* (Cambridge, Mass.: Harvard University Press).

Bettelheim, Bruno (1983), *Freud and Man's Soul* (New York: Knopf).

Bibliothèque Publique d'Information (BPI) (1987), *Censures—De la Bible aux 'Larmes d'Éros'* (Paris: Bibliothique Publique d'Information).

Black, Max (1979), 'More about Metaphor', in A. Ortony (ed.), *Metaphor and Thought* (Cambridge: Cambridge University Press), 19–43.

Blackburn, Simon (1984), *Spreading the Word: Groundings in the Philosophy of Language* (Oxford: Clarendon Press).

Blanchot, Maurice (1953), 'Sade', postface to Sade, *Œuvres* (Paris: Pauvert), 685–732 (repr. from *Sade et Lautréamont* of 1949).

—— (1965), 'L'Inconvenance majeure', preface to Sade, *Français, encore un effort si vous voulez être républicains* (Paris: Pauvert), 9–51.

Bloch, Iwan (1904), Foreword to *Les Cent-vingt Journées de Sodome* (Paris: Club des Bibliophiles), pp. i–iv, 531–43.

—— (1970), *Le Marquis de Sade et son temps* (first published in Berlin/Paris, 1901; Geneva: Slatkine).

Bonnet, Marguerite (1975), *André Breton: Naissance de l'aventure surréaliste* (Paris: Corti).

—— (1987) (ed.), *L'Affaire Barrès* (Paris: Corti).

—— (1988) (ed.), *Archives du surréalisme*, ii. *Vers l'action politique: Juillet 1925–avril 1926* (Paris: Gallimard).

Bouin, Jean-Guy (1986), 'La Loi Lang et le marché du livre', *Les Temps modernes*, no. 475 (Feb.), 58–65.

Bourdieu, Pierre (1982), *Ce que parler veut dire. L'économie des échanges linguistiques* (Paris: Fayard).

Bourdin, Paul (1929), Introduction to *Correspondance inédite du Marquis de Sade* (Paris: Librairie de France), pp. vii–xlix.

Bowie, Malcolm (1987), *Freud, Proust and Lacan: Theory as Fiction* (Cambridge: Cambridge University Press).

—— (1991), *Lacan* (London: HarperCollins (Fontana)).

Boyer, Martine (1990), *L'Écran de l'amour: Cinéma, érotisme et pornographie 1960–90* (Paris: Plon).

Breton, André (1925), 'Pourquoi je prends la direction de *La Révolution surréaliste*', *La Révolution surréaliste*, 4 (July), 1–3.

—— (1932), *Misère de la poésie: 'L'Affaire Aragon' devant l'opinion publique* (Paris: Éditions Surréalistes).

—— (1948), *Poèmes* (Paris: Gallimard).

—— (1967), 'Visite à Léon Trotsky', *La Clé des champs* (Paris: Pauvert with 10/18).

—— (1965), 'Enfin Jean Benoît nous rend le grand cérémonial' (1962), *Le*

Surréalisme et la peinture (Paris: Gallimard), 386–90.
—— (1969*a*), *Les Pas perdus* (first published 1929; Paris: Gallimard).
—— (1969*b*), *Entretiens* (first published 1952; Paris: Gallimard).
—— (1969*c*), *Manifestoes of Surrealism* (Michigan: UMP).
—— (1970*a*), *Point du jour* (contains essays from 1924–33; Paris: Gallimard).
—— (1970*b*), 'Trait d'union' (1952), *Perspective cavalière* (Paris: NRF), 9–12.
—— (1971), *Arcane 17* (first published 1944; Paris: Pauvert).
—— (1972*a*), *Manifestes du surréalisme* (contains texts first published 1924–53; Paris: Pauvert).
—— (1972*b*), *Anthologie de l'humour noir* (first published 1939; Paris: Pauvert).
—— (1975), *L'Amour fou* (first published 1937; Paris: Gallimard).
—— (1982), *Poems of André Breton: A Bilingual Anthology* (Austin: University of Texas Press).
—— (1987), *Mad Love*, (Lincoln, Nebr.: University of Nebraska Press).
—— (1988), 'L'Affaire Barrès', *Œuvres complètes* (Paris: Pléiade), i. 413–33, 1406–13.
Brochier, Jean-Jacques (1967), 'Deux éditions de Sade', *Le Magazine littéraire*, 6 (Apr.), 21.
Brousson, Jean-Jacques (1930), 'Le Dossier Sade', *Les Nouvelles littéraires* (Mar.), 3.
Brown, Andrew (1992), *Roland Barthes: The Figures of Writing* (Oxford: Clarendon Press).
Bruckner, Pascal, and Finkielkraut, Alain (1977), *Le Nouveau Désordre amoureux* (Paris: Seuil).
Burchell, Graham, Gordon, Colin, and Miller, Peter (1991) (eds.), *The Foucault Effect: Studies in Governmentality* (Hemel Hempstead: Harvester Wheatsheaf).
Cameron, Deborah (1985), *Feminism and Linguistic Theory* (Basingstoke: Macmillan).
Carter, Angela (1979), *The Sadian Woman: An Exercise in Cultural History* (London: Virago).
Castoriadis, Cornelius (1978), *Les Carrefours du labyrinthe*, i. (Paris: Seuil).
—— (1986), *Les Carrefours du labyrinthe*, ii. *Domaines de l'homme* (Paris: Seuil).
Caws, Peter (1979), *Sartre* (London: Routledge and Kegan Paul).
Cerf, Madeleine (1967), 'La Censure royale à la fin du dix-huitième siècle', *Communications* 9: 2–27.
Certeau, Michel de (1978), *L'Écriture de l'histoire* (2nd edn., Paris: Gallimard).

Chadwick, Owen (1990), *The Secularization of the European Mind in the Nineteenth Century* (Cambridge: Cambridge University Press).

Chadwick, Whitney (1985), *Women Artists and the Surrealist Movement* (London: Thames and Hudson).

Chapsal, Madeleine (1966), 'Tout Sade est Amour', *L'Express*, 762 (24–30 Jan.), 67–70.

Charles, François (1948), 'Introduction' and 'Justine et Juliette', in *Justine et Juliette* (a book containing extracts from *La Philosophie dans le boudoir* and from *Zoloé*, and these two essays) (Paris: Schmid), 6–65, 69–111.

Chateaubriand, François René, Comte de (1824), *De la censure que l'on vient d'établir* (Paris: Le Normant Père).

Chomsky, Noam, and Herman, E. S. (1988), *Manufacturing Consent: The Political Economy of the Mass Media* (New York: Pantheon Books).

Cixous, Hélène (1972), 'La Fiction et ses fantômes', *Poétique*, 10: 199–216.

Claude, Catherine (1972), 'Une Lecture de femme', *Europe*, 522 (special 'Sade' number, Oct.), 64–70.

Collier, Peter (1990), 'Baudelaire and Metaphor: Work in Regress', *Forum for Modern Language Studies*, 26/1: 26–36.

Communications (1967), *La Censure et le censurable*, no. 9.

—— (1968), *Vraisemblance*, no. 11.

Connerton, Paul (1988), 'Freud and the Crowd', in P. Collier and E. Timms (eds.), *Visions and Blueprints* (Manchester: Manchester University Press), 194–207.

Conroy, Mark (1985), *Modernism and Authority: Strategies of Legitimation in Flaubert and Conrad* (Baltimore: Johns Hopkins University Press).

Constant, Benjamin (1980), *De la Liberté chez les modernes* (Paris: Librairie Générale Française).

—— (1988), *Political Writings* (Cambridge: Cambridge University Press).

Cooper, David E. (1986), *Metaphor* (Oxford: Blackwell).

Cornell, Drucilla (1991), *Beyond Accommodation: Ethical Feminism, Deconstruction, and the Law* (London: Routledge).

Crapouillot (1963), Special number: *L'Érotisme et sa répression: Dans les arts, les lettres, le théâtre et le cinéma*, 62 (Oct.).

Culler, Jonathan (1974), *Flaubert: The Uses of Uncertainty* (London: Paul Elek).

—— (1981), 'The Problem of Metaphor', in T. E. Hope, T. B. W. Reid, R. Harris, and G. Price (eds.), *Language, Meaning and Style: Essays in Memory of Stephen Ullman* (Leeds: Leeds University Press), 5–20.

Darnton, Robert (1979), *The Business of Enlightenment: A Publishing History of the 'Encyclopédie' 1775–1800* (Cambridge, Mass.: Harvard University Press).

—— (1983), *Bohème littéraire et révolution: Le Monde des livres au XVIIIe siècle* (Paris: Seuil).

—— (1984), *The Great Cat Massacre* (London: Allen Lane).

—— and Roche, Daniel (1989) (eds.), *Revolution in Print: The Press in France 1775–1800* (Berkeley and Los Angeles: University of California Press).

Davidson, Donald (1980), 'What Metaphors Mean', in Mark Platts (ed.), *Reference, Truth and Reality* (London: Routledge), 238–54.

DeJean, Joan (1984), *Literary Fortifications: Rousseau, Laclos, Sade* (Princeton, NJ: Princeton University Press).

Deleuze, Gilles (1967), *Présentation de Sacher-Masoch* (Paris: Minuit).

—— and Guattari, Félix (1972), *Capitalisme et schizophrénie*, i. *L'Anti-Œdipe* (Paris: Minuit).

Derrida, Jacques (1967), *L'Écriture et la différence* (Paris: Seuil).

—— (1970), 'La Double séance', *Tel Quel*, 42: 3–43.

—— (1978), *Writing and Difference* (London: Routledge).

Desanti, Dominique (1983), *Les Clés d'Elsa* (Paris: Ramsay).

Desbordes, Jean (1939), *Le Vrai visage du Marquis de Sade* (Paris: Éditions de la Nouvelle Revue Critique).

Desnos, Robert ([1923]), *De l'érotisme: Considéré dans ses manifestations écrites et du point de vue de l'esprit moderne* (Paris: Cercle des Arts, n.d.).

—— (1962), *La Liberté ou l'amour!* (first published 1927; Paris: Gallimard).

Diderot, Denis (1970), 'Lettre historique et politique adressée à un magistrat sur le commerce de la librairie, son état ancien et actuel, ses règlements, ses privilèges, les permissions tacites, les censeurs, les colporteurs, les passage des ponts et autres objets relatifs à la police littéraire' (1763), in *Œuvres complètes* (Paris: Club Français du Livre), 299–381.

—— and d'Alembert (1751–72), *Encyclopédie—Inventaire ou Diction-naire raisonné des sciences, des arts, et des métiers* (Paris).

Dworkin, Andrea (1981), *Pornography—Men Possessing Women* (London: Women's Press).

—— (1987), *Intercourse* (London: Secker and Warburg).

Dworkin, Gerald (1990), 'Equal Respect and the Enforcement of Moral-ity', in E. Frankel Paul, F. D. Miller, Jr, and J. Paul (eds.), *Crime, Culpability and Remedy* (Oxford: Blackwell), 180–93.

Dworkin, Ronald (1985), *A Matter of Principle* (Cambridge, Mass.: Harvard University Press).

Ellis, Richard (1988), 'Disseminating Desire: Grove Press and "The End(s) of Obscenity"', in G. Day and C. Bloom (eds.), *Perspectives on Por-nography: Sexuality in Film and Literature* (Basingstoke: Macmillan), 26–43.

228 *References*

Éluard, Paul (1926a), 'L'Intelligence révolutionnaire', *Clarté*, 4: 27, and 6: 20.

—— (1926b), 'D. A. F. Sade, écrivain fantastique et révolutionnaire', *La Révolution surréaliste*, 8 (Dec.), 8–9.

—— (1968), 'L'Évidence poétique' (first published 1937), in *Œuvres complètes*, i (Paris: Gallimard), 511–21.

Errera, Roger (1993), 'Press Law in France', in *Press Law and Practice: A Comparative Study of Press Freedom in European and Other Democracies* (an Article 19 report), 57–77.

États Généraux du Cinéma (1968), *Le Cinéma s'insurge*, 1 and 2 (June) (Paris).

—— (1969), *Le Cinéma au service de la révolution* (Paris).

Europe (1972), Special Sade number, 522 (Oct.).

Faligot, Roger, and Kaufer, Rémi (1987), *Porno Business* (Paris: Fayard).

Fauskevåg, Svein E. (1982), *Sade dans le surréalisme* ([Toulouse]: Privat).

Favier, Pierre, and Martin-Roland, M. (1990), *La Décennie Mitterrand* (Paris: Seuil).

Fawcett, James E. S. (1987), *The Application of the European Convention on Human Rights* (Oxford: Clarendon Press).

Felman, Shoshana (1987), *Jacques Lacan and the Adventure of Insight* (Cambridge, Mass.: Harvard University Press).

Feminists Against Censorship (1991), *Pornography and Feminism* (London: Lawrence and Wishart).

Flaubert, Gustave (1950), *Madame Bovary* (English) (Harmondsworth: Penguin).

—— (1971), *Œuvres complètes*, i, (including a transcription of the *Madame Bovary* trial), (Paris: Club de l'Honnête homme).

Fontana, Alessandro (1990), *Polizia dell'anima: Voci per una genealogia della psicanalisi* (Florence: Ponte alle grazie).

Forrester, John (1980), *Language and the Origins of Psychoanalysis* (Basingstoke: Macmillan).

—— (1988), Index to Jacques-Alain Miller (ed.), *The Seminar of Jacques Lacan*, trans. J. Forrester and S. Tomaselli (Cambridge: Cambridge University Press).

Foucault, Michel (1963), 'Préface à la transgression', *Critique* (Aug.–Sept.), 751–69.

—— (1973), *Ceci n'est pas une pipe* (Montpellier: Fata Morgana).

—— (1976), *Histoire de la sexualité*, i. *La Volonté de savoir* (Paris: Gallimard).

—— (1984), *Histoire de la sexualité*, ii. *L'Usage des plaisirs* (Paris: Gallimard).

—— (1991), 'Space, Knowledge, Power' (first published in *Skyline* 1982), *Foucault Reader* (Harmondsworth: Penguin), 239–56.

France, Anatole (1881), 'Notice' for Sade's *Dorci: ou, La Bizarrerie du sort* (Paris: Chaveray Frères).

Freud, Sigmund (1953–66), *The Standard Edition of the Complete Psychological Works of Sigmund Freud*, ed. J. Strachey (London: Hogarth Press).

Gabriel-Robinet, Louis (1965), *La Censure* (Paris: Hachette).

Gallop, Jane (1981), *Intersections. A Reading of Sade with Bataille, Blanchot and Klossowski* (Lincoln, Nebr.: University of Nebraska Press).

—— (1982), *Feminism and Psychoanalysis: The Daughter's Seduction* (Basingstoke: Macmillan).

—— (1985), *Reading Lacan* (Ithaca, NY: Cornell University Press).

—— (1988), *Thinking through the Body* (New York: Columbia University Press).

Garçon, Maurice (1963), *Plaidoyer contre la censure* (Paris: Pauvert).

—— (1985), 'Censure', in *Encyclopaedia Universalis* (Paris), v. 202–3.

Gauthier, Xavière (1971), *Surréalisme et sexualité* (Paris: Gallimard).

Gay and Doucé (1881), 'Avis des éditeurs', in Sade, *Les Crimes de l'amour* (Brussels: Gay et Doucé).

Genette, Gérard (1966), *Figures I* (Paris: Seuil).

—— (1969), *Figures II* (Paris: Seuil).

Girodias, Maurice (1962), 'Apology', *Olympia*, 3: 1–2.

—— (1966) (ed.), *The Best of Olympia* (London: Olympia Press).

Goblot, Laurent (1959), *Apologie de la censure* (Rodez: Subervie).

Goldgar, Anne (1992), 'The Absolutism of Taste: Journalists as Censors in Eighteenth Century Paris', in R. Myers and M. Harris (eds.), *Censorship and the Control of Print in England and France 1600–1910* (Winchester: St Paul's Bibliographies), 87–110.

Goldstein, Robert J. (1989), *Political Censorship of the Arts and the Press in Nineteenth Century Europe* (Basingstoke: Macmillan).

Gouges, Olympe de (1986), 'Déclaration des droits de la femme et de la citoyenne' (1791), *Œuvres* (Paris: Mercure de France), 101–12.

Goulemot, Jean-Marie (1966), ' "Divin Marquis" ou objet d'études?', *Revue des sciences humaines* (Oct.–Dec.), 413–21.

—— (1994), *Ces livres qu'on ne lit que d'une main: Lecture et lecteurs de livres pornographiques au XVIIIᵉ siècle* (2nd edn., Paris: Minerve).

Guyotat, Pierre (1970), *Éden, Éden, Éden* (Paris: Gallimard).

—— (1972), *Littérature interdite* (Paris: Gallimard).

Haack, Susan (1988), 'Surprising Noises: Rorty and Hesse on Metaphor', *Proceedings of the Aristotelian Society*, 88: 294–300.

Haarscher, Guy (1989) (ed.), *Laïcité et droits de l'homme—Deux siècles de conquêtes* (Brussels: Éditions de l'Université de Bruxelles).

Habermas, Jürgen (1987), *The Philosophical Discourse of Modernity*

(Cambridge: Polity Press).

Hamelin, Jacques (1935), *Les Plaidoiries de Victor Hugo* (Paris: Hachette).

—— (1956), *Hommes de lettres inculpés* (Paris: Minuit).

Hans, Marie-François, and Laponge, Gilles (1978), *Les Femmes, la pornographie, l'érotisme* (Paris: Seuil).

Harrison, Nicholas (1994), 'Freedom of Expression: The Case of Blasphemy', in G. Raymond (ed.), *France during the Socialist Years* (Aldershot: Dartmouth), 154–71.

—— (1995), 'Colluding with the Censor: Theatre Censorship in France after the Revolution', *Romance Studies* 25: *Confronting the Censor* (spring), 7–25.

Hawkes, Terence (1972), *Metaphor* (London: Methuen).

Heath, Stephen (1982), *The Sexual Fix* (Basingstoke: Macmillan).

—— (1986), 'Realism, Modernism and "Language- Consciousness"', in N. Boyle and M. Swales (eds.), *Realism in European Literature: Essays in Honour of J. P. Stern* (Cambridge: Cambridge University Press), 103–22.

Heine, Maurice (1926), Foreword to *Dialogue entre un prêtre et un moribond* (Paris: Stendhal et cie), 9–32.

—— (1930), Foreword to *Les Infortunes de la vertu* (Paris: Fourcade), 1–34.

—— (1933), 'Chronique sadiste' and 'Le Conteur', in *Œuvres choisies et pages magistrales du Marquis de Sade* (Paris: Trianon), pp. i–lii, liii–lxviii.

—— (1934), 'Hommage', *Documents* 34, NS 1 (June), 26–7.

—— (1950), Foreword to *Contes, historiettes et fabliaux* (first published in 1927) in *Le Marquis de Sade* (Paris: Société du Roman Philosophique) 38–41.

—— (1956), Foreword to *Cent onze notes pour la Nouvelle Justine* (Paris: Le Terrain Vague).

—— (1967), 'Le Marquis de Sade et le roman noir' (first published in *NRF* 1933), in *Justine* (Paris: Cercle du Livre Précieux), iii. 27–48.

Hénaff, Marcel (1978), *Sade: L'Invention du corps libertin* (includes the essay 'Tout dire, ou L'Encyclopédie de l'excès', first published in *Obliques*, 12–13 (1977), 29–37) (Paris: PUF).

Henriot, Émile (1930), 'La Vraie Figure du Marquis de Sade', *Le Temps* (25 Feb.), 2.

Hermann-Mascard, Nicole (1968), *La Censure des livres à Paris à la fin de l'Ancien Régime (1750–89)* (Paris: PUF).

Hertz, Neil (1979), 'Freud and the Sandman', in J. V. Harari (ed.), *Textual Strategies* (New York: Cornell University Press), 296–321.

Hesnard, André (1967), Foreword to *Justine* (Paris: Cercle du livre précieux), iii. 13–25.

Hesse, Carla (1991), *Publishing and Cultural Politics in Revolutionary*

Paris, 1789–1810 (Berkeley and Los Angeles: University of California Press).

Hoffmann, Ernst T. W. (1982), *The Sandman*, in *Tales of Hoffmann* (Harmondsworth: Penguin).

Hollier, Denis (1989) (ed.), *A New History of French Literature* (Cambridge, Mass.: Harvard University Press).

Houdebine, Jean-Louis (1971), 'Méconnaissance de la psychanalyse dans le discours surréaliste', *Tel Quel*, 46 (summer), 67–82.

Hunt, Lynn (1993) (ed.), *The Invention of Pornography: Obscenity and the Origins of Modernity, 1500-1800* (New York: Zone).

Hunter, Ian, Saunders, David, and Williamson, Dugald (1993), *On Pornography: Literature, Sexuality and Obscenity Law* (Basingstoke: Macmillan).

Huston, Nancy (1982), *Mosaïque de la pornographie: Marie-Thérèse et les autres* (Paris: Denoël/Gauthier).

Index on Censorship (1971–95).

Irigaray, Luce (1977), *Ce sexe qui n'en est pas un* (Paris: Minuit).

Itzin, Catherine (1993) (ed.), *Pornography: Women, Violence and Civil Liberties, A Radical New View* (1st edn. 1992; Oxford: Oxford University Press).

Jacob, Paul L. (1870), 'Le Marquis de Sade: L'Homme et ses écrits' and 'La Vérité sur les deux procès criminels du Marquis de Sade' (first published in the *Revue de Paris*, 1837), in *Zoloé et ses deux acolytes* (Brussels: 'Chez tous les librairies' [J. Gay]) pp. i–lxv, lxxvi–cii.

Jacobus, Mary (1993), 'Malthus, Matricide and the Marquis de Sade' (paper delivered in Cambridge, 8 Feb.).

Jakobson, Roman (1975), 'Two Aspects of Language and Two Types of Aphasic Disturbances', in *Fundamentals of Lauguage* (first published 1956; The Hague: Mouton), 67–96.

Jameson, Fredric (1981), *The Political Unconscious: Narrative as a Socially Symbolic Act* (London: Methuen).

Jansen, Susan Curry (1988), *Censorship: The Knot that Binds Power and Knowledge* (Oxford: Oxford University Press).

Johnson, Barbara (1979), *Défigurations du langage poétique: La Seconde Révolution baudelairienne* (Paris: Flammarion).

Jones, Derek, and Platt, Steve (1991) (eds.), *Banned* (produced with the collaboration of Channel 4, the British Film Institute and New Statesman and Society).

Jones, Ernest (1953), *Sigmund Freud: Life and Work*, i (London: Hogarth Press); also ii (1955), iii (1957).

Jones, Malcolm V. (1986), 'Der Sandmann and "The Uncanny": A Sketch for an Alternative Approach', *Paragraph*, 7 (Mar.), 77–101.

Kafker, Frank A. (1964), 'The Effects of Censorship on Diderot's

Encylopaedia', *The Library Chronicle of the Friends of the University of Pennsylvania Library*, xxx.

Kajman, Michel (1990), 'De "l'affaire" au panthéon', *Le Monde*, 23 Nov., p. 22.

Kappeler, Susanne (1986), *The Pornography of Representation* (Cambridge: Polity Press).

Keane, John (1991), *The Media and Democracy* (Cambridge: Polity Press).

Kendrick, Walter (1987), *The Secret Museum: Pornography in Modern Culture* (New York: Viking).

Klossowski, Pierre (1933), 'Éléments d'une étude psychanalytique sur le Marquis de Sade', *Revue française de psychanalyse*, 6/3–4: 458–74.

—— (1962), 'Sade et la Révolution', preface to *La Philosophie dans le boudoir*, in *Œuvres complètes*, iii (Paris: Cercle du Livre Précieux), 349–65.

—— (1967), *Sade, mon prochain* (rev. edn.; first published 1947; Paris: Seuil).

—— (1992), *Sade My Neighbour* (London: Quartet).

Kofman, Sarah (1972), *Nietzsche et la métaphore* (Paris: Payot).

—— (1973), *Quatre romans analytiques* (Paris: Éditions Galilée).

—— (1975), *L'Enfance de l'art: Une interprétation de l'esthétique freudienne* (Paris: Payot).

Krakovitch, Odile (1985), *Hugo censuré—La Liberté au théâtre au XIXᵉ siècle* (Paris: Calmann-Lévy).

Kristeva, Julia (1974), *La Révolution du langage poétique: L'Avant-garde à la fin du XIXᵉ siècle: Lautréamont et Mallarmé* (Paris: Seuil).

—— (1983), *Histoires d'amour* (Paris: Denoël).

—— (1984), *Revolution in Poetic Language* (New York: Columbia University Press).

—— (1987), *Soleil noir—Dépression et mélancolie* (Paris: Gallimard).

—— (1992), 'Identification and the Real', in P. Collier and H. Geyer-Ryan (eds.), *Literary Theory Today* (Cambridge: Polity Press), 167–76.

Kuhlmann, Marie, Kuntzmann, Nelly, and Bellour, Hélène (1989), *Censure et bibliothèques au XXᵉ siècle* (Paris: Éditions du Cercle de la Librairie).

Kuhn, Annette (1988), *Cinema, Censorship and Sexuality 1909–25* (London: Routledge).

Laborde, Alice M. (1990), *Les Infortunes du Marquis de Sade* (Paris: Champion-Slatkine).

Lacan, Jacques (1966), *Écrits* (Paris: Seuil).

—— (1975), *Le Séminaire, i. Les Écrits techniques de Freud* (Paris: Seuil).

—— (1977), *Écrits: A Selection* (London: Tavistock).

—— (1978), 'La Censure n'est pas la résistance', *Le Séminaire, ii. Le Moi dans la théorie de Freud et dans la technique de la psychanalyse* (1954–5; Paris: Seuil), 151–62.

—— (1986), 'Le Paradoxe de la jouissance', *Le Séminaire, vii. L'Éthique de la psychanalyse* (1959–60; Paris: Seuil), 195–281.

—— (1988*a*), *The Seminar of Jacques Lacan*, Book I (Cambridge: Cambridge University Press).

—— (1988*b*), 'Censorship is not Resistance', in *The Seminar of Jacques Lacan*, Book II (Cambridge: Cambridge University Press), 123–33.

LaCapra, Dominick (1982), *Madame Bovary on Trial* (Ithaca, NY: Cornell University Press).

Lacey, Nicola, Wells, C., and Meure, D. (1990), *Reconstructing Criminal Law* (London: Weidenfeld and Nicolson).

Lachaume, J.-F. (1989), *Droit administratif: Les Grandes Décisions de la jurisprudence* (Paris: PUF).

Lakoff, George, and Johnson, Mark (1980), *Metaphors We Live By* (Chicago: Chicago University Press).

Laplanche, Jean, and Pontalis, J.-B. (1967), *Vocabulaire de la psychanalyse* (Paris: PUF).

—— (1988), *The Vocabulary of Psychoanalysis* (London: Karnac Books).

Lavers, Annette (1982), *Roland Barthes: Structuralism and After* (London: Methuen).

Lazar, Marc (1986), 'Les "Batailles du Livre" du Parti Communiste Français (1950–52)', *Vingtième Siècle: Revue d'histoire*, 10 (Apr.–June), 37–49.

Le Brun, Annie (1965), 'Les Premiers Romans noirs, ou L'Ébauche d'une scène révolutionnaire', *La Brèche: Action surréaliste*, 8 (Nov.), 31–5.

—— (1986), *Soudain un bloc d'abîme, Sade*, Introduction to Sade, *Œuvres complètes* (Paris: Pauvert).

—— (1991), *Qui vive: Considérations actuelles sur l'inactualité du surréalisme* (Paris: Pauvert).

Leclerc, Yvan (1991), *Crimes écrits: La Littérature en procès au XIXᵉ siècle* (Paris: Plon).

Lee, Simon (1990), *The Cost of Free Speech* (London: Faber and Faber).

Legendre, Pierre (1974), *L'Amour du censeur: Essai sur l'ordre dogmatique* (Paris: Seuil).

Lély, Gilbert (1938), *La Sylphide, ou L'Étoile carnivore* (Paris: Le François).

—— (1948*a*), Foreword and introductory essay ('Tableau de l'objectivité de Sade'), to *Morceaux choisis de D. A. F. Marquis de Sade* (Paris: P. Seghers), pp. vii, xi–xxxviii.

—— (1948*b*), 'A huit rais d'or', poem serving as introduction to *Eugénie de Franval* (Paris: Georges Artigues).

Lély, Gilbert (1950), Foreword to Heine, *Le Marquis de Sade* (Paris: Gallimard), 9–24.

—— (1967), *Ma civilisation* (expanded; original version 1954; Paris: Pauvert).

—— (1971), Foreword to *Les Crimes de l'amour* (Paris: 10/18), 7–21.

—— (1982), *Vie du Marquis de Sade* (revised and augmented; 1st edn. 1952–7; Paris: Pauvert aux Éditions Garnier Frères).

Lemaître, Maurice (1965), 'Le Boudoir de la philosophie', special number of *Lettrisme*, 5 (July–Aug).

—— (1989), *Œuvres supertemporelles de polémique créatrice d'anti-censure* (pamphlet: no publication information).

Lichtman, Richard (1982), *The Production of Desire: The Integration of Psychoanalysis into Marxist Theory* (New York: Free Press).

Liseux, Isidore (1884), 'Avertissement', in *Justine* (Paris: Liseux), 5–7.

Littérature 9 (Nov. 1919), 10 (Dec. 1919), 11 (Jan. 1920), and 12 (Feb. 1920).

Long, M., Weil, P., and Braibant, G. (1984), *Les Grands Arrêts administratifs*, (8th edn., Paris: Sirey).

Losfeld, Eric (1980) (ed.), *Tracts surréalistes et déclarations collectives (1922/1969)*, presented by José Pierre (Paris: Le Terrain vague).

Lotringer, Sylvère (1990), *Overexposed—Treating Sexual Perversion in America* (London: Paladin/Grafton).

Lyotard, Jean-François (1971), *Discours, figure* (Paris: Klincksieck).

Maarek, Philippe J. (1979), *De mai 68 . . . aux films X: Cinéma, politique et société* (Paris: Dujarric).

—— (1982), *La Censure cinématographique* (Paris: Librairies Techniques).

MacCabe, Colin (1981) (ed.), *The Talking Cure: Essays in Psychoanalysis and Language* (Basingstoke: Macmillan).

McGrath, William J. (1986), *Freud's Discovery of Psychoanalysis: The Politics of Hysteria* (New York: Cornell University Press).

McGuinness, Brian (1982) (ed.), *Wittgenstein and his Times* (Chicago: Chicago University Press).

MacKinnon, Catherine (1987), *Feminism Unmodified: Discourses on Life and Law* (Cambridge, Mass.: Harvard University Press).

—— (1994), *Only Words* (London: HarperCollins).

McNay, Lois (1992), *Foucault and Feminism: Power, Gender and the Self* (Cambridge: Polity Press).

Marcuse, Herbert (1987), *Eros and Civilization: A Philosophical Inquiry into Freud* (1995) (London: Ark).

Marcuse, Ludwig (1965), *Obscene: The History of an Indignation* (London: MacGibbon and Kee).

Marre, Jean-Luc (1991), 'Classé X—Cinéma porno ou cinéma engagé', 7 *à*

Paris (22–8 May), 22–7.

Marx, Karl (1975*a*), 'Comments on the Latest Prussian Censorship Instruction' (1841), in *Collected Works of Marx and Engels* (London: Lawrence and Wishart), i. 109–31.

——(1975*b*), 'Debates on Freedom of the Press' (1842), in *Collected Works*, i. 132–81.

——(1975*c*), 'The Holy Family' (1844), in *Collected Works*, iv. 3–211.

——(1979), 'The Eighteenth Brumaire of Louis Bonaparte' (1852), in *Collected Works*, xi. 99–197.

Maulnier, Thierry (1947), Foreword to *Les Infortunes de la vertu* (Paris: Jean Valmont), pp. ix–xii.

Mauriac, Claude (1953), *Hommes et idées d'aujourd'hui* (Paris: Albin Michel).

May, Georges (1963), *Le Dilemme du roman au XVIIIe siècle* (Paris: PUF).

Merck, Mandy (1991), 'From Minneapolis to Westminster', in L. Segal and M. McIntosh (eds.), *Sex Exposed: Sexuality and the Pornography Debate* (London: Virago Press), 50–62.

Miller, Nancy K. (1975), '*Juliette* and the Posterity of Prosperity', *L'Esprit Créateur*, 15/4 (Sade number), 413–24.

Mitchell, Juliette (1986), *Psychoanalysis and Feminism* (Harmondsworth: Penguin).

Mitton, Fernand (1928), Introduction to *Zoloé et ses deux acolytes* (Paris: Éditions d'Art de l'Intermédiaire du Bibliophile), pp. iii–xviii.

Monnerot, J.-M. (1933), 'A partir de quelques traits particuliers à la mentalité civilisée', in *Le Surréalisme au service de la révolution*, 5: 35–7.

Morange, Jean (1993), *La Déclaration des Droits de l'Homme et du Citoyen* (3rd edn.; Paris: PUF, Que sais-je?).

Moreau, Jacques (1989), *Droit administratif* (Paris: PUF).

Mouvement contre le Racisme et pour l'Amitié entre les Peuples (MRAP) (1987), *Évolutions et adaptations de l'extrême-droite en France (1945–87)* (Paris).

Moyen, François (1991), *Le Petit Livre rose à l'usage des Mitterrandophiles, Mitterrandophobes, Mitterrandolâtres* (Paris: La Table Ronde).

Muller, John P., and Richardson, William J. (1988) (eds.), *The Purloined Poe—Lacan, Derrida and Psychoanalytic Reading* (Baltimore: Johns Hopkins University Press).

Nadeau, Maurice (1947), 'Exploration de Sade', in Sade, *Œuvres* (Paris: La Jeune Parque), 8–58.

——(1964), *Histoire du surréalisme* (first published 1944; Paris: Seuil).

——(1978), *The History of Surrealism* (Harmondsworth: Penguin).

Nelson, Cary, and Grossberg, L. (1988) (eds.), *Marxism and the Interpretation of Culture* (Basingstoke: Macmillan).

Nerval, Gérard de (1986), *Les Faux Saulniers* (first published in *Le National* 1850; Paris: Larousse).

Nietzsche, Friedrich (1976), *The Portable Nietzsche* (Harmondsworth: Penguin).

Noël, Bernard (1975), *Le Château de Cène, suivi de L'Outrage aux mots* (first published, under a pseudonym, in 1971; Paris: Pauvert).

Le Nouvel Observateur (1991), special number on Mitterrand, 1382 (2–8 May).

Obliques (1977), 12–13, 'Sade'.

Ortony, Andrew (1979) (ed.), *Metaphor and Thought* (Cambridge: Cambridge University Press).

Paulhan, Jean (1930), 'Les Infortunes de la Vertu', *NRF* 204 (Sept.), 414–17.

—— (1945), 'Sade, ou Le Pire est l'ennemi du mal', *Labyrinthe*, 11 (15 Aug.), 1–2.

—— (1946), Introduction to *Les Infortunes de la vertu* (Paris: Point du Jour), pp. ii–xliii.

Pauvert, Jean-Jacques (1953), 'Le Marquis de Sade, l'histoire et la littérature', in Sade, *Œuvres* (Paris: Pauvert), 1–63.

—— (1963), *L'Affaire Sade: Compte rendu exact du procès intenté par le Ministère Public* (first edn. 1960; this edn. includes the court of appeal decision; Paris: Pauvert).

—— (1971), 'Le Vrai problème de la censure', preface to Y. Belhomme, *L'Enfer du sexe* (Paris: Pauvert).

—— (1981), *Anthologie des lectures érotiques* (Paris: Pauvert).

—— (1982), 'Histoire d'O ou mes démêlés avec la censure', *Le Matin* (24 Nov.), 32.

—— (1994), *Nouveaux (et moins nouveaux) visages de la censure, suivi de L'Affaire Sade* (Paris: Les Belles Lettres).

—— and Le Brun, Annie (1986), 'Avis des Éditeurs', *Œuvres complètes du Marquis de Sade*, i(b), 7–10.

Perceau, Louis (1921), Foreword (anon.) to *Le Bordel de Venise* (extract from *Juliette*) (Venice[?]).

—— (1930), 'Notice bibliographique' for *Léonore et Clémentine, ou Les Tartufes de l'Inquisition* (extract from *Aline et Valcour*) (Paris: Cabinet du livre).

—— ([1948]), 'Le Marquis de Sade et son œuvre' (under pseudonym Helpey), in *La Philosophie dans le boudoir* ('Sadopolis': Société des études sadiques), 5–40.

Péret, Benjamin (1944), 'La Pensée est Une et indivisible', *VVV* 4 (Feb.), 9–13.

—— (1956), *Anthologie de l'amour sublime* (Paris: Albin Michel).

—— (1991), *Mad Balls* (*Les Couilles enragées*, 1924; first published 1954) trans. J. Brook (London: Atlas Press).

Phelps, Guy (1975), *Film Censorship* (London: Victor Gollancz).

Phillips, Eileen (1983), *The Left and the Erotic* (London: Lawrence and Wishart).

Pia, Pascal (1926), 'Le Divin Marquis', in *Ernestine* (from *Les Crimes de l'amour*) (Paris: Cabinet du livre), pp. i–iv.

—— (1963), 'Sade au XXe siècle', *Carrefour* (24 July), 20.

—— (1978), *Les Livres de l'Enfer* (Paris: Coulet et Faure).

Pierre, José (1990) (ed.), *Recherches sur la sexualité, janvier 1928–avril 1932* (Paris: Gallimard).

—— (1992), *Investigating Sex* (London: Verso).

Place, Jean-Michel (1976) (ed.), *Le Surréalisme au service de la révolution [SASDLR]: Édition complète* (Paris: J.-M. Place).

Platts, Mark (1980) (ed.), *Reference, Truth and Reality* (London: Routledge).

Pompidou, Georges (1966), Interview in *Figaro Littéraire* (1 Sept.), 8–9.

Post, Robert C. (1988), 'Cultural Heterogeneity and Law: Pornography, Blasphemy and the First Amendment', *California Law Review*, 76: 297–335.

Pottier, Jean-Michel, and Berthet, Roger (1992) (eds.), *Anastasie, Anastasie: Groupement de textes sur la censure* (Troyes: Centre Régional du Livre de Champagne-Ardenne).

Prendergast, Christopher (1986), *The Order of Mimesis* (Cambridge: Cambridge University Press).

Proverbe (1920), 1 (1 Feb.).

Queneau, Raymond (1965), 'Lectures pour un front' (1950), *Bâtons, chiffres et lettres* (Paris: Gallimard), 157–220.

Queyranne, Jean-Jack (1985), 'Les Socialistes et l'avenir de l'audiovisuel', *Film Échange*, 32: 55–61.

Réage, Pauline (1975), *L'Histoire d'O* (illustrated edition; 1st edn. 1954; Paris: Pauvert).

Revel, Jean-François (1968), 'Les Succès du moi—variations autour de la tentation de parler de Sade', *Preuves*, 208 (June–July), 45–50.

La Révolution Surréaliste, 1 (1924), 2 (1925), 3 (1925), 8 (Dec. 1926), 9–10 (Oct. 1927), 11 (Mar. 1928), and 12 (Dec. 1929).

Ricœur, Paul (1975), 'La Métaphore et la sémantique du discours', *La Métaphore vive* (Paris: Seuil) 87–128.

Rieusset, Isabelle (1986), 'Acte métaphorique et sujet de l'énonciation: Les transports de sens dans le texte', D. Kelley and I. Llasera (eds.), *Cross-References—Modern French Theory and the Practice of Criticism* (Oxford: Society for French Studies), 45–56.

Rist, Ray Charles (1975), *The Pornography Controversy* (New Brunswick: Transaction Books).

Robinson, Paul A. (1970), *The Sexual Radicals: Wilhelm Reich, Geza Roheim, Herbert Marcuse* (first published as *The Freudian Left*, 1969; London: Temple Smith).

Roger, Philippe (1976), *Sade: La Philosophie dans le pressoir* (Paris: Bernard Grasset).

Rogers, Robert (1978), *Metaphor: A Psychoanalytic View* (Berkeley and Los Angeles: University of California Press).

Romane, Cécile (1989) (ed.), *De l'horrible danger de la lecture: Aide mémoire à l'usage des intolérants* (Paris: Balland).

Rorty, Richard (1980), 'Freud, Morality, and Hermeneutics', *New Literary History*, 12 (autumn), 177–85.

Rose, Margaret A. (1978), *Reading the Young Marx and Engels: Poetry, Parody and the Censor* (London: Croom Helm).

Ross, George, Hoffmann, S., and Malzacher, S. (1987) (eds.), *The Mitterrand Experiment* (Cambridge: Polity Press).

Rougemont, Denis de (1989), *L'Amour et l'Occident* (first published 1939; Paris: France Loisirs).

Rousseau, Jean-Jacques (1977) *Du Contrat social* (1762; Paris: Seuil).

Sade, D. A. F., Marquis de (1966–7), *Œuvres complètes* (Paris: Cercle du Livre Précieux).

—— (1987), *The One Hundred and Twenty Days of Sodom* (New York: Grove Press).

—— (1991), *Juliette* (translation) (London: Arrow).

—— (1992), *Osons le dire. Choix et présentation de J.-J. Pauvert* (Paris: Les Belles Lettres).

Saïd, Edward (1988), 'Identity, Negation and Violence', *New Left Review*, 171 (Sept./Oct.), 46–60.

Sainte-Beuve (1843), 'Quelques remarques sur la situation en littérature', *La Revue des deux mondes*, 3 (July), 5–20.

Sanouillet, Michel (1965), *Dada à Paris* (Paris: Pauvert).

Sartre, Jean-Paul (1943), *L'Être et le néant: Essai d'ontologie phénoménologique* (Paris: Gallimard).

—— (1948), *Qu'est-ce que la littérature?* (Paris: Gallimard).

—— (1969), *Being and Nothingness* (London: Methuen).

Schama, Simon (1989), *Citizens: A Chronicle of the French Revolution* (Harmondsworth: Penguin).

Schorske, Carl E. (1981), *Fin de siècle Vienna: Politics and Culture* (Cambridge: Cambridge University Press).

Segal, Lynne, and McIntosh, M. (1991) (eds.), *Sex Exposed: Sexuality and the Pornography Debate* (London: Virago Press).

Shackleton, Robert (1975), *Censure and Censorship: Impediments to Free*

Publication in the Age of Enlightenment (Austin: University of Texas Press).

Sollers, Philippe (1970), 'La Lutte idéologique dans l'écriture d'avant-garde', in *La Nouvelle Critique*, 39*b*: *Littérature et idéologies: Colloque de Cluny II, 2–4 April 1970*: 74–85.

—— (1971), 'Thèses générales', *Tel Quel*, 44 (winter), 96–8.

—— (1991), 'Nouvelle inquisition, nouvelle censure (A propos de Genet)', *L'Infini*, 36: 3–8.

—— (1992), *Sade contre l'Être suprême* (Paris: Quai Voltaire).

Sontag, Susan (1969), *Styles of Radical Will* (London: Secker and Warburg).

Stone, Alec (1992), *The Birth of Judicial Politics in France: The Constitutional Council in Comparative Perspective* (New York: Oxford University Press).

Stora-Lamarre, Annie (1990), *L'Enfer de la IIIe République—Censeurs et pornographes (1881–1914)* (Paris: Imago).

Strauss, Leo (1952), *Persecution and the Art of Writing* (Glencoe, Ill.: The Free Press).

Suleiman, Susan Rubin (1990), *Subversive Intent: Gender, Politics and the Avant-Garde* (Cambridge, Mass.: Harvard University Press).

Tel Quel (1967), 'La Pensée de Sade', 28 (winter).

—— various other issues (references given in body of text).

Toubiana, Serge (1988), 'Censure, danger immédiat', *Cahiers du cinéma* (Nov.).

Uzanne, Octave (1878), Foreword to *Idée sur les romans* (Paris: Librairie ancienne et moderne Édouard Rouveyre), pp. v–xliii.

Vartier, Jean (1989), *Barrès et le chasseur de papillons* (Paris: Denoël).

Voltaire, (1971), *Correspondance*, in Œuvres complètes, xviii, ed. T. Besteman (Banbury: Voltaire Foundation).

Weber, Samuel (1982), *The Legend of Freud* (Minneapolis: University of Minnesota Press).

Webster, Richard (1990), *A Brief History of Blasphemy—Liberalism, Censorship and the 'Satanic Verses'* (Southwold, Suffolk: Orwell Press).

Wheeler III, Samuel C. (1989), 'Metaphor according to Davidson and DeMan', in R. W. Dasenbrock (ed.), *Redrawing the Lines: Analytic Philosophy, Deconstruction and Literary Theory* (Minneapolis: University of Minnesota Press), 116–39.

Williams, Bernard (1979), *The Williams Report on Obscenity and Film Censorship* (HMSO Command Papers LXVI, no. 7772).

Williams, Linda (1989), *Hard Core: Power, Pleasure and the Frenzy of the Visible* (Berkeley and Los Angeles: University of California Press).

Williams, Raymond (1958), *Culture and Society (1780–1950)* (London: Chatto and Windus).

Wing, Nathaniel (1986), *The Limits of Narrative: Essays on Baudelaire,*

Flaubert, Rimbaud and Mallarmé (Cambridge: Cambridge University Press).

Wright, Elizabeth (1984), *Psychoanalytic Criticism* (London: Methuen).

Yvert, Benoît (1990) (ed.), *Dictionnaire des ministres (1789–1989)* (Paris: Perrin).

Index

❧